OEDIPUS AND THE COUPLE

OEDIPUS AND THE COUPLE

Editor

Francis Grier

KARNAC

LONDON   NEW YORK

First published in 2005 by
H. Karnac (Books) Ltd.
6 Pembroke Buildings, London NW10 6RE

Reprinted in 2006

British Library Cataloguing in Publication Data

A C.I.P. for this book is available from the British Library

ISBN: 1 85575 922 5

Edited, designed and produced by The Studio Publishing Services Ltd, Exeter EX4 8JN

Printed in Great Britain

10 9 8 7 6 5 4 3 2 1

www.karnacbooks.com

CONTENTS

This book is dedicated, with gratitude, to Betty Joseph

CONTRIBUTORS

Andrew Balfour originally trained as a Clinical Psychologist at University College London, and then as a Psychoanalytic Psychotherapist at the Tavistock Clinic. Subsequently, he trained as a Couple Psychoanalytic Psychotherapist at the Tavistock Marital Studies Institute. He currently works as a Senior Clinical Lecturer and Couple Psychotherapist at the Tavistock Marital Studies Institute, and as a Consultant Clinical Psychologist at the Tavistock Clinic.

Sasha Brookes studied English Language and Literature at Oxford University, and, later, Psychology at London and Durham. She taught in higher education and worked as a Relate counsellor before training as a Couple Psychotherapist at the Tavistock Marital Studies Institute, and as an Individual Psychotherapist with the Arbours Association. She has now retired from clinical practice and is engaged on a study of some of the works of Henry James, of which this chapter forms a part. *The Invisible Matrix*, which she co-edited with Pauline Hodson, was published by Karnac in 2000.

Francis Grier is an Associate Member of the British Psychoanalytical Society. He is also a Full Member of the Society of Couple

Psychoanalytic Psychotherapists. He is a Visiting Research Lecturer at the Tavistock Marital Studies Institute, where he was previously a Senior Marital Psychotherapist and Clinical Lecturer. He has a private practice for individuals and couples. He edited *Brief Encounters with Couples: Some Analytical Perspectives*, which was published by Karnac in 2001.

Monica Lanman is a Psychoanalytic Psychotherapist who works with individuals and couples. She is the Clinical Co-ordinator at the Tavistock Marital Studies Institute. She is the author of a number of papers on working with couples, and outcome research in couple psychotherapy. She is a Full Member of the Tavistock Society of Psychotherapists, the British Association of Psychotherapists, and the Society for Couple Psychoanalytic Psychotherapy.

Lisa Miller is a Consultant Child Psychotherapist in the Child and Family Department at the Tavistock Clinic. She is particularly interested in early development and for many years she organized the Under Fives' Service at the Tavistock. Until recently she was Chair of the Child and Family Department. She is the Editor of the *International Journal of Infant Observation*. She has been heavily involved in training child psychotherapists for many years.

Mary Morgan is a Senior Clinical Lecturer and Couple Psychotherapist at the Tavistock Marital Studies Institute and a founder member of the Society of Couple Psychoanalytic Psychotherapists. She has taught extensively in this country and abroad on the theory and practice of couple psychoanalytic psychotherapy. She has a private practice in psychoanalytic psychotherapy and is a candidate at the Institute of Psychoanalysis.

Viveka Nyberg is a Full Member of the British Association of Psychotherapists and has a part-time private practice in psychoanalytic psychotherapy. She is currently undertaking the clinical training in Couple Psychoanalytic Psychotherapy at the Tavistock Marital Studies Institute. She is the Arts Review Editor of the *BAP Journal*, and she has active interest in training and supervision.

Joanna Rosenthall is a Senior Marital Psychotherapist and Clinical Lecturer at the Tavistock Marital Studies Institute. She also has a private practice. At TMSI she used to be the Organizing Tutor for the Couple Psychotherapy Training Programme. More recently, she has focused on developing training and clinical work with couples within the public sector.

Stanley Ruszczynski is a Principal Adult Psychotherapist at the Portman Clinic (Tavistock and Portman NHS Trust, London), an outpatient forensic psychotherapy clinic. He is a Full Member of the British Association of Psychotherapists and is in private practice as a psychoanalytic psychotherapist. He was previously a senior clinician at the Tavistock Marital Studies Institute, holding the posts of Deputy Director and both Clinical and Training Co-ordinator, and is a Full Member of the Society of Couple Psychoanalytic Psychotherapists. He has edited and co-edited four books, including *Intrusiveness and Intimacy in the Couple* (Karnac, 1995) and *Psychotherapy with Couples* (Karnac, 1993), and is the author of over twenty book chapters and journal articles. He is currently the Joint Editor of the *Journal of the British Association of Psychotherapists*.

Margot Waddell is a Member of the British Psychoanalytical Society. She works in private practice and is a Consultant Child Psychotherapist in the Adolescent Department, Tavistock Clinic, London. She teaches and lectures widely both in Britain and abroad. The second edition of her most recent book, *Inside Lives: Psychoanalysis and the Development of the Personality*, was published by Karnac in 2001.

There has been a long tradition associated with the Tavistock of working psychoanalytically with couples, dating from the formation of the Family Discussion Bureau in 1948. The present volume belongs at the heart of this time-honoured service. The editor and most of the contributors to *Oedipus and the Couple* are past or present members and associates of what, in 1993, became known as the Tavistock Marital Studies Institute.

The book reflects the experience and learning of this tradition, but its specific focus both extends and deepens marital work itself, and also makes an important contribution to wider areas of theory and of clinical practice. For, in revisiting the great Oedipus myth, as told by Sophocles and drawn on by Freud, the respective authors explore not only ways of working with oedipal issues as they arise in the clinical setting and with the cross-generational impact of such issues, but also some of the less well-worked aspects of the story. In doing so, they illuminate new dimensions of couple and family life, and the intricacies and obstructions that derive from negotiating or failing to negotiate the oedipal situation.

The supporting theory, as worked and reworked in successive chapters, is steeped in a broad range of psychoanalytic perspectives and raises some current and important questions. What, for example, determines the choice of a life-long partner? What are the internal conditions necessary for even contemplating such a choice? Other questions are ones that underlie not only work with couples, but also contribute important dimensions to the understanding of individual adult states of mind, children, adolescents, and families.

The distinctively focused chapters complement each other in rich and instructive ways, both theoretically and clinically, and also artistically and culturally. Between them they make an important contribution to a deeper understanding of the oedipal myth itself and to the field of couple therapy more generally.

Margot Waddell
Series Editor

Introduction

Francis Grier

For over 100 years the myth of Oedipus has been mined by generations of psychoanalysts for the insights it offers into the deep levels of the human mind. Following Freud, the emphasis for the most part has been on gaining understanding into the mind of the individual. Couple psychoanalytic psychotherapists find the theory of the oedipus complex as valuable as do their colleagues engaged in clinical work with individuals, and yet no book has been specifically devoted to this core subject. This book, then, is an attempt to remedy the situation and to fill an obvious gap. It is an attempt to think primarily about couples from the perspectives afforded by contemporary developments in theories of the oedipus complex. Foremost among these, and much quoted in the following chapters, is a publication that has gained almost classic status, *The Oedipus Complex Today* (Steiner, 1989), in which a leading group of Kleinian psychoanalysts show how the concept of the oedipus complex is still at the vital core of analytic work.

In the myth of Oedipus we are confronted with a number of couples. First, there is the couple of Laius and Jocasta, the king and queen of Thebes. They are immediately presented to us as a couple who cannot cope with a threesome relationship. As soon as their first child is born they feel under deadly threat; their equilibrium is fatally undermined. A catastrophe is foreseen. The myth does not tell us whether they had been content as a twosome, but they certainly feel they do not have the resources to cope with the far more complicated emotional situation when two becomes three. As Canham (2003) illustrates, it seems the parents could not cope with their infant son's projections of envy and jealousy and murderous hatred. Or, perhaps, it was their own projections of these emotional qualities into their son and into their new threesome relationship that brought about a situation of such intensely persecutory anxiety that the couple felt they could no longer tolerate it. They appear not to have been able to think about the situation; to allow the more difficult and complex relationship to compel them to develop emotional maturity in response to its demands. Instead, they felt driven to drastic action to wipe out the hated threesome. They attempted to avert what they felt to be certain catastrophe by trying forcibly to turn the clock backwards, to go back to their previous twosome situation. In order to do this, however, they had to commit murder, which was their conscious intention when they commanded the shepherd to expose Oedipus on the mountainside. The myth goes on to tell of Oedipus's survival. If we allow ourselves to imagine that their strategy had succeeded, and that the baby Oedipus had actually been killed, we can see that it is very unlikely that Laius's and Jocasta's long-term plan of returning to an idyllic twosome could actually have succeeded, due to the appalling persecutory guilt from which they would undoubtedly have suffered. Presumably, they would then have conspired for the rest of their lives to erect increasingly manic and possibly psychotic defences against actually knowing in depth and owning what they had done.

So, even in its very opening, the Oedipus myth evokes in detail how appalling the dilemma of going from two to three can appear; how some couples feel inescapably driven towards drastic measures, including the enormous temptation to try violently to turn the clock of development backwards, and yet how impossible in psychic reality it is for their attempt to be successful.

The culmination of the myth famously concerns the tragic adult couple of Oedipus and Jocasta. They believe themselves to be happily married, and indeed produce children apparently without too much emotional turbulence. However, they gradually make the discovery that in fact they are an incestuous couple, and that therefore what had previously had the appearance of integrity and love had all the while actually been based on denial, lies, deceit, greed, jealousy, hatred, arrogance, envy, murderousness, and possessive lust. These revelations lead inexorably to the tragic outcome. This climax of the narrative illustrates the universal tendency to "turn a blind eye" (Steiner, 1993, Chapter 10) to what we do not want to know. It also evokes the terrifying unconscious phantasy that, although we may think we have successfully broken free from our families of origin in choosing our sexual partners, we may be duping ourselves. At a deeper level, perhaps we are merely employing strangers to stand in for father, mother, brother, sister— those closest family members we "really" desire incestuously. For some couples, the breaking through into consciousness of this underlying phantasy, perhaps through dreams, can be devastatingly shocking, and can be felt to threaten their adult relationships with catastrophe. Often enough, such couples feel compelled to employ extreme defensive measures, such as stopping all sexual contact, or only having sex "illicitly", out of the marriage (paradoxically felt unconsciously to be more, not less, "licit", because such relationships would be with persons felt *not* to represent close family members), or getting into a cycle of regularly divorcing and marrying new partners.

There is, however, another adult couple in the myth that is virtually never commented upon—the king and queen of Corinth. They were the childless couple to whom the shepherd brought Oedipus, whom they then adopted and brought up. There are no details about this part of Oedipus' life. However, the story implies that they were a stable enough couple and that he was happy enough with them because, on hearing that the Oracle had foretold that he would kill his father, Oedipus chose to leave Corinth in order to forestall and frustrate the prophecy and spare the man he thought to be his father.

So we have two arenas of couple functioning, located in two different cities—the apparently well-functioning couple in Corinth, and the pathological couples in Thebes. I suggest that the myth splits apart two psychological levels that actually belong together. The "Corinthian" is the more externally orientated, more rational,

more reality-based, though often more superficial, level of functioning. The "Theban" is the deeper, much less conscious, more
irrational and instinctual level, containing the more intense currents
of love and hate. All couples could be viewed as having "Corinthian" and "Theban" dimensions. What makes each couple different and particular is the greater or lesser intensity of the different
elements of these two levels of functioning. All couples need to
achieve at least some minimal degree of "Corinthian" functioning,
otherwise they would not be able to function at all as a couple. The
vast majority of couples aspire to achieve stability and good enough
day-to-day functioning in the external world. But this level in isolation can be rather dry and unimaginative, at worst dull and boring.

Perhaps this level also always involves at least some measure of
semi-conscious deception of self and other, represented in the myth
by the Corinthian royal couple's not disclosing to Oedipus that they
were his step-parents. Instead, they fostered the illusion—perhaps
more comforting for themselves as well as for him—that they were
his real parents. Margaret Rustin has suggested (personal communication) that perhaps what Oedipus feared, and was protecting his
adoptive parents from when he decided to leave Corinth, was his
own hatred of them for deceiving him and not disclosing his true
identity—thereby robbing him of his true story. The relationship
appears to have been a dangerously idealized one, of the defensive
"happy families" variety, not a truthful one that was strong enough
to contain the painful and conflictual emotional realities of its
members.

Inner emotional and imaginative life comes from the "Theban"
level but, somewhat like Pandora with her box, most couples
discover that when they wish to help themselves to the pleasures of
love they get a lot more than they bargained for. They get embroiled
in currents of love imbued with a passionate intensity that can
threaten to devour them and, much as they might wish to enjoy
love without hate, hatred nevertheless insists on coming out of the
box too. The eruption of these explosive feelings can, and theoretically, should, promote growth and development in the couple as
they try to face these difficult challenges, coming together to think
and struggle over how to resolve them over time. But there has
probably never been a couple whose emotional functioning has not,
from time to time, been severely rocked and at least dented by such

challenges, and this will always result in some symptoms expressive of this internal turbulence in their external functioning.

It seems, moreover, that the sum of a couple is more than the addition of its parts. Even when there are just two people involved, there already exist, on what one might call an elemental level, at least potential conflicts between a view of the partnership as comprising two "free" individuals on the one hand, and a view of the partnership as an entity of its own—an item, a couple—on the other. The needs and the rights of the partners as individuals and as a couple will always be potentially in tension with each other.

One of the most common sources for such disruptions is the arrival of children, when the couple expands to become a threesome. Such was Laius's and Jocasta's initial situation. But the troubling third party need not be a person. Each partner, over time, may feel moved to take up new interests or develop particular aspects of their personality. The new interest or development can be experienced by the other partner like a third party, often enough like a symbolic child, which comes between the couple and threatens the closeness, intimacy, and exclusiveness of their relationship, opening the door to hatred and jealousy.

Just as Oedipus wished to spare the man he thought was his father, and so took avoiding action but, in fact, was unable to avoid fulfilling the Oracle, so it often happens within couples that a partner will have intimations that the particular current developing in his or her mind—a new job, a new interest, a new friend—has the potential to unsettle or even damage the relationship. Evasive action is taken, designed to lessen the impact of the new development, or even to stop it in its tracks. However, the very fact that there has been a movement in the soul means that the clock can never quite be put back. Many couples find that, even if they have succeeded superficially in putting the brakes on any external developments that they fear might disturb the equilibrium of their partnership, it is precisely that balance which, at a deeper internal level, has nevertheless been unsettled. Of course, on many occasions brakes are not applied, and couples find themselves thoroughly destabilized by the actual developments that they have put into motion in space and time, and that have thrown them into disarray.

Nor is it is just the developments of individuals that threaten the couple's equilibrium. It can happen *vice versa*, *mutatis mutandis*. The

developmental movement can happen within the couple dimension, and it can be the individuals who feel threatened. A very
common example would be when there arises in the couple a feeling that the time is organically approaching for them to begin to
have children, although each of the individual partners is still
wedded to his/her individual life and, indeed, to each other as
exclusive partners. Within such couples, each partner may feel
threatened by the idea of a baby, whom they fear would undermine
all this, including their being the other's exclusive partner. Love
would have to be shared with a child, which can intensify narcissism and bring up feelings of jealousy and fears of exclusion, and
can also stimulate sadistic excitement about the possibility of
making a weak third party suffer. Defences mount against such
horrible feelings even before a child has been conceived, and the
irony is that the two individuals can collude and cooperate in such
defences, as it were *against* the desires and intentions of the very
couple that they themselves comprise. One might wonder, for
example, whether this was a hidden part of Laius's and Jocasta's
dilemma: that they wished to conserve the narcissistically gratifying aspects of their individual sexual relationship, but hated and
resisted its developmental, procreative couple aspect. When the
feared child arrived, their hatred and murderous hostility were
perhaps directed not only towards him, but also towards the
"developmental couple" dimension of their own relationship.

I would suggest that, in the broadest outline, the three adult
couples of the Oedipus myth present three elemental couple
themes. First, there is the move—developmental or potentially
catastrophic—from two to three. Second, the destabilizing effect of
learning through experience that one's adult emotional and sexual
relationships are intimately and inevitably connected with, indeed
map more or less closely on to, one's earliest relationships of love
and hate with each of one's parents and siblings. Finally, there is the
need to construct a good-enough, reality-based mode of couple
functioning. This, however, if defensively disconnected from
contact with the deeper emotional currents of love and hate, may
become a dry wilderness, stifling life rather than promoting it.

The following chapters are sufficiently diverse for each to stimulate reflections and responses from readers in the particular area
upon which the author has chosen to focus. The authors share

enough common ground—broadly speaking, a contemporary Kleinian/object-relations psychoanalytic base—for readers to feel that there is also enough of an underlying unity to facilitate meaningful links between ideas and themes in different chapters.

The ten chapters have been organized into three sections. The first three chapters, by Mary Morgan, Stanley Ruszczynski, and Andrew Balfour, are primarily theoretical. The second section comprises chapters by Margot Waddell, Viveka Nyberg, Sasha Brookes, and Monica Lanman, who make use of artistic and cultural themes from the worlds of literature and film to explore oedipal couple issues. The final section consists of chapters by Lisa Miller, Joanna Rosenthall, and myself, and these are specifically clinical. The manifest focus in most chapters is on the couple, but there are variations on this theme. Margot Waddell examines how individuals ripen developmentally to the point where they can look for and engage with another person to form a couple, a point also central to Mary Morgan's chapter. Sasha Brookes and Viveka Nyberg explore the developments of a girl and a boy, respectively, whose disturbed and unconventional youths are characterized by their forming the third point in differing triangles with parental and quasi-parental couples to the point where each of them, too, might be ready, as a young woman and a young man, to participate, or avoid such participation, in forming a couple of their own. Lisa Miller's chapter focuses on all three elemental players together— both parents and child—in the oedipal drama as they presented themselves to her in differing clinical situations.

Whenever the authors have made use of clinical material, they have restricted themselves to using only those aspects of their patients' cases that are strictly relevant to the particular themes under discussion, and they have disguised the material as far as is possible while conserving necessary and salient features.

I think it will be seen that the authors repeatedly find themselves investigating the ramifications of the oscillating, and never entirely comfortable, relationship between the "Corinthian" and "Theban" levels in couples' functioning, and how the three broad problem areas are repeatedly raised, albeit in infinitely varied and particular manifestations. Conflicts are engendered when there is movement from two towards becoming three; the disturbing emergence of very early "incestuous" desires and hatreds, and there is a constant pull from, and flight towards, a so-called sensible and rational way of relating (which never quite delivers what it promises), away from feeling tilted in the direction of emotional drought or tilting in the other direction, towards being flooded with too much and too intensely turbulent and potentially destructive emotion.

CHAPTER ONE

On being able to be a couple: the importance of a "creative couple" in psychic life[1]

Mary Morgan

> "The idea of a couple coming together to produce a child is central in our psychic life, whether we aspire to it, object to it, realise we are produced by it, deny it, relish it, or hate it"
>
> Britton, 1995, p. xi

Couples coming for therapy show us just how difficult it can be to develop and sustain an intimate, adult couple relationship. This begs the question, what is an intimate, adult couple relationship? Clearly some important earlier psychic developments occur that make it possible to become a couple. In my opinion, a crystallization of these psychic developments occurs, which becomes a part of the individual's psychic structure and helps to sustain him or her in a couple relationship. I shall refer to this as the internalization of a "creative couple" (Morgan & Ruszczynski, 1998). This development brings about a state of mind and way of relating, to oneself and to the other, that is a change from earlier kinds of psychic development. Because of the vagaries of life the psychic development may or may not be manifested in an actual couple relationship. Without this psychic development

9

couples in a relationship have difficulties, or the relationship is severely limited.

My intention in this chapter is twofold. First, it is to make explicit the process of psychic development as I understand it, and illustrate how two particular areas—the negotiation of the oedipal situation and adolescence—are crucial precursors to the development of a capacity to form part of a creative couple. I will also address the anxiety involved in psychic change.

My second intention is to describe key aspects of a creative couple state of mind and way of relating to another. In particular, I suggest that once an individual is part of an intimate adult couple relationship, if this development has taken place, then the creative couple as a psychic object can be turned to as a "third position" (Britton, 1989, p. 87), to help the individuals sustain their relationship when it is vulnerable. I hope also to show how creative this relationship can be, both internally and as part of a relationship with another; and how, through this relationship itself, further psychic development is possible.

Epistemophilia and the couple in psychic development

First, I will try to put the development of a creative couple as a psychic object within the context of psychic development as a whole. From the beginning of life the infant is struggling to make sense of experience and has an innate expectation of there being an object. Klein (1930a,b) stressed Freud's (1916–1917) assertion of an epistemophilic instinct, the urge to know or understand, as a component instinct of the libido. In her view, all instinctual urges involved objects, external or internal (Klein, 1952a). In her work with young children she could see inhibitions of epistemophilia and consequent learning difficulties, because the frustration that stimulated the urge to know could also give rise to sadistic impulses inhibiting it. Bion (1962b) saw the epistemophilic instinct in terms of the emotional links between objects, which he formulated as being either 'L' (loving), 'H' (hating), or 'K' (the wish to know the other). He described truth and understanding as food to the mind. Similarly, Britton conceives of the desire for knowledge as existing alongside love and hate: "Human beings have an urge to love, to hate, to know, and a desire to be loved, a fear of being hated and a wish to be understood" (Britton, 1998a, p. 11).

These theories about the human being encompass the idea of an infant who is trying to make emotional links with an object, and to make sense of experience from the beginning of life. Although the newborn infant is not fully aware of the mother as a separate object, it does seem that the infant is born with an innate preconception of there being an object and, therefore, of coupling or linking. The idea of there being an object is very important because it means that there is, in the baby's mind, the idea of an "other" into which something can be evacuated, from which something can be taken in, or with which he can split off or link up. Following this, as Money-Kyrle (1971) has stated, it is also probable that the idea of a couple coming together sexually is derived from innate knowledge. At the beginning of life the infant seeks the mother's breast, the nipple and the mouth forming a vital link, both real and symbolic. There is a development of this imperative later in life in the drive to create a sexual couple, symbolized and sometimes actualized by the link between penis and vagina. From this beginning of linking up with an object (the mother) to linking up with another in an intimate adult relationship, much changes and has to be struggled with and negotiated. The important point about this model of development is that there is a process in human development where changes occur using what is already known, albeit often in an entirely new configuration. It also places psychic development within the context of a relationship.

Physiological changes in the individual and environmental responses stimulate psychic development, but such development may also be resisted. It may be possible to form an adult couple relationship without the development that occurs through relinquishing the primary object and negotiating the oedipal situation, but it will be fraught with difficulties. Intimacy, for example, instead of being based on knowledge of the reality of the separateness of the other, and the wish really to know the other, can be based on an expectation of omnisciently knowing the other and/or being known by the other; an experience closer to intrusion (Fisher, 1995; Morgan, 1995). Many couple relationships contain aspects of a regressive wish to be the infant with a mother who can provide everything; emotional, physical, and mental.

The oedipal situation

From Freud onwards, psychoanalysis has fruitfully employed the myth of Oedipus to show the complex centrality of the primary triangular relationship between a mother, a father, and a child. That relationship is considered to be crucial in psychological development because the meanings and patterns the child experiences in that situation are likely to influence all subsequent relationships made in the journey through life.

What is it that is so significant about this early triangular relationship? The child is involved in a nurturing relationship with a mother and with a father, and in a relationship with the mother and father as a couple, including their sexual relationship and their capacity to produce new life. (This is no less true in the situation of an absent mother or father, or in the absence of the actual parental relationship.) By having a relationship with a mother and/or father, coming to observe and, if all goes well, to tolerate the special link between the parents, the child becomes aware of the experience of being included and excluded, and of there being different types of relationships. He also learns that there are generational boundaries (Britton, 1989). In other words, it has a structuring role in the personality. In coming to tolerate these vagaries of relating, the child has to contend with an affront to his or her narcissism and omnipotence. The child is not always at the centre of good relationships, and is needy of something that is creative and outside him or herself which, if his envy and narcissism can bear it, he can draw on. It is only by relinquishing the omnipotent phantasy of becoming part of a sexual couple with mother or father, and by recognizing and tolerating the special link between them, that the child will introject the parents-as-a-couple as a psychic object. The seed of the possibility of forming his or her own adult sexual couple relationship is sown.

As indicated earlier, working through the oedipal situation does not simply enhance the capacity to form a couple relationship but contributes in an essential way to a growing, intrinsic knowledge of what being part of a couple means. There are many aspects of this. Facing the oedipal situation requires the capacity to manage loss, as the idea that one could be the grown-up partner to either parent, and that one could prevent the parents being a couple together, has to be relinquished. If not achieved, it will be impossible to fully invest in one's own intimate couple relationship. Couple psychotherapists frequently see couples in which one or both partners are still too enmeshed in a relationship with a parent, either as primary object, or as an oedipal object. In this situation there is a lack of emotional investment in the spouse, and the children can be drawn into a relationship with a parent as support or confidant, severely undermining the marriage and the children's own oedipal development. If the boundary around the parental couple's relationship is accepted, it becomes possible to see the difference between the parents as a couple and the child's relationship to the parent. Later in adulthood the situation is reconfigured, as the individual becomes part of an intimate couple and can bear to exclude the children from aspects of the relationship. It is easier, not simply because of having had that experience in relation to the parents as a couple but because the experience is internalized, effecting all kinds of other developments—physiological as well as psychic—occurring in the individual. As Money-Kyrle describes it:

> Where there has been a favourable development, and the concept of the first good object is well established, together with the capacity to remember it with love, there is far less difficulty in being able to recognise the parental relation as an example of the innate preconception of coitus as a supremely creative act—especially if this is reinforced by the memory of a good relationship between the nipple and the mouth . . . and after a renewed period of mourning for the child–parent marriage that can never be, to internalise and establish a good concept of parental intercourse as the basis of a subsequent marriage which may in fact take place. [Money-Kyrle, 1971, p. 105]

Adolescence

The unconscious introjection of the parents as a couple in an object relationship to the child aids later psychic development, such as that occurring in adolescence. For example, this triangular configuration helps the adolescent take ownership of his own body and mind, because he can be the one who chooses to exclude himself from the couple and develop his own identity (Laufer, 1975). The typical adolescent then develops a sense of independence that is seen as the ideal. However, this is also a state of mind in which independence is diametrically opposed to the young infant's absolute dependence on the mother. If relationships are seen as one of these two kinds, utterly dependent or completely independent, then it is easy to see how such a state of mind would be extremely problematic, once in an adult couple relationship, should further development not occur. There is sometimes a tendency for the young adult to believe that his development is over and that he has succeeded in becoming "independent". Usually, this period of experiment with oneself and one's identity ends because of the impact of a new developmental imperative to form a couple. To some adults this can feel threatening, as if being part of a couple means the loss of this hard-won independence. It may therefore be avoided for some time, and sometimes forever. This adolescent idea of independence is an illusion because it denies a fact of life, namely that we all need help. Money-Kyrle (1971) conceptualizes this as the "recognition of the breast as a supremely good object", something that is innately known and discovered as part of experience, though something that can also be turned away from or denied. This is different from a regressive wish for dependence such as the infant had with mother. Both the idea of a relationship with the ideal object (mother) and the idealization of independence as in the adolescent state of mind are deeply problematic for the individual in a couple relationship.

The potential we have as individuals depends upon having the idea of being able to form a couple with another individual. Furthermore, though actually being part of a couple may be the desired state, not every individual chooses or achieves this due to any number of circumstances. More important is the belief in relationships as a source of creativity, and this may be concretely realized through becoming part of a couple from some other source; for example, through contact with colleagues, friends, and even good internal objects. The creativity of practising psychotherapists and psychoanalysts surely stems from an internal dialogue with such good objects.

Everyone struggles in coming to terms with the oedipal situation and, actually, the struggle seems to be an inevitable part of the experience. It is, moreover, not a once and for all development.

Negotiating the oedipal situation is not the same thing as resolving it, and difficulties in triangular situations (for example, becoming parents and incorporating a third into the couple), in being part of a couple, and in thinking, may continue in some form or emerge at times of stress. However, for some people there is a fundamental problem in this area of psychic development. Britton has described two areas of difficulty. The first is where the patient cannot allow a couple to come together in his or her mind, or in that of the analyst. The second is an "oedipal illusion", in which "the parental relationship is known but its full significance is evaded" (1989, p. 94).

The first situation Britton describes leads to serious difficulties in thinking, and is the diametrically opposite situation to the creative couple state of mind, in which it is possible to allow two thoughts to come together with a creative outcome. This process is reinforced by the experience of being in a relationship with another person with whom thinking can take place. The analytic situation that Britton describes is one in which any evidence that the analyst is having this experience inside his own mind, or between him and the patient, is felt as too threatening. He suggests that this is due to an earlier failure of maternal containment. The oedipal couple becomes equated with linking-up an idealized mother and her split-off hostility that threatens a precarious relationship to the primary object:

> The idea of a good maternal object can only be regained by split-ting off her impermeability so that now a hostile force is felt to exist, which attacks his good link with his mother. Mother's goodness is now precarious and depends on him restricting his knowledge of her. . . . The hostile force that was thought to attack his original link with his mother is now equated with the oedipal father, and the link between the parents is felt to reconstitute her as the non-recep-tive deadly mother. The child's original link with the good mater-nal object is felt to be the source of life, and so, when it is threatened, life is felt to be threatened. [Britton, 1989, p. 90]

Britton shows how difficult an analysis with such a patient is, because the patient needs a relationship with the analyst in which there is no psychic intercourse.

One might think that individuals who require this kind of relat-ing would find being in an intimate adult couple relationship extremely difficult. Often this is the case, or it becomes the case. However, sometimes, for a while, such a couple feel they have found a way of relating that relieves them of the anxieties they would experience if there were more psychic intercourse. This relationship requires the kind of intercourse described by Britton with his patient: "We were to move along a single line and meet at a single point" (1989, p. 88). I described this kind of relationship in a previous paper on "projective gridlock", from which I quote the example of Tom and Rachel:

> Rachel reflected on how she and her husband Tom always did everything together: they studied together, shared the same interests and operated as one. He would chose clothes for her, and when they went to parties Tom would speak for both of them. It never occurred to her that she might have a different point of view. She often felt that when they talked to each other, he would lose awareness of her presence, and it seemed that she, for her own unconscious reasons, had gone along with this. For a long time she felt quite content in this situation, except that she had never enjoyed sex with Tom. Tom said that looking back, what had felt awful about having sex with Rachel was that he worked out what she thought, felt, and wanted to such an extent that it was like having sex with himself; paradoxically, he had not really known what was going on for her at all. [Morgan, 1995, p. 44]

In the second situation Britton describes, the oedipal illusion is felt to protect the individual from the psychic reality of their phantasies of the oedipal situation. This evasion has serious consequences for the individual's mental and emotional life. The patient Britton describes had difficulty in bringing things together in his mind, which affected the clarity of his thinking, and there was a pervasive sense of unreality and feeling of unfulfilment in his life, as well as a quality of non-consummation in all his relationships and projects in life.

Some couples come for therapy with the problem that they are unable to move forward, to make a commitment together (live together or marry with the possibility of having children), or to separate. This can be quite a desperate problem, particularly if the female partner is reaching the end of her fertile years and if one partner longs for children.

One such couple presented their problem as an inability to decide to get married, sometimes expressed by James and at other times by Ellie. They felt they probably would marry at some point, but they didn't know when that would be or how they would be able to make the decision. Sometimes they felt comfortable in this position, and sometimes they felt in an acute state of anxiety. James was in his late forties and, although he had had previous long-term relationships and, in fact, had been engaged twice, he had never married. Ellie was in her early forties, and this was her first committed relationship. Neither of them had more than a rudimentary sense of a creative couple in mind, and they were frightened of repeating the dynamic of their respective parents' relationships, which were sado-masochistic in nature. In fact, their stalemated situation had a sado-masochistic aspect to it, of which they were unaware. There was a dynamic in the sessions that felt like treading water as, even when there was a sense of some intercourse taking place between them, or between them and me, it didn't seem to lead to any outcome. In one session they reported feeling that they had had a good discussion over the weekend with friends they had been away with, and they felt that this was progress. They had talked about the future, where they would live when they were married, in particular Ellie's hope that they could move closer to her sister, how many children they would have, including the fact they both secretly hoped to have a boy. The content of their discussion felt very new, and the therapist initially also heard this as progress. However, as they shared more of the details, the therapist became aware of how defensive this thinking was. It began to take on the quality of a flight away from the painful reality of not actually knowing whether they could be together or not in the future. It was as if they had by-passed that difficult problem and taken up residence in a fantasy world of being married, of being parents, and of being able to resolve things without conflict.

Many couples coming for help present similar difficulties rooted in problems with facing or working through the oedipal situation. The difficulties may be narcissistic in nature, as I have described in the "projective gridlock" (Morgan, 1995). In this situation, like Tom and Rachel, two different and separate people cannot come together, feeling that there is only room for one in the relationship. Alternatively, as with the "oedipal illusion" in James and Ellie's case, there is room for two, but they can produce nothing much between them, resulting in the feeling of non-consummation that Britton describes.

Anxieties aroused by development towards creative couple relating

The movement towards feeling oneself to be part of a couple in which two minds come together to create something can challenge both partners' narcissism and omnipotence, which are rarely, if ever, relinquished without regret, shame, sadness, and opposition. However, the internalization of the creative couple as a psychic object also provides the container within which the regression often associated with the first phase of the capacity to experience something new can be contained.

As with every new stage of psychic development, there are anxieties about giving up what previously felt known and secure in order to step into something new and not yet known. As discussed earlier, many individuals on the verge of making a committed relationship feel full of loss about giving up their independence and autonomy. There is tremendous anxiety about giving up what was previously regarded as being the achievement of a "mature" position. This may be because, following the earliest developments as part of a mother–baby couple, all subsequent developments have been largely about becoming more separate and independent, and the achievement of this relative independence is often felt to constitute maturity. Becoming part of a couple again often stirs up anxieties about losing this independence, raising fears of having to fit in, and feelings that it will not be possible to be fully oneself in a relationship. Some couples come for help in a battle, each wanting to hold on to their omnipotent individuality, and seeing a relationship as a situation where their partner should fit into their view of how things should be. At its most extreme, such couples have no idea that a relationship could be anything else.

Building on Klein's work, Bion (1970) has conceptualized how changing one's way of thinking and relating involves dismantling previous views and theories, which can have the quality of a psychic catastrophe—a going to pieces (Grier, Chapter 10, herein). In Klein's (1946) terms, this is a move into the paranoid–schizoid position. The subsequent reforming of a new set of views and theories is a synthesizing move into what Klein described as the depressive position (Klein, 1935, 1940). Creative effort can therefore be viewed as a process, on a small scale, of movements to and from the paranoid–schizoid and depressive positions. The tolerance of a degree of disintegration, without resorting to omnipotent, primitive defence mechanisms, or turning back to a previously held position, is essential for creative thinking and living. At each point of development, fluctuations between the paranoid–schizoid and depressive positions will occur.

Britton (1998) develops these ideas, describing the process of moving from the depressive position to what he calls a post-depressive position. This entails moving from a situation of integrated understanding into a new situation of uncertainty and incoherence, a new paranoid–schizoid position, before moving on to a new and, as yet, unimaginable resolution incorporating the new facts; a new depressive position. Ruszczynski (1995) has referred to this, in terms of the couple relationship, as allowing inevitable and necessary regressions, at times towards more narcissistic relating, even in a couple relationship that has the capacity for more mature relating.

Both these writers are describing the fact that regressive states of mind and behaviour are not to be considered simply as psychopathological states, nor as only the products of disruptions caused by life transitions and environmental impingement or traumas, but that such states are unavoidable, even necessary, as a result of the inevitability of psychic disruption occurring at points of new learning and growth. Once the new learning is established, an internal reintegration takes place and there can then be a move forward to a new depressive position.

Paul and Anna, married with a young baby, had fallen into a pattern familiar to many couples seeking help, in which they were leading quite separate and independent lives. The husband was very involved in his work, a new business he was developing, and the wife was very involved with their baby, who had been conceived after several years of infertility treatment. It was his affair with a close friend of hers, shortly after the birth of their child, which exposed something between them and led them to apply for therapy. They were both sceptical about therapy. Anna had once had counselling in connection with the infertility problems but hadn't found this helpful. Paul thought therapy would be about putting him on the right track and imposing a bland alternative to his more exciting, though (he also felt) destructive, existence.

In the early sessions, Paul was brutally honest to Anna, saying that he wasn't in love with her any more and that he was unsure if he wanted to stay in the relationship, though he felt devoted to their baby. Anna was extremely hurt and angry with Paul. However, at this stage she was much closer than he was to a belief in the possibility of their establishing a more creative couple relationship. She dealt with his rejection by becoming emotionally and sexually withdrawn. They both sought refuge from their painful situation, he in his work, and she in a rather idealized relationship with their baby.

In the course of the therapy it became apparent that there had been rejection upon rejection from the beginning of the relationship. One partner would risk showing vulnerability and great need of the other, and the second partner, relieved of these feelings via projection of them into the first partner, would turn away with renewed feelings of self-sufficiency and independence. One of the things that contributed to the shift in this couple's way of relating was their feeling of dependence on the therapist, which took them both by surprise. On one occasion the therapist had to cancel a session at short notice. In the following session the couple denied that this event mattered at all, nor did it matter if they had to miss a session for any reason. The therapist felt, though, that they had been quite disturbed by the event. It was only several sessions later, when the issue came up in relation to something else, that the couple could let themselves, and the therapist, know how angry they had been. Once their need for another could be grasped, initially in relation to the therapist, they began to risk being more open with each other. Both began to share very deep anxieties about their inadequacies in a number of areas, particularly in relation to sex.

As the couple began to feel safer with the therapist and with each other, they discovered something that neither had been able to envisage earlier. Simply put, they began to feel that they had a "relationship"; a third that they were invested in nurturing, but that also contained them. They were, of course, still sometimes in conflict, particularly when they felt let down by each other. However, this conflict began to be contained within their relationship, and was less at risk of being acted out outside the relationship in an affair, or inside the relationship in emotional withdrawal. They also discovered that conflict, if containable, could lead to solutions. Paul came to understand that only when he did not have the "relationship" was he capable of destructive acting out, as he had done in becoming involved in the affair. At the same time he rued the loss of his earlier freedoms, which were accompanied by a phantasy of not being in a relationship. Through mourning this loss he became able to discover something else—a deep love for his wife. Towards the end of therapy, the couple had been to see a play in which one of the central themes was about the exploitation of indigenous peoples. Suddenly, in the middle of the play Paul had a revelation. He realized he had treated the woman he'd had the affair with as a "lesser human being", summoning her when he felt depressed or inadequate and, at the same time, debasing his wife and himself. When he'd been with his mistress he was in a state of mind in which he no longer felt contained by the relationship with Anna.

As the end of the therapy approached, Paul said to his wife, "Look, if we're going to stay together as a couple, there may be difficult things we'll have to face together. Maybe we won't be able to have more children, we'll both get older—there may be illnesses, and there will be losses." This couple could only contemplate facing these facts of life because of the strength derived from discovering a creative couple relationship, which provided a container, in the sense that they could imagine facing difficult things.

As is often the case, this couple had come for therapy at the point of psychic disintegration, in the sense described by Bion and Britton. Their previous way of being was no longer functioning adequately as a container. They had to let it go, without yet knowing what a future different psychic state could be.

Aspects of creative and non-creative relating

I will now describe some aspects of creative and non-creative relating that manifest in the couple relationship. My purpose is to illustrate the movement between more, and less, creative relating in any one couple, and to show how some couples find themselves situated much more in one position or the other. This may prove useful diagnostically, and it also relates to the aim of couple psychoanalytic psychotherapy, which could be conceptualized as helping the couple towards more creative couple relating. Perhaps I should first reiterate that the "creative couple" is primarily a psychic development, one in which it is possible to allow different thoughts and feelings to come together in one's mind, and for something to develop out of them. This capacity obviously has a major impact on an actual couple relationship. If one can allow this kind of mating within oneself, it becomes more likely that one can allow it to occur between oneself and one's partner. I wish to clarify that, when writing about the creative couple state of mind, I refer to a level of psychic functioning of which individuals become capable, even though they may not always achieve it. Fisher's (1999) conceptualization includes an oscillation between what he calls the psychic state of marriage and something more narcissistic. What marks this out from a more overall narcissistic relating is that this creative couple state of mind has been discovered, and can be recovered.

The relationship as the third position

The development of the depressive position goes hand in hand with the oedipal situation, as Britton (1998) has so clearly pointed out. With the awareness of mother as a separate object, with relationships that can exclude the child, comes development of triangular space and three-dimensional thinking. As well as being an observer of a couple from which he is excluded, the child can start to develop an idea of himself in a relationship excluding a third, and being observed by a third. Eventually this third becomes internalized as an aspect of himself, the capacity to observe himself in his own relationship. This development, what linguistics calls the "meta" position, is crucial for the individual in an adult, couple relationship.

In the creative couple state of mind, the concept of the relationship provides a third position for the two individuals in the relationship. The capacity for a third position is central to the creative couple, and the oedipal triangle now becomes a template for understanding oneself as part of a couple. The oedipal situation provided the opportunity to develop one's capacity to observe one's internal intercourse, and now the concept of oneself as a couple provides the vantage point from which to observe oneself in a couple relationship. When a breakdown occurs in one's relating to the other, one can take up the position of the relationship as a third, and observe oneself within the relationship (Figures 1 and 2).

In this position the different, or sometimes opposing, perspective of the other is not felt to obliterate one's own view, but can be taken in to one's psyche, and allowed to reside there and mate with one's own thought. In this way, the individual's psychic development is enhanced through an actual creative couple relationship with another person. This creativity becomes possible because a state of mind has been achieved in which two minds, as well as two bodies, can come together and create a third.

Simon and Karen, a young and very affluent couple with an eleven-year-old daughter and a nine-year-old son, approached therapy in utter despair. Simon thought his wife was so angry and irrational as to be on the point of madness. Karen was despairing of the fact that, in her eyes, her husband fell acutely short of her idea of what a husband should be. She had previously been married and it appeared that there had been little sexual contact in the relationship, which had lasted only a short time before her husband had left her. Although angry with her ex-husband, Karen held a conviction that, had it continued, this would have been the

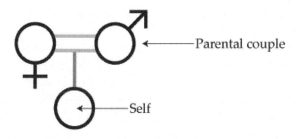

The oedipal triangle, at the end of a healthy development; the individual feels him/her self to be in a positive relationship to the parental couple and can experiment with occupying all the different roles either including or excluding the other(s).

Figure 1

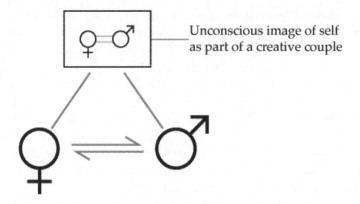

Unconscious image of self
as part of a creative couple

Each individual perceives him/her essentially to be part of a couple,
therefore, in the relationship, each feels 'contained' by a shared
unconscious concept - the creative couple.

Figure 2

ideal relationship. At the beginning of therapy, her disappointment
with what she and Simon had in comparison to her previous, idealized relationship fuelled her anger. It was only much later in the
therapy that the non-attainment of the ideal began to be mourned,
and Karen could become in touch with some of what she did have
with Simon.

There was a long phase in the therapy in which the couple had
no contact with the idea of a creative couple relationship, and therefore did not have the kind of relationship that they could turn to as
a third position. Consequently they rapidly became very dependent
on the therapist as a third party who could keep the relationship in
mind. The therapy was marked by a conflict in which Karen would
berate Simon for falling so far short of the mark, and Simon would
attempt to be reasonable and to pacify her. Karen related to her
husband as someone who should relieve her of pain, anxieties, and
depression. In order to do this he had to understand exactly how
she felt, and why she felt like it. Simon was a man who had difficulty in knowing about his own feelings, and frequently failed
adequately to understand those of his wife. This dynamic between
them, which was experienced time and time again in their relation-

ship, left Karen feeling she had no husband, no other to turn to, and left Simon feeling impotent and a failure. There was pressure on this relationship to be a more of an infant–mother coupling, set up as one of the partners to be contained by the other, rather than an adult sexual relationship in which the two individuals can come together and think.

There was probably a narcissistic structure in Karen that provided her with an illusion that actually she could manage by herself, a situation common in individuals seeking help as part of a couple. This was, of course, by definition, an anti-relationship, psychically quite active, which could manifest itself quite destructively between the couple. The relationship was founded on an attack on relating. Against the background of often being emotionally let down by her husband, Karen would also, on occasion, actively destroy those times when Simon was capable of offering her something that she wanted or needed. Becoming aware of Simon's capacity to meet some of her requirements terrified her, because she experienced knowing about her dependence as an attack on her illusory self-sufficiency. At worst she felt this to be tantamount to an annihilation of her self.

Karen described, in a desperate way, how Simon was simply "not there". In the consulting room this was, at first, rather difficult to see. Simon presented himself as a reasonable man, on the face of it always trying to do things and to make things better for Karen. However, in a more fundamental sense, Karen was right; her husband was not there for her. Simon didn't let her know how he felt about anything, and sometimes was quite secretive about what he actually did contribute to the relationship. This increased her difficulties in a number of ways. She didn't have someone else's feelings to come up against, to take into account and to act as a limiting factor to her own feelings; she didn't have the opportunity to be the one able to think about him when he was distressed, as she was always seen to be the irrational one; but, even more importantly, she felt that she was not in a relationship with another person.

Simon could understand some of this and its impact on his wife. The problem for him was that he did not feel in touch with his own feelings and anxieties, which were connected to his early experience of relating to an object similarly cut off from feelings. Moreover, he was so frightened of his feelings, which were powerful and violent—primitive because they had never been processed—that he was invested in leaving Karen with all the feelings in the relationship, and in unconsciously and sadistically allowing them to escalate. Therefore, although on the face of it Karen was the irrational one, the therapist was aware of how invested Simon was in getting Karen to express feelings that he was too frightened to contemplate in himself.

After quite some time in therapy moments slowly began to occur in which the couple began to discover their relationship as a resource. For example, later in the therapy, their son developed a condition that required a lot of medical intervention and would possibly require one of them to take a period of time off work, or even to leave their job. In a rare moment, instead of taking up their opposing positions on the subject, they were both able to own and share with each other their anxieties. They also began to get themselves into a third position, and to see how they had been dealing with their anxieties by attacking each other. They could then move towards something more supportive. It was an important experience for them to discover that this could lead to a creative solution as their collaborative thinking emerged—an outcome that neither had considered a possibility at the beginning.

The degree of conscious and unconscious relating

The way a couple deals with their emotions is an indication of whether or not they are relating as a creative couple. The couple relationship is a very emotional one, regardless of whether, or how, emotion is expressed. This is due to the intimacy of this relationship, which either breaks down, or threatens to break down, boundaries, including defences. Primitive emotions, such as dependency, envy, love, and hate, are evoked. In addition, earlier internal object relationships become re-enacted as the drive to work through unresolved inner conflicts takes hold.

It is not true that in the creative couple there is no fighting between the individuals. There will inevitably be differences, disagreements, frustrations, anger, and hatred. However, in the creative couple relationship there is a sense that the relationship can survive attacks that each individual makes on the other, and hope that, out of disagreement, understanding may eventually come. In this way the relationship is subjectively experienced as a resource, something the individuals in the relationship can turn to in their minds, with the whole being greater than the sum of the parts. This is tremendously helpful to a couple that is having a difficult time together because somewhere there is a belief that the relationship can withstand it. Of course, not all arguments have the potential to be creative, and sometimes it is quite the opposite. In the creative couple relationship, however, the individuals find it possible, enough of the time, to process their own emotional experiences and to think about them, sometimes with the help of their partner. This capacity for reflection, for being able to think about one's own feelings as well as a partner's, is, as described earlier, an important part of psychic development.

In what one might describe as a destructive argument there is the tendency to rid oneself of what feels emotionally unmanageable, and to project it into the partner. Intimate relationships are a fertile arena for projections. Partners are obvious objects into which to project, both because of their proximity and because the boundaries between intimate couples are more permeable. Many couples seek help in a state of mind where they feel unable to think about their own and their partner's unmanageable feelings, nor can they think about what is happening between them. They feel the impact of their own emotions, but are overwhelmed by them and, in this primitive state of mind, are unable to think about them. On top of this they often feel, like young infants, that the reason they are feeling so overwhelmed is because they are being attacked from outside by the partner. As described earlier, the idea holds sway that the partner is responsible for both one's happiness and one's unhappiness.

Psychic separateness

In a creative couple relationship it is possible to be psychically separate within the context of an intimate relationship. This is different from the early relationship between mother and baby. There, mother and baby are not psychically separate, and this is quite appropriate—in fact, this symbiotic relationship is a crucial part of psychic development, with the infant needing to be dependent on a mother to meet his needs. But, even for an infant, psychic

separateness soon becomes essential to his being and the development of his personality, as Winnicott pointed out:

> It is only when alone (that is to say, in the presence of someone) that
> the infant can discover his own personal life. The pathological alter-
> native is a false life built on reactions to external stimuli. When
> alone in the sense that I am using the term, and only when alone,
> the infant is able to do the equivalent of what in an adult would be
> called relaxing. [Winnicott, 1958, p. 418]

One of the dilemmas many individuals encounter when they
become part of an intimate, adult relationship, is how to be psychically separate and, at the same time, intimate. If the developments
referred to earlier have not taken place, then the individual may
have the merged mother–baby model unconsciously in mind as a
mode of relating. Although I refer to this as a difficulty, it is of
course quite common for couples to seek and aspire to a merged
state of mind, feeling this to be the essence of being in love. However, true and sustaining love comes only with the disillusionment
of this idea of merger as the ideal. The relinquishment of the ideal
object goes hand in hand with the development of the wish really
to know the other, not by magically becoming "one", but from the
outside, with all the limitations and frustrations that this involves.
The feeling of merger in the being-in-love state is so powerful
because one feels just like the baby with mother, i.e. fused with an
ideal maternal object. If the ideal of merger can be relinquished,
then the attractions of difference can be discovered. Once the couple
has given up the idea of merger as the ideal that they have to strive
for, it becomes more possible from time to time to move into that
state spontaneously, for example during sex, and to enjoy the
intense feeling that it arouses; and it is also more possible to move
out of it again, without too much regret.

If, however, the ideal of merger is not relinquished, and yet
becomes harder to sustain, difficulties will arise in the relationship.
Sometimes the couple are quite aware of this problem, and one or
both describe the feeling of not having a separate existence within
the relationship. Most commonly, one partner feels that the other's
behaviour is responsible for his or her happiness. Conflict arises
around not being able to see the other as separate, as one partner

tries omnipotently to control the other, to make them into the kind of object they want or need them to be, or to impose their own version of reality on the other as if theirs is the only true version. The one, more or less tyrannically, requires of the other certain forms of behaviour so that life may be bearable.

Conclusion: a sense of containment

In this chapter I have tried to show how I understand psychic development as it relates to the couple; where it founders, and where, sometimes with the help of psychotherapy, the awareness of creative intercourse can be discovered or recovered.

In living through the oedipal situation the infant has the beginnings of an idea of a couple who together, as a function of their relationship, "contain" the baby (Bion, 1959, 1962a). What the child does with this experience and information goes through some transformations on the way to his or her developing the idea of a creative couple relationship. As an adult, this is encompassed in the idea of a couple relationship, which can contain not only actual children, but also, when needed, each partner in the relationship. It is also the beginning of the idea that this couple relationship can be creative, symbolized by the possibility of actual children, and realized through new thoughts, ideas, and other possibilities.

In the creative couple state of mind, the couple feels they have something to which they both relate, something they can turn to that can contain each of them as individuals. It is something they have in mind, and they can imagine the relationship as something that has them in mind. With couples in treatment it is observable both when this third element is absent and when it starts to develop. The latter can be a profoundly moving experience, as in the case of Paul and Anna.

Once this capacity to create a relationship is secure, it can then help contain the regression that inevitably arises at life transitions, at points of crisis or of new learning, or just in trying to manage the ups and downs of everyday life, all of which are likely temporarily to undermine more mature relating. It allows room for ambivalence and the toleration of the inevitability of conflict and tension. This is the kind of relationship in which creative solutions are sometimes possible—solutions that neither of the individuals would have imagined or found on their own. One can notice this development in couples in treatment, as in Simon's and Karen's case, when previously stuck situations become loosened up, as perhaps some things can be relinquished, and possibilities for different ways forward start to emerge.

Note

1. My thanks to Philip Stokoe, with whom I formulated the idea of a creative couple in psychic life in 1998. This formed the basis of a paper which Stanley Ruszczynski and I gave at The Tavistock Marital Studies 50th Anniversary Conference later that year.

CHAPTER TWO

Reflective space in the intimate couple relationship: the "marital triangle"*

Stanley Ruszczynski

> "The vital process that drives men and women to each other,
> to love each other, then create life, and thus achieve continu-
> ation of the human race Freud called the oedipus complex"
>
> Rey, 1994, p. 4

Britton's (1989) paper "The missing link: parental sexuality in the oedipus complex" has, in a short space of time, come to influence much psychoanalytic thinking and practice with individual patients. Britton delineates the significance of the infant's relationship not only to each of the parental couple individually, as mother and as father, but crucially to the parental couple *as a couple*, for individual psychic development. He develops Bion's (1962b) two-body, container–contained concept to that of a

---

*This is a revised version of a paper titled, "The 'marital triangle': towards 'triangular space' in the intimate couple relationship", first published in the *Journal of the British Association of Psychotherapists*, 34(3) Part 1, January 1998, and, in Italian, in *Interazioni: Clinica e Riecrca Psicoanalitica Individuo-Coppia-Famiglia Vol. 2 1996/8* (Naples 1997).

triangular space within which observation, reflection, and thinking can take place.

In this chapter I want to show how, in my view, the conceptualization offered in Britton's paper is equally useful in both theoretical thinking about, and psychoanalytic treatment of, couples. This is perhaps no great surprise, given that the nature of the intimate couple relationship is unconsciously determined by the nature of the two partners' relationships to their parents: imbued with projections, internalized, and enacted in their internal and external object relationships (Dicks, 1967; Ruszczynski, 1992). I will briefly review some of the central concepts set out in Britton's paper, and show how they may be applied to offer further understanding of the dynamics in the intimate, adult couple relationship that, as a result, provides an arena for continued reworking of unresolved oedipal dilemmas.

Waddell has described how, in late adolescence, re-working oedipal issues is of central significance to a person's eventual capacity to enter into and sustain an intimate couple relationship. She says that probably at no other developmental stage other than infancy and young childhood are the demands of the oedipus complex as prominent as during adolescence. Waddell states that "among the central tasks of the period are those of separation, of tolerating frustration, of living with disillusionment, of struggling between the pleasure principle and the reality principle" (Waddell, herein, p. 75). What strikes me about this description is that very similar tasks seem to be present in the process of sustaining a healthy couple relationship. These issues concern separateness and attachment, disillusionment in relation to the original and necessary idealization of the chosen partner, struggles about what is desired of the other and of a shared life, what is possible in reality, and, inevitably, frustration, relinquishment, and the capacity for ambivalence. Waddell recognizes that these struggles are, of course, lifelong. She writes, quoting Britton, that they have to be "reworked in each new life situation, at each stage of development and with each major addition to experience or knowledge" (Britton, 1992, p. 38; in Waddell, herein, p. 74).

I want to explore how engaging in a couple relationship offers the partners an opportunity to rework oedipal issues and potentially develop the *capacity to be a couple*, a capability fundamentally dependent on the reasonable achievement of depressive position capacities. The capacity to be a couple might, in itself, be seen as a developmental stage in its own right (Morgan, 2001; Morgan & Ruszczynski, 1998), as a result of which the possibility of true intimacy might emerge (Fisher, 1995).

As stated explicitly by Britton, but inherent in the writings of Klein, her colleagues, and those who followed her, the link between the oedipal situation and the depressive position, and hence the capacity for more mature object relationships, is well recognized. Britton states it simply: "we resolve the oedipus complex by working through the depressive position and the depressive position by working through the oedipus complex" (Britton, 1992, p. 35). This tandem resolution, though a life-long struggle and never actually completed, creates the capacity for, and hence the possibility of, healthy relationships—including intimate couple relationships.

A detailed description of what exactly is meant by mature relating is not easy to give but, following Money-Kyrle, it would certainly have to include the toleration of what he described as certain irrefutable facts of life. These are the reality of dependence, the multiple aspects of the oedipal situation, including the differences between the sexes and the generations, the supreme creativity of parental intercourse, and the inevitability of ageing and death (Money-Kyrle, 1971, p. 443). Inherent in all of these is the toleration of the loss of narcissism and omnipotence, the capacity to be included and to tolerate being excluded, knowing about one's loving and hating feelings, bearing guilt, and experiencing gratitude. These are aspects of depressive capacities that come to predominate against the pull of more paranoid–schizoid defences and functioning. The difficulties in making this transition mark the borderland between more narcissistic and more mature functioning. If found intolerable, various defensive mechanisms might be aroused, including perverse and sometimes violent resolutions involving sado-masochistic enactments in relation to both internal and external relationships (Ruszczynski, 2003).

To illustrate some of these dynamics, I shall give some brief details about Mr and Mrs Jones (as I will call them). They are an attractive and intelligent couple in their early thirties, who came for treatment because of a growing sense of non-specific discomfort, tension, and argumentativeness between them. They described an increasingly frequent oscillation between cooperative and loving contact with each other, and increasingly aggressive and explosively angry exchanges. They work in the same profession, though not together, and have a three-year-old child whose care they share by both working part-time.

From my first contact with them there was a rather disturbing sense that their marriage might be based on a narcissistic structure, with a very subtle but discernible struggle by each for dominance and control in their relationship. Both partners seemed to function significantly by splitting and projective identification; each trying to control the other, and fending off a perceived fear of being controlled. They were able to have periods of loving emotional contact, but these were usually brief, often highly sexual, and quickly followed by a scramble for a position of control and domination. Each seemed to be frightened of dependence but also feared being excluded, and for each, the other had to be little more than a narcissistic extension of themselves. Dismissal of the separateness and integrity of the other, often quite overtly in the service of gaining a sense of superiority and power, was a more common feature than cooperation.

In their professional lives each felt a sense of powerlessness and envy towards the other, again leaving them feeling threatened and, as a consequence, driven to attempt to gain a sense of dominance and superiority over the other. For example, Mrs Jones was beginning to have some of her work published and Mr Jones would often quietly, but in a very calculated way, undermine her achievements by questioning the worthiness of her material and ideas. At the same time, his wife often enviously challenged Mr Jones about his greater flexibility at work, one that she would dearly love to have. Both openly flaunted their own work situations and attacked that of the other.

Something similar took place in relation to the care of their child. Each argued that the other's parenting was poor—too rigid or too lax were the usual criticisms—and that he or she was the better parent. The shared parenting arrangement was quickly exposed as being highly competitive, based on a desperate wish to be seen as superior at parenting, and on an implied criticism of the other; rather than a result of considered, appropriate division of labour. There were also times when, in quite a distressing way for their child, each would desperately try to hand over the child to the other, feeling, it seemed, overwhelmed and threatened by his needs and demands and anxious to retain their own autonomy.

In the transference both Mr and Mrs Jones often related to me as if I were a wise sage whose every word was profound. Both would see me as a preferred partner, and I was competed for in the three-person dynamics of the consulting room, sometimes in quite blatant ways. Behind this idealization, however, lay barely hidden denigration and contempt, which was regularly exposed at the end of sessions. The couple would leave the consulting room and, outside the door, would noisily giggle and excitedly whisper to each other, positioning me as the "listener in" to their apparently enviable intimacies and pleasures. In the counter-transference I initially found myself feeling seduced by one or the other of them, and would then feel shocked and disturbed by a sense of being suddenly rejected by their conspiratorial coming together on leaving the session. Occasionally, the couple would spend much of a session telling me in detail about their sexual activities over the previous weekend. It would be difficult for me to make any comments or observations without being experienced as if I was spoiling their pleasure, and I was forced into a position of being a witness to, and observer of, their intimacies and excitement. It was as if any form of coupling brought with it an excluded, envious victim.

We can see that, with this couple, pairing with another is greedily desired, and hence pursued, or feels threatening, and so is avoided. Relating to a pair is found to be unbearable because the pair is felt to be excluding and provoking of feelings of persecutory envy. The idealized contact or persecutory abandonment of me in the transference suggests a difficulty with the toleration of both dependence and separateness and difference. In the transference there appears to be either an idealized two-person relationship or an idealized couple with an abandoned and rejected child. The couple did have some capacity to join cooperatively, and they referred to that as being part of their marital history. But it seemed to be a manic coming together, as if constituting a desperate defence against the anxieties of an intrusive other, or a recognition of a separate other. It was rare that I heard about, or experienced in the consulting room, a real capacity to function or to think together as a couple made up of two separate people.

As their history unfolded in the treatment it became clear that the sense of disruption, anxiety about their status in their relationship and outside, and the growing argumentativeness and striving for control, had followed the birth of their child. Their capacity to sustain a reasonably benign and cooperative couple relationship was at best fragile, and became increasingly disrupted by anxieties over their interactions with each other and their child. For this couple the threesome relationship with their child marked a fracture in their capacities to function more cooperatively, and more paranoid functioning was beginning to emerge, with an increasing tendency towards sado-masochistic interactions.

In terms of family histories Mr Jones was an only child. His parents ran a business together and travelled abroad for work purposes, leaving him with an aunt and uncle and their four children. Mr Jones often felt marginalized, he said, both in his own home and when with his aunt and uncle and their children. Mrs Jones was the first-born, followed by a brother who was born when she was six years old. Her special place was dramatically disrupted by this unexpected (though for the parents very welcome) new arrival. For both Mr and Mrs Jones some of the residual dynamics of their respective early family lives seem to have been reactivated by the arrival of their child, resulting in each of them defensively turning to more narcissistic ways of relating.

It is not difficult to imagine that the intimate couple relationship will recreate some of the oedipal conflicts first experienced in childhood, but requiring continuing working through. Issues relating to dependence and independence, being included and excluded, sexuality, procreation, and the toleration of ageing and death are inevitably at the heart of all couple relationships. Much of the psychic working through of these realities takes place naturally, mostly unconsciously, in the everyday relationship of the couple. If this proves insufficient, and the couple find themselves seeking psychotherapeutic help, then their attention becomes consciously focused on these dynamics, both in their relationship to each other and in the transference–counter-transference relationship that develops.

Britton (1989) has shown that for the infant and child, psychic development requires the ability to relate not only to individual others (i.e., to each of the parents), but to others in a relationship (i.e., to the parental sexual couple). Coming to terms with the reality of this triangular oedipal situation leads to the developmental move from narcissistic to more mature object relationships and heralds, in the adult, the capacity for true intimacy. This capacity might be defined as the ability to tolerate both one's separateness and one's need to relate to a valued and separate other, a tension at the heart of every intimate couple relationship (Fisher, 1999; Ruszczynski & Fisher, 1995).

When two people join together to form a relationship, they do so substantially for unconscious as well as conscious reasons, via mutual projective and introjective processes and identifications that are sufficiently congruent to create a "marital fit". By accepting the other's unconscious projections, each partner gives the other an initial feeling of recognition and acceptance and, as a result, of attachment. By unconsciously creating an equilibrium in the mutuality of their projective and introjective identifications, the couple are likely to form a relationship on the basis of shared unconscious phantasies, defences, and conflicts—especially those relating to the internal couple—that become externalized and enacted in their marital relationship (Ruszczynski, 1992). A new opportunity is created for unresolved internal conflicts to emerge and be attended to, creating the possibility of further emotional development and growth.

Couple relationships can, of course, be used more defensively: one partner will be obliged to carry projected undesired or feared aspects of the other, with no real intention of re-introjecting them in some mediated form. Here, projective identification is used primarily for defensive evacuative purposes, in the way initially described by Klein (1946). For all couples some of the time, and for some couples all of the time, the nature of their interaction is such that they become psychically gridlocked (Morgan, 1995). Their relationship is in danger of becoming a psychic retreat (Steiner, 1993), unconsciously defending against the feared pain and anxieties associated with such emotional work.

All relationships are a complex and fluid mix of both developmental and defensive dynamics and interactions. The important issue is whether there is the flexibility within the structure to allow appropriate attention to both partners' individual needs, and to the needs of the relationship that they aspire to. The tension and conflict that this provokes is inherent in every intimate relationship.

It tests the partners' capacities to manage love and hate, be included and excluded, to give up idealization and tolerate ambivalence, and mourn that which has to be relinquished and lost.

Britton draws on Klein's (1945) theories of the early oedipal situation, and on Bion's (1962b) notion of container–contained. Britton highlights how the young infant, driven by natural curiosity, is confronted by a dim recognition of a *link* between the parents, and of a *difference* between the relationship each of them have with him and with each other. Theirs is a sexual relationship and it produces new babies, certainly so in phantasy even if no new babies are born (Segal, 1989). This knowledge has to become tolerable to the child's mind: otherwise it will give rise to feelings of abandonment, envy, and deprivation and may be defended against by more primitive or perverse solutions. If this knowledge can become tolerable and integrated, it heralds the relinquishment of narcissism and omnipotence, resulting in the possibility of maturer, whole-object relating, including the capacity for ambivalence and the essential task of mourning.

The toleration of this knowledge of the special link between parents provides the infant with the experience of an object relationship in which he is *not a participant*, but an "observer". This gives rise to a very important capacity required for healthy relating. Britton writes,

> A third position then comes into existence from which object relationships can be observed. Given this, we can also envisage *being* observed. This provides us with a capacity for seeing ourselves in interaction with others and for entertaining another point of view whilst retaining our own, for reflecting on ourselves whilst being ourselves. [Britton, 1989, p. 87]

The development and integration of the capacity for self-reflection and awareness of another, achievements of some substantial psychological maturity, also show a developing capacity for containment—to emotionally manage the complex varieties and vicissitudes of human relating. According to Britton,

> The closure of the oedipal triangle by the recognition of the link joining the parents provides a limiting boundary for the internal world. It creates ... a "triangular space" i.e., a space bounded by

the three persons of the oedipal situation and all their potential relationships. [Britton, 1989, p. 86]

Segal stresses a crucial difference between Britton's concept of triangular space and Bion's earlier description of the container and the contained. She writes,

> In the original situation the child is a participant and a beneficiary of that [container–contained] relationship. Recognizing the parental couple confronts him with a good container–contained relationship *from which he is excluded.* It confronts him with separateness and separation as part of the working through of the depressive position. [Segal, 1989, pp. 7–8, my italics]

It also introduces the infant to the reality of *different types of relationships,* some of which he will be included in, some of which he will be excluded from, and some of which he may create for himself in future.

I would like to suggest that Britton's conceptualization of triangular space might be *adapted* so as to be seen to have a potential for a *symbolic* existence within the intimate couple relationship. The triangle in the couple relationship—I have called it the "marital triangle"—is made of the two individuals of the partnership and *their relationship as the third element.* The relationship may be said to have a dynamic identity of its own, in addition to the identity of each of the two partners. Clearly, because the relationship is made up of these two same individuals, a symbolic triangle is being referred to rather than one that could be drawn between a child and two parents.

Kernberg discusses the notion of a couple relationship as an object in its own right. He describes how "the couple becomes the repository of both partners' conscious and unconscious sexual fantasies and desires and of their consciously and unconsciously activated internalised object relations". Consequently, the couple acquires *"an identity of its own in addition to the identity of each of the partners"* (Kernberg, 1993, p. 653, my italics). He describes, for example, how over time, the interaction of the partners' superegos results in the forging of a new system, which he calls the "couple's superego" (p. 653). He proposes that:

The enactment of the mature superego functions in both partners is reflected in each having the capacity for *a sense of responsibility for the other and for the couple*, of concern for their relationship, and of protection of the relationship against the consequences of the unavoidable activation of aggression as a result of the inevitable ambivalence in intimate relationships. [Kernberg, 1993, p. 655, my italics]

Kernberg is describing healthier relating, based on the internalization of a benign internal couple. In less healthy relationships, rigid sado-masochistic enactment between the partners in their interaction suggests the unconscious sharing of a more perverse relationship with the internalized couple, which is intrusive, humiliating, and based on coercion and subjugation. In both cases, however, there is an internal couple in the minds of the two partners with which they unconsciously identify, and which strongly influences the nature of the coupling they themselves produce.

The significant issue in relation to the couple relationship as an object in its own right is that, just as the child needs to learn to tolerate the fact that the parental relationship, at times, and for its own legitimate purposes, excludes him, so too the individual partners in an intimate relationship have to tolerate the fact that *for the purposes of their relationship* they may sometimes have to give up needs, interests, and aspects of themselves, and tolerate doing so, however ambivalently. As for the infant, for the adult partner too, this relinquishment has developmental potential. If one partner refuses to accept a projection (as happens occasionally in all but the most disturbed or gridlocked marriages), the projector is obliged to take back and accommodate their own previously disavowed aspect, and accept a reality other than the one previously constructed. This is a developmental move away from a more narcissistic way of relating, based on projective identification, towards one based on a greater degree of recognition of the separateness and integrity of the other.

Participation in a reasonably healthy intimate couple relationship obliges each partner to be re-united with feared aspects of the self, previously split off and projected into the ever-present other. This loss of a previous psychic equilibrium may feel undesirable, traumatic and possibly disturbing; it may cause instability in the relationship and be defended against by sado-masochistic solutions. However, if it can be contained by the more mature aspects of the partners and their relationship (or by the psychotherapeutic process), then omnipotent projective identification and narcissistic relating may be slowly relinquished, and lost parts of the self regained. This leads to the greater integrity of each of the partners and so to a more mature interaction between them as a couple.

For this development to take place there is a need to relinquish narcissistic ways of functioning and to do the work of mourning that this requires. Steiner has described the painful necessity of experiencing the mourning process that arises through reclaiming parts of the self from the other, and how this takes place in the transference whenever the analyst is experienced as acting independently, outside the patient's control (Steiner, 1990). I suggest that exactly the same process arises in the couple relationship when a partner refuses to accept a projected attribute and acts independently of that projection. Steiner writes that if the independence of the analyst can be tolerated—and this is also true of the marital partner's independence—the loss of what he calls "the possessive relationship" can be mourned, a degree of separateness results, and disowned parts of the self are regained, enriching the ego. This is a difficult process, eliciting anxiety, guilt and mental pain, but if this can be borne, "the sequence can proceed and further separateness is achieved by progressive withdrawal of projections. *More realistic whole-object relationships result*" (Steiner, 1990, p. 89, my italics).

In the couple relationship the process of relinquishing projections will never be fully realized. Some degree of narcissistic relating is inevitable, and necessary, to sustain an intimate relationship that, unlike an analysis, at least promises to be interminable, for better and for worse. Ordinary life transitions, such as birth and child-rearing, sexuality, and ageing and death, together with unexpected events and traumas, buffet all relationships. They provide lifelong opportunities to confront fears and anxieties, hopes, and aspirations, and hence rework intrapsychic and interpersonal object relations. A couple able to do this emotional work will go on developing a relationship based on more realistic knowledge and awareness of themselves and the other.

In as much as this can be achieved, a space is created—which I have called the "marital triangle"—where the couple can reflect on their own needs, the needs of the other, and on the needs of the relationship. Often and inevitably, these various needs will be in conflict and require reflection, possible relinquishment, and tolerable, though ambivalent, resolution.

The *capacity* to achieve this state, to create the space within the marital triangle and to be a creative couple, if achievable, could be said to be a developmental stage in its own right (Morgan & Ruszczynski, 1998; Morgan, 2001). As Britton has pointed out, there are often narcissistic problems in sharing space. Psychic space and physical space overlap, he says, and both can feel to be intrusively occupied by the other, arousing both claustrophobic and agoraphobic anxieties (Britton, 2003). What is required to allay these anxieties, he says, is not necessarily agreement, which is likely to require domination and subjugation or identification, but rather a capacity for reflection and understanding (Britton, 1998, 2003). This capacity for reflection and thought requires the triangular space that Britton has highlighted, and the capacity to make links. The ways in which an individual experiences his own thoughts and reflections emerging and coming together, and how these are then perceived to be, and actually are, received and experienced by the other, will be determined by how each partner experiences their internal parental couple coming together in their phantasies; with liveliness and pleasure, with destruction and aggression, or not at all.

What the intimate adult couple therefore requires is *the capacity for symmetry*, a capacity for the two partners to recognize their separateness and difference, but to achieve a balance or congruity in their interaction. Linking can only take place across a space. The capacity to achieve linking suggests the ability to recognize and tolerate there being two separate, though "equal", claimants to the benefits of the relationship and guardians of the relationship's needs. How possible this is will partly be based on the partners' internalized perception of the nature of their parents' interaction and their capacity for harmony and symmetry. However, it may also relate to the internalization of the nature of the inevitably rivalrous, but also loving, sibling relationships, and to how these were experienced and managed. The achievement of this capacity for symmetry—which I am not suggesting can ever be complete and unproblematic, as tension and conflict are inevitably part of life—

may be part of the developmental possibilities within the intimate, adult couple relationship.

Evidence that the "marital triangle" exists is most clearly demonstrated by the ways in which an *actual* third is incorporated into the couple relationship. I have in mind, perhaps most obviously, a child, but also other "intrusions" such as, for example, professional demands or demands from external family. I also have in mind less concrete factors such as an illness, or a preoccupation, or a particular interest, or simply a thought in the mind of one of the partners. Is there a thinking space within and between the couple and a capacity for symmetry, which enables them jointly to reflect on the impact and meaning of this "third" on each of them— as individuals and on their relationship? A "real" third will most likely be accommodated within the space offered by the symbolic marital triangle, irrespective of how it might actually be managed on a day-to-day basis. The likely relinquishments and losses will be mourned and become tolerable, perhaps with some ambivalence. On the other hand, if the thinking space is absent, more psychotic anxieties are likely to arise, and coercion and subjugation will emerge rather than cooperation. Here, the "third" is experienced as intrusive and persecutory, disruptively imposing itself into the relationship. In the absence of the capacity for symmetry, it might be experienced as being hijacked by one of the partners at the expense of the other, or as kept at a distance from or abandoned by one partner, forcing the other to accommodate it or take responsibility for it. This difficulty in finding the necessary triangular space in the relationship could produce shared agoraphobic and claustrophobic anxieties, and result in the defensive use of sado-masochistic interactions as attempted solutions (Ruszczynski, 2003).

The clinical work with a couple that I will call Mr and Mrs Brown illustrates some of what I have been describing. Both are actively involved in their work situations, and they have an eight-year-old child. In some ways, they have remarkably similar histories. Both describe distant and rejecting fathers and over-attentive mothers, who were narcissistically and dependently attached to them as children. One important difference was that Mrs Brown had a number of siblings with whom she had good relationships and who offered each other a refuge from their parents. By contrast, Mr Brown was an only child, and he described how his only escape from his parents was by retreating into "a secret place in my head".

In the clinical work, Mr Brown's profound level of anxiety and paranoia emerged quickly and he related on the basis of a high degree of passive aggression, projecting his angry and violent feelings into his wife and into me. Mrs Brown also functioned narcissistically, with denial and projective identification, but she could, at times, be more sensitive to her husband and child, although this was inconsistent. The couple came into treatment following severe bullying and suspected abuse of their daughter at school, after which their relationship seemed to break down dramatically as they struggled in vain, individually and as a couple, to give their child the emotional support and care she required. Such a trauma would test any couple and family, but the immediacy of the collapse, their inability to recover, and the recriminatory and violent atmosphere between them marked this couple. Even at those moments when Mrs Brown could have some degree of sensitivity to her daughter's situation, she became overwhelmed by a sense of fury, rather than feeling enabled to attend to her child.

What emerged in the clinical situation was that they had a marriage and a parenting style based on pseudo-independence, rather than on any capacities to manage dependence and independence. They could not differentiate the appropriate level of care for their daughter, whom they often described as if she was no different from them. It sounded as if, in an effort to manage this lack of generationally appropriate parental attention, the daughter had developed a degree of precocity that, unfortunately, confirmed her parents' view of her as mature and independent. When, after the trauma, their daughter needed real emotional care, the parents were incapable of offering it, individually or as a couple. Later in the treatment the extent to which both Mr and Mrs Brown were themselves identified with a very vulnerable and needy child, with no internal picture of a caretaker, became clear. Consequently, they unconsciously experienced their daughter's vulnerability primarily as a threat to their own psychic equilibrium.

Some of the dynamics emerging in the transference–countertransference relationship indicate the primitive oedipal themes active within and between this couple. I often found myself struggling to make any contact with either of them as individuals, and it could feel almost futile to talk with them as a parental or sexual couple. I wondered whether this showed, as indicated by their history, the depth of their own difficulties in relating to their parents in their own early histories. In addition, on occasion, I felt an enormous pressure to make some sort of emotional contact with the very suspicious and anxious Mr Brown. I eventually came to realize that in my counter-transference this was a pressure to strengthen and enliven him and to diminish his paranoid view that I might be critical of him or bully him. This counter-transference feeling of being a bully was very interesting, given that their daughter had been badly bullied at school—as if care and bullying were, in some perverse way, linked.

I came to wonder whether this very strong counter-transference was a projection from the couple of their shared unconscious desire to reach and enliven the distant father, and bring him to life with the desire that he should contain the mother's anxieties. The wished-for result would be the creation not only of a functioning mother and father but also of a functioning parental couple. This wish, however, is accompanied by an anxiety that to make emotional demands of the father would be tantamount to bullying and attacking a weak and vulnerable man. This may be an illustration of the healthy part of the child needing to create or unite the parental couple, in an unconscious acknowledgement of the importance of this in the oedipal situation (Feldman, 1989; Fisher, 1993), without which healthy sexual relating might be difficult, if not impossible (Grier, this volume, pp. 201–219).

The possibility of establishing a triangular space in the mind for this couple, however, was very difficult. The central wish to unite the parental couple was in itself the main problem area. For both Mr and Mrs Brown, the search seemed to be for a father–man who is neither weak nor a bully—but it was this that seemed impossible. What was problematic and clinically challenging was to discern whether each had an internal relationship with a narcissistic mother, thereby establishing a narcissistic identification which actually worked against securely finding a place for the father (in the transference, me). If they were to have done so, they would be deprived of their illusory, narcissistic autonomy, and pseudo-independence. Alternatively, they might have been deprived of the triumph of being their mother's primary object of affection. The sabotage of this developmental step was likely to have been actively provoked, because if a good father were to have been found, he would have stepped in and spoiled this illusory mother–child oedipal couple by reclaiming the mother. In doing so he would have constructed a generationally appropriate oedipal situation. The relinquishment that this would have required, in the acknowledgement and toleration of the primacy of the parental couple, could have felt unbearable. In the transference, therefore, there was a constant attack on any possibility of making use of me, constantly relating to me as if I was bullying and persecuting, or weak and impotent. My attempts to interpret this dynamic were treated contemptuously as abstract, and unrelated to them—the idea of a functioning, thinking capacity could only be perceived, at best, as an abstract possibility, rather than something which might relate to them emotionally.

Summary

In this chapter I suggest that, given that the intimate adult couple relationship is likely to recreate some of the couple's shared, unresolved oedipal conflicts, a symbolically similar process can take place within the dynamics of that relationship itself. By withdrawing the narcissistic and omnipotent projective identifications from each other, the couple not only move towards a greater degree of integration between themselves, but their relationship is allowed to develop along the lines of more whole-object relating in its own right and become established as a symbolic, third object. This creates the possibility of what I have called a "marital triangle", within which there is the reflective and thinking space to address the appropriate needs and requirements of each of the partners in the couple, and of their relationship.

Couples who seek psychoanalytic treatment vary in the degree to which they are capable of reworking their unresolved oedipal conflicts. In the clinical situation, the psychotherapist is drawn into re-enactments of the oedipal struggles, but also holds the potential for being the third object to be contended with. The therapeutic role is to conserve the psychoanalytic stance: to maintain a capacity to observe, reflect, and comment on the dynamics in the relationship between the partners and in the transference–counter-transference relationship between the couple and therapist. The therapist's task is to attend to each of the two individuals and to their relationship, while retaining a thinking mind so as to comment on this transferential involvement. This attempt enacts the very struggle at the heart of the triangular oedipal situation, reconstituted in the intimate dynamics of the couple relationship.

CHAPTER THREE

The couple, their marriage, and Oedipus: or, problems come in twos and threes

Andrew Balfour

T here can be few more relevant concepts to coupling than the oedipus complex which, though it is associated with three-somes, might also be said to be about the difficulty of the twosome. Current thinking about the oedipus complex reveals its importance in helping us to understand the difficulties adult couples experience in sustaining a shared "psychic space" (Britton, 2000), an integration of two different psychic realities in a couple relationship. In this chapter, I will explore a particular constellation of anxieties that have their origins in the oedipal situation, and are observable in psychotherapeutic work with adult couples. In this constellation, the individual in close relationship feels caught between fears of engulfment, and fears of abandonment. This has been termed the "claustro-agoraphobic dilemma" (Rey, 1994), and I will outline how analysts from the three different groups in the British Psychoanalytic Society have described such anxieties in similar terms. Each group links difficulties in the infant's earliest relations with mother to particular problems in the oedipal situa-tion, leaving a legacy of claustro-agoraphobic anxieties in the adult. These contemporary psychoanalytic accounts of the oedipus complex are important in psychotherapeutic work with couples for

understanding the profound difficulty that close emotional involvement with a partner presents to many of our patients.

Theoretical background

The oedipus complex has never been simply to do with sex and
rivalry, as "pop" psychology may have it. Freud's account was
central to the development of his theory of the mind. His theory
offered the beginnings of an account of the processes of internalization and introjection, and the development of different agencies
within the mind, particularly that of the ego ideal, which later
became an aspect of the superego. In the history of psychoanalysis,
the understanding of the oedipus complex is one of the central
developmental points for the beginning of a theory of internal
object relations.

Klein's work took this aspect of the oedipus complex further.
She emphasized what she termed the "oedipal situation" (Klein,
1928), including the sexual relation between the parents, which
Freud had considered in the context of the primal scene. Klein
developed this thinking in her work, based on the close observation
of young children. She positioned the developmental importance
of the conflict inherent in the oedipal situation much earlier in an
individual's life than Freud had.

Klein saw the essential features of the oedipal conflict, the difficulties of the "three-cornered situation", as being experienced by
the infant in oral and anal terms as well as the later genital stage of
Freud's original formulation. This leads to a view of the oedipal
situation as concerned with relations between objects, as they are
coloured by unconscious phantasy. Of course, this anticipates the
development in psychoanalysis over recent decades from the classical emphasis on the distribution of energies to a theory of internal
object relations.

Contemporary accounts of the oedipal situation

Both post-Freudian and post-Kleinian thinkers have subsequently
made further developments to Klein's thought. Britton (1998)

describes how certain individuals have difficulty with triangular, oedipal relations because they threaten chaos and fragmentation. For Britton, there is a particular aetiology underlying oedipal problems, which explains the difficulty of triangular, three-person relationships in the context of the coupling between mother and infant. According to this view, a failure of containment in the mother–infant relationship leads to splitting, where the phantasy of the ideal, understanding, primary object is maintained at the cost of projecting into the third. This is generally the father, who is then experienced as the source of "malignant misunderstanding" (Britton, 1998, p. 54). Therefore, parental union threatens the engulfment of the understanding object with the misunderstanding one. Consequentially, parental intercourse is experienced as catastrophic; creating a combined figure that personifies contradiction, meaninglessness, chaos, and fragmentation. Steiner (1996) and Segal (1988) have described the oedipal situation in similar terms.

Britton (1989) describes how, in working through the oedipal situation, it is crucial to establish a third position whereby one can know that one is excluded from the couple, and yet still know that one is loved by the parents. According to Britton, such a relatively successful negotiation of the oedipus complex allows the possibility of empathic engagement with the subjectivity of the other, while also having a vantage point from which to view this relating, to think about it. Britton pointed out that, as development proceeds, then at best, the infant is able to achieve the capacity to be involved in relating, and to reflect upon that relating, or to take up an empathic position. This position is based on subjective experience of contact with the other, and having the mental space to think more objectively about what is going on. Hence Britton's is an account of developing the capacity for a linked separateness, a third position in relation to the object, and an account of the consequences of the failure to achieve this. Failure is associated with difficulties in sharing psychic space with another person, as though it is felt as a severe threat to psychic existence. Britton gives an account, in developmental terms, of the perceived catastrophic consequences for the infant of the link between the parents. Similarly, he describes how, for the individual, the legacy is the anxiety that psychic intercourse, the bringing together of two psychic realities, will be catastrophic.

Writing as a contemporary psychoanalyst from the Independent Group, Birkstead-Breen (1996) also describes how the failure to face oedipal reality confronts the individual with the threat of internal fragmentation and chaos. Birkstead-Breen takes as her starting point the notion that internalizing the linkage between parents provides the individual with an internal, bounded, three-dimensional space (what Britton calls "triangular space"), and a concept of being linked to, but separate from, their objects. She describes this using the language of part objects, in terms internalizing what she calls the linking function of the penis, to link and encompass the two worlds of the parents. The "penis-as-link" is seen as the elemental symbol of the relationship between them, of the completion of the oedipal triangle. In her view, then, failure to internalize the penis-as-link results in the individual facing the threat of chaos and fragmentation, due to the lack of the internal structure of a bounded, internal, three-dimensional space. Instead, the individual inhabits a binary world. Oedipal reality is evaded, difference is not recognized, the capacity for symbol formation is under-developed, and what is known as "symbolic equation" (a failure to distinguish between the symbol and the thing it symbolizes, resulting from a defensive fusion of self with object, or object and symbol) is dominant (Segal, 1957). Birkstead-Breen describes how, for individuals without such an internal structure, there is an oscillation between fears of claustrophobic invasion, and agoraphobic dislocation. She outlines how a defensive "solution" to this can be based on internalizing an omnipotent "phallus", instead of the penis-as-link. The former offers the phantasy of completion without need, based on a denial of difference, a narcissistic avoidance of recognizing the reality of parental intercourse. Although she writes more in part object terms, her account is similar to Britton's, particularly in the emphasis upon the claustro-agoraphobic anxieties associated with oedipal difficulties. What is crucial here is that Birkstead-Breen and Britton show how, for such individuals, coupling or linking with another person can be felt to threaten catastrophe. Hence, lacking a capacity to be separate but linked to their objects, a "triangular space", they are caught in what is described as a claustro-agoraphobic dilemma.

From a Contemporary Freudian perspective, although not writing specifically with the oedipus complex as the focus, Glasser

(1979) describes a very similar clinical picture of claustro-agora-phobic anxieties arising in the earliest relationship between infant and mother. He describes a "core complex"; a conflict the infant faces between an intense desire for contact with the mother—a wish, ultimately, to merge with her—and the fear of engulf-ment, with the annihilation of the self a merger would entail. He describes how the infant mobilizes aggression in response to this "annihilation anxiety", with the aim of self-preservation, to defend itself from the threat of engulfment. The consequent withdrawal and wish to destroy the mother are then associated with the converse fear, that of abandonment. He sees the core complex as a "pre-oedipal" phenomenon, part of the struggle of the two-person relationship between mother and infant. This reflects the Con-temporary Freudian view that the oedipus complex and tripartite relations are an issue only later in the infant's development. Glasser describes how a mother who is unable to take in might either exacerbate the anxieties associated with the core complex, or respond appropriately to the infant's needs. For example, if the infant experiences the mother as unable to manage its feelings, projection may increase and, as aggression is projected into the mother, she may become, in the infant's mind, more frighteningly engulfing or devouring. This increases the infant's fear of anni-hilation and further fuels the need to withdraw or destroy her, further exacerbating the fear of abandonment. According to this account, lack of containment in the mother–infant relationship might amplify the anxieties associated with the core complex, increasing the infant's aggression and so further increasing the claustro-agoraphobic anxieties.

Glasser describes the distorting effects that the difficulties of the core complex can have on the infant's oedipal development. In particular, he describes how the infant may invest the father with the dangerous attributes originally experienced in relation to the mother, in order to preserve the relationship with her. This has much in common with Britton's account. However, Glasser's view that the oedipus complex is an issue only later in development, means that the relation between the parents does not have the importance that it does in Britton's. For Glasser, subsequent diffi-culties in oedipal development are *underpinned* by the individual's attempt to manage this claustro-agoraphobic dilemma of early infancy. Oedipal difficulties, according to Glasser, may at root reflect earlier difficulties, associated with the core complex, and with claustro-agoraphobic anxieties arising in the infant's earliest relations with its mother.

Summary

These accounts have the common view that a failure of containment in the infant's relationship with its mother leads to difficulties in negotiating the oedipal situation, associated specifically with claustro-agoraphobic anxieties. They describe how such difficulties leave the individual in a position that is more akin to a straight line than a triangular space, where there is no happy point between the two polarities of "too close" and "too far apart". According to Britton, the consequence of developing triangular space is that the individual is held in a tension in relation to the other, where closeness to the object (what Britton calls the "subjective" state) is held at one point of the triangle, while at another point is the more objective "otherness" of the object. The idea of triangular space is that one has freedom to move within it, without losing touch with the other two points, and without becoming lost in the engulfing world of the subjectivity of the other, or in the lonely dislocated world of the "objective" other. With the collapse of triangular space, or the failure to develop it, one is caught between fears of engulfment and agoraphobic abandonment. The claustro-agoraphobic dilemma is familiar to us clinically, particularly with borderline states, and has been described by a number of psychoanalytic writers representing the Kleinian, Independent, and Contemporary Freudian groups (e.g., Birkstead-Breen, 1996; Britton, 1989, 1998, 2000; Glasser, 1979). As one might expect, such anxieties make a very difficult business of establishing stable, intimate relationships, and so an understanding of this area is important for the psychotherapist working with couples.

Each of the following clinical examples is an amalgam of different cases, which I hope gives a picture of what I am describing and retains a truth to the underlying psychic experience of the couples involved.

Clinical example 1

This couple highlighted the threat of annihilation of individual identity, an intense sense of claustrophobia, and the associated threat of explosive violence.

Philip and Susan presented tremendous difficulties over disagreements between them, which might start off as small issues of misunderstanding, but which quickly seemed to become matters of life and death. It was as if they shared a conviction that there was only room for one point of view. Within the sessions, I felt that I was walking on eggshells, that it was almost impossible to link the experiences of the two. Instead, I felt caught in a dilemma: that I could only understand one partner at the expense of the other. If one were understood, the other would feel misunderstood. Susan described this as an "inverse relationship", that one person's gain was another's loss. For example, they frequently fought during the session over which partner's experience of the chain of events leading up to a row would prevail. Although sometimes beginning ostensibly in a spirit of wanting to repair or to understand the conflict, such discussions would quickly escalate in intensity as details were disputed. As the atmosphere became more charged I felt helpless to be able to intervene in any helpful way. Susan, in particular (although at other times, Philip too) would become increasingly shrill and they would start to shout very loudly, as though trying to force their words through their partner's "deaf ears". If I gave one person's account, I was felt to be giving it credence and so negating the other's experience of events. Both partners were in earnest, and the other one, if they had a different version, must either be lying, or else mad. Or they were felt to be cynically trying to drive the other mad, misrepresenting the truth to deny the other's experience.

The pattern was one of beginning to discuss a recent point of disagreement, and then each individual insisting, increasingly vehemently, that their way of seeing things was "right", and complaining that they were hitting a brick wall. Each partner seemed to feel that the other, whom they felt utterly unable to get through to, was wiping out their sense of reality. When this happened during the sessions, the atmosphere became claustrophobic and there was a suffocating feeling in the room. On one occasion, Susan found her husband's quiet disagreement with her unbearable, and ran out of the room, having to get away physically. This echoed her behaviour on other occasions, jumping out of cars during arguments, or physically withdrawing from her husband in other dramatic ways. She had smashed things when in this state of mind and seemed to withdraw in order to obviate the possibility of violence. She described a feeling of "total misunderstanding" that might overwhelm her, "but I won't let it". (This links to Britton's description of the fear of engulfment by the "misunderstanding" object, a psychic catastrophe that one must escape from.) Such rows became unbearable for both partners, as each tried to assert their views—fighting, increasingly desperately, not to have their way of seeing things negated. It felt that their very identities were at stake, and that either one or the other had to prevail. There was no sense that they might "agree to disagree", or tolerate the idea that their partner might have a different perspective on the same thing. There was no perspective possible, no "third position" from which their respective experiences could be reflected upon. Instead, there was a bloody battle over who would prevail, fought out repeatedly within the sessions. The desperation and threats of violence emerging when they were in this state of mind seemed to link to the claustrophobic atmosphere; the threat of engulfment by "malignant misunderstanding", and the response of trying to smash out of it with violence or violent withdrawal.

This case contains many echoes of Glasser's account of the violence that may be mobilized when the individual feels threatened by engulfment, and wishes to destroy the object. Generally, it was Susan who expressed this, and her husband and the rest of the family who were left in the lonely, dislocated position, following her frequent walkouts during rows. The couple had tremendous difficulty in tolerating the therapeutic situation, and, unable to sustain the therapy, withdrew in a dramatic walkout from a session at a point when tensions were running high.

The example of this couple brings home very powerfully what it means to lack a third position, where two separate minds can co-exist together. One person's view is felt to exist only at the expense of the other, with the ever-present threat of one psychic reality being engulfed by the other. This is linked to a palpable feeling of claustrophobia. The violent reaction, expressed ultimately in withdrawal, leaves the couple in an agoraphobic position, isolated and cut-off from one another. This pattern seems to link to Glasser's idea that mobilizing aggression in response to the threat of the annihilation leaves the same individual facing the converse fear of abandonment. The specific fear demonstrated in this example is the fear of engulfment by "total misunderstanding", as Britton (1998) describes. Both partners fight desperately against this, reflecting the shared conviction that they inhabit a binary world, where there can be only two positions—engulfment and abandonment—that they constantly oscillate between.

Case example 2

The following clinical material illustrates how a deep difficulty of two people allowing any sustained emotional involvement with one another underlies the difficulties in three-way relationships that this couple presents.

Jorge and Montse met relatively late in life, having both already built successful careers. He is a both a practising lawyer and an academic, she a film-maker. He, but not she, had already had considerable experience of therapy in his country of origin. They had both apparently wanted to come to this country to develop in their chosen fields, though shortly after they arrived, Montse became pregnant. They have a young son, aged eight, and they emphasized from the outset how their difficulties seemed to have begun at around the time of his birth. They had had no sexual contact since his birth, and lived a life where they looked after their son but had little or no emotional contact with one another. I had the impression of two people who were more or less alongside one another—looking away from one another towards some other involvement or commitment.

From the start of therapy, I found it difficult to think of comments or interpretations that included both of them. It was very difficult to think of them as a couple, with a joint contribution to their difficulties. I was pulled now towards his position, now towards hers, and I found myself quickly becoming involved with one of them, while the other became an onlooker. Initially, this mostly followed the pattern of my thinking that Jorge had joined me as a co-therapist, with Montse in the position of the vulnerable patient with difficult feelings. When I was able to notice this, and to put my observation into words, the situation quickly switched. Now I found myself intensely involved in long exchanges with Jorge, leaving Montse as an outsider looking on.

In the room with them I often felt a lack of physical space, a feeling of being cramped. Metaphorically speaking, it felt as if there was nowhere to sit between them. At other times, I could feel miles away from them. They often began sessions in silence, keeping their eyes averted from me, occasionally exchanging small glances of what seemed like mutual understanding. At such times I felt very much on the outside, trying to guess at what might be going on inside them, feeling I had no way in. The early sessions were characterized by their mistrustful challenges to me. I found myself trying very hard, striving to give them "good" and insightful interpretations. As time went on, the atmosphere over these early months changed from one of awkwardness to a warm and easy one. In some ways, it felt as if useful work was done during this time. However, after sessions I often felt a nagging uneasiness that, though at moments the work was painful and difficult, everything mostly seemed to come very easily. My counter-transference experience was very comfortable; I started to look forward to the sessions, and afterwards sometimes noticed myself feeling rather pleased with myself for doing such good work.

During this period a number of themes emerged. In sessions the couple often commented on how far apart they had been during the week—working separately, taking turns to look after their son, functioning in some ways as a "team", but miles apart from one another emotionally. They were, individually, good parents to their child, but almost never seemed to be together as a family, as a threesome. There was an idealized quality to the contact with their son. Occasionally, each described intensely good experiences of involvement with him, and the other felt excluded. Mostly, Jorge was the excluded one, although this could suddenly switch and Montse felt left out. They each seemed to have made a separate, absorbing link with their son, to the exclusion of any corresponding link with one another. The quality of the idealization of their individual links with him went alongside their denigration, and loss of the idealization, that had characterized their relationship at the start, leaving their marriage in a devalued position.

Each of them described longing to get back to the "golden time" of the first period of their relationship, when it had been just the two of them. Of course, like many couples at the start of a relationship, this was at a time when they were not living together, and so they had an actual physical gap separating them, mediating their contact with one another. Jorge commented that it was rather like the arrangement Woody Allen and Mia Farrow made, in famously trying to solve their difficulties with one another by each having their own apartment on opposite sides of Central Park. Indeed, Jorge and Montse also conveyed a fear that, should they try to get close again, they would be terribly disappointed. Moments of better contact or involvement with one another quickly collapsed into disappointment, and a feeling of mutual recrimination. They conveyed how, while each of them seemed to be able to have intense involvements, for example, with their son, with myself, or with their careers, they could sustain none of these for long.

This issue appeared to be linked to their difficulty in sharing "psychic space", in integrating their two different psychic realities, as Britton (2000) puts it. The couple expressed this in a number of ways. One was the conflict between them over the time they could give to developing their careers, the struggle over their own development as individuals, and the needs of the family. Jorge, in particular, feared the "pull" of family demands, and that if he did not keep his working life separate, keep the ideas he was working on a secret, his creativity would in some way be "sucked out of him". He would often speak of how, when trying to work at home, he only ever had a few minutes before he was pulled away by the demands of the family. He spoke of how painful this experience was for him, and how he feared that something essential in him would be "snuffed out". He held his hand over his mouth at that moment, mimicking the act of suffocation. Montse also shared this worry. It was as if, for each of them, there was an idea that their individual careers and needs might be swallowed up by the other, and that only one person's needs could exist at any one time. They conveyed, I felt, how ultimately their very identities were at stake. Montse commented on how difficult she found living with Jorge and having to be "available" to him emotionally. He tended to work in a converted shed in the garden of their house, she in the attic. If they were in the "shared" part of the house, Jorge might intrude on

Montse at any moment. On one occasion, when she was describing one of the familiar rows between them over such an episode, she began talking about a recent hijacking that had received a lot of news coverage at the time. It felt to me that she was conveying how her experience was that her mind had been "hijacked" by Jorge, overtaken by his needs and preoccupations, and her own thoughts killed off. They discussed how, in concrete terms, they might get the right distance from one another, and find a "protected space". How could they arrange the house, in terms of "his" and "her" areas?

They seemed to share an underlying phantasy that something vital in them, their very psychic life, would be "squeezed out" by the other one—that one identity would take over the other. While the fear, or underlying phantasy, appeared to be the same, their defences against it differed. Montse tried to organize, on a diary sheet, the times she was prepared to be available for involvement with the family and contact with Jorge. The times when she was "off limits" were sacrosanct to her, and terrible rows ensued if she felt that Jorge had breached these "demarcation areas", as they called them. By contrast, Jorge set great store on his right to "spontaneous freedom"; to withdraw suddenly from the family if he felt "creative", or, at other times, to seek contact or involvement with them if he felt in need of it. His re-entry into the family tended to happen after a period of withdrawal, in which he would suddenly become anxious about being alone and cut-off from his wife and son. Such episodes were difficult for Montse to cope with, and she complained that she and their son had become used to Jorge's absence, and then felt he was, in her words, "crashing back in". Although apparently very different, such behaviour seemed to reflect each partner's attempt to manage the fear of "psychic take-over". While it is true to say that each of them was creative and successful, they idealized their "creativity" and the importance of their own "reflective life". This actually seemed to illustrate what Steiner calls a psychic retreat (1996, p. 435), away from the anxieties associated with the living link between them.

Although much of the material that emerged during this early period with them was, on the face of it, very rich, I had a doubtful feeling, at moments, about it being a little too easy. What was missing, I felt later, was any room for differences of view. My comments or interpretations made sense to them, but did not seem to be anything particularly new. One might say that the therapeutic situation of couple psychotherapy, the presence of the couple plus the therapist, in some way has the potential to represent the oedipal situation of a couple and a third object. At times, as I have described, there were different permutations of this coupling—one or other of them joining with me and the other seeming to be the excluded one, either the onlooker onto a therapeutic coupling, or a co-therapy team dealing with one individual patient. However, during this period I think that I was in some ways joined with them. Taking Britton's formulations into account, one might say that I was closely involved in a subjective contact, a close empathic link that was ultimately undifferentiated. What was lacking was a third position, in which I was more separate and able to think *about* what was happening between us in the room. The loss of this position was reflected in my lack of anxiety and my relative sense of comfort and ease when I was in the room with them. A comfortable situation seemed to be one where oedipal anxieties, which might be elicited by the therapist's third position, were to some extent avoided.

This situation changed, rather dramatically, some months into the therapy. Jorge and Montse came to a session describing how they had united together the previous week to deal with several difficult situations. There followed examples of uniting together against the "madness" of other people that each of them had had to deal with. Jorge, in particular, was preoccupied with a battle with a senior colleague who, though normally referred to as a very supportive and benign figure, had unusually suggested that Jorge radically revise some of his recent work. Jorge was outraged by this suggestion, describing his colleague's views as "deranged". These accounts had a dramatic quality, and I started to feel under pressure to support and agree with the rather triumphant position that the couple had taken up in relation to the people they described. My counter-transference at that moment was that it felt dangerous not simply to be swept along with this prevailing view. It was very hard for me to put anything back to them—all the disturbance and difficulty had to be lodged outside of them, and I started to feel under fire for implying anything different. When I ventured a comment about how they were joining together to this end, Jorge reacted by telling me that I had "submerged him" because my comment was also addressed to her. By including them both, I seemed to have dissolved his differences from Montse.

At the next session, this situation had intensified. I was told I had behaved in a "procrustean" way, that I had fitted their experience into my way of seeing things. At the time, I was struck by their use of this word. After the session, I looked it up. *Longmans Dictionary* describes its origins in a mythical robber of Ancient Greece, who forced his victims to fit a certain bed by stretching them, or lopping off their legs. I felt that the violence of this image conveyed the experience of how my linking their own experience to my way of seeing things entailed the mutilation of their own psychic reality. During the session I felt they were telling me that if I was not with them, I was against them. I could keep up a position of atunement to their feelings, their way of seeing things, but I should not think about this. I should not offer my own thoughts, based on my own experience, as it differed from their way of seeing the situation. It seemed at that moment as if the "irreconcilable gulf" that they often described between them now lay between this couple and me. I found myself full of self-doubt. Had I lost touch with them and simply "got it wrong"? Had I been pushing an over-valued idea at them? As I struggled with these doubts, I tried to continue working with them in the session. Faced with a stony silence from Jorge, and Montse's apparent struggle to come up with something, I was treated first as though I was criticizing her effort and then as though I was intruding into his silence. It felt as if there was a powerful attack on any more hopeful contact, or wish for a link. This produced a very difficult counter-transference. I felt myself to be in the presence of a united couple, implacable and impenetrable, as if I was the one left feeling small and humiliated. The couple had united against the anxieties of the oedipal situation, which, apparently, they projected very powerfully into me.

Afterwards, when the heated feelings of the session had begun to cool, I felt that what had happened reflected a dynamic that reverberated in the different relationships that the couple had previously described. In the session, they seemed to have united in a coupling that depended upon all the badness being lodged outside—first in the other people they described, then in the transference, in relation to me. This took shape when I took up a different position from the one that I felt pressured to conform to. How much they also unconsciously pushed me to do just that, to enact the underlying dynamic of their uniting against the denigrated others is an interesting question. As I have stated, Britton, Segal, Steiner, and others have described one particular dynamic that can characterize the oedipal situation. The infant's idealized contact with mother is preserved through experiencing what is outside the couple (the third object) as correspondingly bad. This could be the father, or, in this example, it was my linking with my own thoughts, based on my wider professional experience. The intense couplings that Jorge and Montse established conveyed a similar quality. Ambivalence was intolerable within the relationship, and intense idealization maintained through denigration of what lay outside the pairing. This pattern appeared repeatedly in different combinations.

Jorge and Montse gave numerous examples of absorbing couplings that they excluded one another from; their intense, exclusive involvement with their careers, with friends from work, with their child, and with myself. What they present is an unstable situation of idealized, yet unsustainable couplings. As I have said, such coupling only seemed to be possible in an idealized state, with badness split-off and projected. Segal (1988) and Steiner (1996) describe how the "bad object" is perceived as a malignant and powerful one, intruding into the idealized, blissful coupling of mother and infant, and bringing the return of the projected "badness". I think that this couple demonstrated constant efforts to recreate this idealized "blissful" union, with all badness projected into a third object, which then threatens the ideal with intrusion; a precarious situation to maintain. In my early experience of myself as a very good therapist in a relationship with very good patients, one can glimpse how the couple tried to enlarge the "blissful" union to include everyone in the immediate circle—one another, their child, and myself. This precarious situation repeatedly broke down, so that they started to experience first me as the "bad one", and then each other.

Underlying the idealized coupling that they each seemed to have in their minds, there appeared to be a fear of allowing close emotional contact, as if it might lead to a wiping out of their own "reality" or identity. Britton (2000) describes this as the terror of bringing two psychic realities together. To manage this fear they kept themselves, as they put it, on two separate planets, and felt lost and isolated from one another much of the time. They came together for a while, but as I have said, could not sustain it for long. "Ideal" periods of closeness were quickly followed by something more explosive, and they would be apart again. The instability of the situation was conveyed in the fast-shifting couplings—the changing pattern of alliances that I heard about in their home life, and reflected in my experience of them in the room, when I would often feel involved with one partner to the exclusion of the other. Instability and sudden changes seemed to reflect the difficulty of any sustained emotional contact between two people, associated with anxieties to do with "claustrophobia", the swallowing up or engulfing of one identity by another. In my encounters with the couple I also experienced the difficulty of introducing another position or perspective, the pressure to be alongside, or in tune with them, and not to move to a third position of thinking about what was going on. When I did hold on to a different perspective, it provoked a massive attack. Initially, this brought the feeling of a gulf in understanding opening between us, a feeling echoed in their accounts of being miles apart, on opposite sides of the world from one another. This experience was also associated with considerable anxiety over being lost, and cut off from the other one—what we might term "agoraphobic anxiety".

Case example 3

Finally, I will describe another couple who, when they first sought help, seemed to have settled on a very rigid split between them of the two poles of claustro-agoraphobia. At first sight, she appeared to hold all the anxiety about being submerged or wiped out by the other (the claustrophobia), and he to hold all the anxiety of being left alone and out of contact (the agoraphobia).

James and Mary sought help following the revelation of Mary's homosexual affair. They separated soon after this but had regular contact, ostensibly around the care of their daughter. Although there was a physical separation, they continued to be very involved with one another, and continued in psychotherapy. Within the therapy Mary presented her homosexuality as an untouchable fact. The marriage was over and she could not give further explanation, for that might draw back her into an emotional contact with her husband. From the beginning, at a conscious level, she was coming to therapy in order to be helped to separate from her husband. All of the wish to carry on with the relationship and the sadness at its end seemed to be lodged, by both partners, in James. She presented herself as guilty of the "destruction" she had wrought, but with nothing to add. The fact of her newly discovered homosexuality acted as a full stop on any further enquiry, representing a barrier between the partners that could not really be breached. Over time, as Mary allowed a little more involvement, she described how she had to leave the marriage in order to escape from her husband's "moulding" of her. She conveyed the impression that involvement with James felt like a psychic annihilation, as if it wiped out her identity. By contrast, James conveyed an utter desperation to have his wife back at all costs, and appeared to have no conscious ambivalence about this, no more mixed picture. The two horns of the claustro-agoraphobic situation seemed to be rigidly divided between them. The psychic annihilation that Mary's withdrawal represented for James was conveyed, I felt, by his description of how the revelation of her affairs felt like a "bomb going off, a complete demolition". He linked this to his experience of driving to the session, and witnessing the demolition of two adjacent tower blocks.

Although their positions were polarized, with James as the excluded partner, over time it became clear that this was a shared difficulty. What became apparent was how, in fact, Mary could act to provoke his sense of exclusion. At times, her own feelings of exclusion were more directly evident. For example, on one such occasion, when she had felt shut out of the family home, she secretly had her own set of keys cut. At other times she would complain in the session that he expected her to be available twenty-four hours a day. She then revealed that she had decided to check if it was the same the other way around, and had telephoned to check up on James' movements.

Mary's account of the marriage before separation conveyed her feeling that she had always been very good and dutiful, but had compromised herself and her own needs entirely in order to fit in with James. Her attitude tended to be superior, and there was a hint of martyrdom in her sense of long-suffering forbearance. This reflects what has been described by Britton (2000) as one defensive solution to the fear of being taken over or annihilated by another person's mind—the individual's exaggeration of their capacities for tolerance, lowering their expectations of others, a greed for virtue, and avoidance of any situation that might provoke internal jealousy or envy. According to Britton, such individuals expect very little from their partners: "An unconscious sense of moral superiority is more important to them than what they might get from another person" (2000, p. 12).

This is close to Morgan's (2001) observation that one way for couples to manage anxiety about sharing psychic space is to make an unconscious agreement that only one partner's psychic space will exist. The point of conflict that emerged for this couple seemed to be over whose it would be. James agreed that Mary had subordinated herself to him before. Now, however, he felt that, having gone along with him for so long, she was turning the tables, forcing him to fit in. Now, he felt, she was getting what she wanted, her freedom. Having previously felt like the winner, he now felt like the loser, he said. One way of thinking about this is that it reflects their experience that one person's need, or psychic reality, must always dominate the other's. The account of their marriage suggested that difference was denied through her suppression of herself, fitting herself in, so to speak, to him and later, through his subordination of himself to her. They seemed to have been drawn to one another on the basis that only one psychic reality would exist, so avoiding both partners' anxieties about bringing two different minds together. They appeared to have settled on a "solution" to their oedipal anxieties in which psychic differentiation was denied. In this sense, psychically, their marriage was a "homosexual" one, in that there was no differentiation of two separate minds in a situation of give and take between them, a more "heterosexual" pattern of relating.

Over time, the reality of their differences resurfaced, underscored by their physical differences. One outcome of this was that they conceived a child. It was at this point that their shared defensive "solution" broke down, and they described the onset of their overt marital difficulties from the birth of their child. It was after having the child that Mary began having homosexual affairs, and, from this point, when their differences re-emerged, she was driven internally to form a physical relationship that more truly matched her psychic defensive solution. These affairs were not hidden from her husband, and they functioned to push him into struggling now to please her and to keep her in the marriage, to put her into the dominant position. Effectively, the same dynamic persisted in their marriage, with the roles simply reversed. This time he was to be the one who submitted himself to her domination. However, he contested the situation and conflict emerged. It was at this point that they presented for help. The catastrophic breakdown of their shared defensive "solution" was conveyed in James' description of the demolition of the two tower blocks. However, rather than aiming to establish a relating that included both of their different minds, what he tried to do was to re-establish the former relationship in which he was dominant, she submissive; there was not to be give and take, but only one dominating mind. For example, when Mary allowed a more flexible contact with her husband, by letting him in a bit more on her feelings, he quietly turned it into something else in his mind. It was confirmation, he said, that his agenda for their reconciliation would win out, if he just bided his time. My understanding of this was that he had experienced her as opening the door a little and that he had then, in his mind, quietly colonized the space that he felt had opened up. He revealed that he had immediately started to build up in his mind a fantasy of a happy ending, a re-uniting. For her part, Mary conveyed that she felt she had opened the door to her husband a little and then immediately felt controlled by him. She experienced him as intrusively wanting to pursue her. At first sight, then, this couple looked as if they were caught in a particularly rigid split. For Mary, leaving the marriage seemed to be associated with psychic survival, whereas for James it appeared to mean psychic death. What emerged over time, however, was that, underlying this, each partner was trying to subjugate the other's "psychic reality" to their own, attempting to "resolve" their anxieties about sharing psychic space by ensuring there was only one.

One way of understanding this couple's situation might be that it reflects the "solution" to oedipal anxieties that Birkstead-Breen describes, of erecting and worshipping the omnipotent phallus. In this case, initially James was to be the dominant one, the phallus, to which Mary should submit. As time went on, it seemed that she could not sustain this, and so she tried to make *herself* the phallus, to which *he* must submit. The image of the demolition of the two skyscrapers appears to represent the "demolition" of this shared defensive arrangement, of the "homosexual" marriage, of psychic non-differentiation. When the differences between them re-emerged, there was possibility of a "heterosexual" conflict, through which the couple could be differentiated. However, they were unable to envisage the relationship which Birkstead-Breen describes as "penis-as-link", where they might relate to each other as two different people who are linked, producing all kinds of thirds, including their own child. Instead, the pressure was to restore the familiar regime, each now competing for the dominant position. This seems to reflect an internal situation that both partners shared—a belief that coupling with another person will not lead to a situation of give and take, based on a linked separateness. Instead, it will lead only to a tyrannical relating, where one partner dominates and the other is tyrannically colonized. Birkstead-Breen's account outlines how this reflects an attempted defensive "solution" to the anxiety of the individual who has evaded the reality of the oedipus situation, and failed to internalize the "penis-as-link". What emerges for this couple is that where both partners each defensively seek to dominate the other, then these underlying fears are given flesh, as each partner confirms the other's fears.

As with the previous cases, this example conveys the difficulties experienced by the couple for whom there is no sustained triangular space, but instead an unstable situation where there is the threat of engulfment or abandonment. The associated sense of psychic annihilation seems to be expressed each partner's desperation, and their attempt to split the roles so rigidly. The way in which both partners' hatred of exclusion can underpin the situation was revealed, at moments, by each of them. The attempted defensive "solution" in this case involves each individual trying to dominate their partner, reflecting their shared phantasy that one "psychic reality" must prevail. In this way, the couple enacts their shared, underlying fear of psychic take-over.

Conclusion

Situations involving a third object often bring couples into treatment. It could be that the birth of a child triggers difficulties, as with two of the couples I described, or a new career, or an affair, or any number of other issues. As such, we often see couples presenting with ostensibly oedipal problems, and of course, the very situation of couple psychotherapy, the presence of a couple and a therapist, gives representation to the oedipal configuration. The oedipus situation might be said to be at the centre of our psychotherapeutic work with couples. What I have tried to highlight is that contemporary psychoanalytic accounts show how the situation is more complex than simply a difficulty in encompassing three-way relationships. These accounts describe how the psychotherapist's struggle is not just to understand the couple's difficulty in managing the threesome, but also to think about how these link with the difficulties of the twosome. I have focused particularly on the legacy of claustro-agoraphobic anxieties that can originate in the oedipal situation.

In thinking about the second couple that I described, for example, one might say that, on the face of it, they were pulled into intense absorbing one-to-one contacts but could not manage any relation to a third object. However, as I have tried to show, if one looks more closely at the situation, it becomes apparent that they are not simply happy being in twosomes, and only encounter difficulties in relating to a third. What they present is an unstable situation, of intense idealized couplings, which cannot be sustained for long. The difficulties they presented around the third object seemed to concern the use of that object in their attempts to sustain intense, idealized couplings, reflecting their shared difficulty in maintaining emotional contact with one another.

By contrast, the first couple I described only presented problems in relation to one another, without reference to a third object. However, what they seemed to lack was a "third position" (Britton, 1998), due to unresolved oedipal difficulties leaving a legacy of profound anxieties, described here as "claustro-agoraphobic". Consequently, their ability to form any stable, sustained emotional link with one another was severely impaired.

The third case illustrates, I think, how the couple might present a situation in which the partners appear to be bringing something very different: his agoraphobia, her claustrophobia. However, I have described that what emerged was how both partners were defending against these claustro-agoraphobic anxieties in similar ways. This reflects something of the complexity of the situation that can face the psychotherapist who is working with the couple. Of course, from a psychoanalytic perspective, the patient who is agoraphobic is also, at some level, claustrophobic too, though this part of them may not be consciously known. Couples are drawn together, at an unconscious level, because of shared or complementary unconscious phantasies. How they represent one another's fears, or project their anxieties into one another, is important in understanding how they act on one another to sustain and perpetuate their shared difficulties. The third couple I described demonstrates how each partner's defences can also form part of an enactment of a shared underlying phantasy. In this case, their shared fear was of "psychic take-over", so that between them, they confirm each other's worst anxieties. This presents difficulty both for the psychotherapist and the couple involved, but, at best, offers an opportunity for these anxieties and defences to be struggled with and understood in a very alive way in the therapeutic setting.

My interpretation of the clinical material is that it supports the link between claustrophobia and agoraphobia as two sides of the same constellation, linked to difficulties in the oedipal situation described in the theoretical accounts I have outlined. Overall, these case examples highlight the instability that seems to be part of the clinical picture associated with claustro-agoraphobic difficulties, and the problems when couples have no resting place between the anxieties associated with being too close, and those over being too far apart. For individuals with particular difficulties in this area, coupling, or linking with another can be felt to threaten catastrophe. The theoretical accounts of the oedipus complex given here are of profound relevance to working with couples. They describe the nature of the feared catastrophe, and the unstable oscillation, which we can witness in the consulting room, between fears of engulfment and abandonment. I have tried to illustrate how the desperation and threat of annihilation associated with a claustro-agoraphobic situation can give it a deadly quality when it is enacted between the partners in a marriage.

Bion (1961) describes man's struggle to be linked to the wider social group without losing his own individual identity as a fundamental human conflict. Man is, he says, "a group animal, at war with his own groupishness". The legacy of unresolved oedipal difficulties can leave the adult couple in a similar dilemma: terrified of being cut-off from one another, and yet terrified of being engulfed. Often, the couples we see in the consulting room could be said to be drawn together and yet repelled; each partner a "couple animal" at war with their own "couple-ishness".

CHAPTER FOUR

Coming into one's own: the oedipus complex and the couple in late adolescence*

Margot Waddell

I t is now recognized that there is an indivisible link between the oedipus complex and the depressive position as it figures in Klein's later work and in post-Kleinian writing. If one can sufficiently know and bear the experience of the oedipal situation and of the depressive position, centrally important developments can take place. A creative couple can be internalized, and the capacity strengthened for discrimination, in psychic reality, between the generations and the sexes.

Thought of in these terms (Britton, 1989, 1992; O'Shaughnessy, 1989), the oedipus complex puts fundamental issues of sexual identity into context with more general issues concerning the "whole process of engendering, disguising, attacking, and tolerating meaning" (Rusbridger, 1999, p. 488). In this model we see the child presented with the painful necessity of separating, with the accompanying feared, yet also alluring, possibility of actual separateness. This situation presents the child with the potential to be him or herself, based on a growing feeling of integration, a sense of becoming *one-self*.

---

*This chapter has formerly been published in the *Journal of Child Psychotherapy*, 29(1): 53–73, 2003.

At this point the child has psychically to accommodate the reality of a "creative relationship of which he is the product and from which he is excluded" (Rusbridger, 1999, p. 488). He or she has to tolerate the impossibility of claiming and winning one parent at the expense of the other, and to endure the position of being the observer of a relationship in which he or she does not belong. This is a position of being, in other words, at the lonely point of the triangle; of having to acknowledge the existence of a different *kind* of relationship from that available with either parent, unless perversely or abusively.

Much hangs on the negotiation of depressive position anxieties, which are bound with paranoid—schizoid states of mind. On pain of limiting or foreclosing development, such negotiation must stay reasonably independent of defensive procedures. Only in this way can a person "progress fully towards developing a capacity for symbol formation and rational thought" (Britton, 1992, p. 37). In the case where such negotiation fails, paranoid—schizoid anxieties and defences in the form of excessive splitting and projection, denial, concretization, mindlessness, and omnipotence, will flood in and swamp the personality's efforts to grow.

These struggles are not limited to the infantile years (the Kleinian early oedipal situation), or to early childhood (in both Klein and Freud). They are lifelong. Struggles of this kind have to be "re-worked in each new life situation, at each stage of development, and with each major addition to experience or knowledge" (Britton, 1992, p. 38). Much will depend, in this process, on the relative strength or fragility of previous developmental struggles, ones that leave a legacy either promotive or subversive of engagements yet to come. Contemporary theories emphasize the extent to which the ability to bear relinquishment fundamentally affects the course taken by this oedipal working-through. How well did the young child tolerate ceasing to be the sole possessor of the love-object? How well did the older child or young person tolerate other losses—those consequent upon infidelity, for example, or involving personal or professional displacement, or those of having to give up a cherished ideal?

When it comes to establishing a sustained, intimate partnership, the implications of these questions are quite clear. Individual capacity for relationship depends on coming to terms with the discrepancies between perception of the chosen, and usually briefly idealized, love-object (for such is "falling in love"), and the actual characteristics of that same love-object that become apparent. Whether the disappointment, disillusionment, rage, and frustration are felt to be bearable will depend on the outcome of myriad attempts to work through previous loves and losses. The first among these, perhaps, is a baby's discovery that the external world (in the sense of extra-uterine) does not offer unlimited provision of the "stuff of life". The infant's experience was that sometimes the breast was absent when it was desperately needed; sometimes it was intrusively present when hunger was not the source of discomfort; sometimes the milk itself was too thin, or too slow in coming, or too rich and gushing. Confusingly, the breast was sometimes offered without interest, or lacking the usual accompanying feelings of passionate love and comfort, or else it brought disturbing feelings of excitement and over-stimulation. Such manifold physical sensations can scarcely be separated, moment by moment, from their psychic accompaniments. These become more complex as experiences of the object, both externally and internally intensify, are exaggerated or modified, whether in love or in hate, and the psychological mechanisms of projection and introjection come into play.

There is possibly no other stage of development, beyond infancy and young childhood, where the demands of the oedipus complex and the inextricable challenges of the depressive position are more absolute, more disturbing, and more categorical than during adolescence. Among the central tasks of the period are those of separation, of tolerating frustration, of living with disillusionment, of struggling between the pleasure principle and the reality principle. In short, as hard-won depressive capacity strains against the pull towards paranoid–schizoid defences, the whole oedipal situation has to be constantly re-worked. At this time, the ever-oscillating shifts between the paranoid–schizoid and the depressive positions are occurring with especial force and intensity. Under the impact of powerful hormonal changes and newly discovered senses of self, every aspect of life is renegotiated, both of inner and outer life. Amid all this, the young person's experience of his or her changing identity becomes of paramount importance. Its contours are shaped and re-shaped—as they have forever been—through relationships with others, but now in different ways. The child's oedipally freighted relationship with the actual parental couple, and with its many internal versions, is diffused, displaced, and distorted. This happens first in the group-dominated existence of early adolescence, and then is re-focused and intensified in the pairing relationships of the later adolescent years.

These are the years that I am addressing—a time of life not necessarily limited chronologically to being a teenager, but the time, whenever that turns out to be, when adolescent states of mind are being renegotiated. The "teens", however, *are* the years that are developmentally appropriate for such negotiations. These years are inevitably laden with historical and cultural weightings that are seldom fully consonant with the course of any single person's psychosexual development, as he or she struggles to find an inhabitable place in the adult world. These are years when there is a simultaneous drive towards integration and also towards fragmentation; years characterized by drastic defences against the psychic turmoil involved; years when there is a strong pull towards pairing relationships of a kind that can represent a vast range of diverse internal states. For example, establishing an early "long-term" relationship *may* indicate an unusually mature capacity for intimacy. It may just as possibly signify an avoidance of oedipal disturbance by means of a projective, pseudo-adult identification with "being-a-couple". By contrast, an apparently promiscuous approach to sexuality may represent just that—a reliance on multiple sexual experiences as a defence against the felt impossibility of integrating "the sensual and the tender" (Freud, 1905b)—again a failure of oedipal working-through. However (to put the matter equally schematically), such an approach *may* indicate an exploratory and constructively experimental struggle to resolve the adolescent's oedipal dilemma (how can the feeding and nurturing mother also be the sexual mother?). Thus, serial sexual partners could be a way of seeking a relationship with that mother/partner, not so much through mindless erotic adventures but through the capacity to risk loving and losing in the name of fully engaging with life. There are, of course, innumerable positions in between.

My exploration of these issues falls into two very distinct parts, the first being rather general. I will refer to certain classic literary texts, including aspects of the nineteenth-century novel and Shakespeare's comedies. These provide a non-pathological illustration of how the constellation of feelings and defences constituting the depressive position can both enable and inhibit the constant, necessary re-working of the oedipal situation—ultimately leading to the possibility of establishing a profound commitment to a couple relationship.

Second, I shall focus on some detailed clinical material to show the deeply pathological consequences of an incapacity to cope with oedipal struggles, in turn based in the nature of the earliest mother–baby relationship. The context is that of a late adolescent's unsuccessful struggle to engage with his depressive anxieties and his inability to work through a very early-established oedipal *impasse*. Each part of the paper focuses, therefore, in contrasting ways, on the developmental significance of the capacity, or lack of capacity, for introjective identification with a loving, thinking figure or figures—whether embodied in a fictional character, or in elements of actual experience as explored in dreams and in the transference. This capacity is central to the original theorizing of the oedipus complex. The task was always to relinquish the external parents, in favour of their internal representations, and to find ways of psychically accommodating these representations, which may be so heavily imbued with projections that there remains little similarity with the actual figures.

At best, adolescence is a process of becoming; literally, of becoming an adult, and of doing so by becoming a "thinker". This is achieved by gaining and possessing a degree of self-knowledge, through engaging with the process of "engendering, disguising, attacking, and tolerating meaning"—an essential part of becoming mature. It is a process of constant recasting and assimilation, involving repeated reorganization through new identifications and altered object relations. A good outcome to adolescence depends on the capacity to allow for this continuous evolution of the personality, for the transitions from one state to another. This takes place by way of depending on, and being able to take in, the functions and qualities of a benign good-object, in contrast with attempting to master experience projectively through imitation, impersonation or pseudo-identification. The process is one of retrieving projections to support a more integrative thrust towards being one-self, towards "coming into one's own", however mixed a picture that turns out to be.

This major transition from one state to another is traditionally marked by the readiness to form a deep emotional attachment, conventionally represented by the change from being unmarried to being married. In this sense, "marriage" could be described as emblematic of the symbolic realization of internal capacities that have been developing over the years, whether as actually lived or as traced in a work of drama or fiction. The central relationships, as experienced or explored, promote these internal capacities so that, eventually, a shift can be described as having taken place from an initial *idea* of marriage, often culturally and contractually framed, to a final *capacity* for marriage. The latter represents a profound achievement. It is partly based on having established one's own place in life, rather than that assigned by social convention, and partly on having worked through the two necessary oedipal undertakings of rivalry and relinquishment (Britton, 1989, p. 95). The two undertakings are inextricably interrelated.

The novels of, for example, Jane Austen, George Eliot, and Charlotte Brontë share a developmental thrust towards an ability to engage fully with a true partner. This ability is a consequence of having slowly, and often painfully, developed the internal capacity to be committed to a life-long and creative relationship, one implicitly encompassing the renewal of life itself.[2] For, as in the great Shakespearean comedies, whatever may be the underlying strains of melancholy, the spirit, ultimately, is one of rebirth and of hope. The mythic significance resides in the ultimate acceptance of an internal couple that makes possible an external relationship of passion and implied procreativity. The much-maligned "happy ending" is a necessary expression of individual growth and of generational potential. For with the final "marriage", the narrative moves up a generation. The continuity of the social fabric is ensured by the regenerative power of love. The painful acquisition of self-knowledge in the process of finding a partner in life confers "heroic" status on these individuals and equips them to become the parents of generations to be.

The myriad possibilities of social and familial interaction, of public and intimate entanglement and resolution, of political critique and cultural observation, interweave as warp and woof in the canvas of the nineteenth-century novel. However, the adventurous engagement underlying the internal development towards marriage constitutes a central thread, the one in relation to which the action takes place. It is arguable that the actual external marriages are not always adequate statements of the individuals' respective capacities to establish an internal place, and a space, in which the fantasy of fruitful intercourse can occur. But it must be clear that the capacity for marriage and actual marriage are not necessarily meant to be perceived as being consonant with one another. Indeed, nineteenth-century novels are full of people who are married to each other but do not have what I am describing as an internal capacity for marriage. Nor do the partners in such relationships have the capacity *not* to be married.

Contractual marriage clearly functions quite as much as a social or financial convenience, as a defence against separation and intimacy, or as the perpetuation of an unresolved oedipal constellation, as, by contrast, a mature expression of separateness and internal resolution. Jane Austen's novels, in particular, both wittily and painfully depict any number of bad marriages. These relationships are wholly distinct from the central thrust, in which internal development proceeds as the protagonists engage ever more deeply with their lives, loves, and losses.

In *Middlemarch* as, for example, in Jane Austen's *Emma*, or Charlotte Brontë's *Jane Eyre*, there is a central developmental axis: the heroine "grows up". In this sense, each novel depicts the struggles of young women, late adolescents, to reach maturity—a state of being that is implicitly synonymous with acquiring a capacity for intimacy. The compelling aspect of these three books, as of so many of this period, is the nature of the internal odyssey that is embarked upon. Each novel portrays a movement towards inner orientation and integration. Over time, the main characters begin to be able to learn from the experience of having had to confront the truth about themselves. They suffer, endure, weather self-deception and, in terms of the oedipal issues under review, most significantly and importantly, face and survive the experience of rivalry, jealousy, and supposed loss.

Middlemarch begins and ends with a marriage—the contrast between the two measuring the development of young Dorothea (a central protagonist) in the course of the book. The first marriage is to the desiccated pedant, Casaubon. Dorothea is described as wholly caught up in her own youthful ideas, as one whose nature is "altogether ardent, theoretic and intellectually consequent" (Eliot, 1872, p. 51). She is "imbued with a soul hunger to escape from her girlish subjection to her own ignorance and the intolerable narrowness and purblind conscience of the society around her" (ibid., p. 60). This is a wonderful evocation of the adolescent's omnipotent wish to by-pass the pains of ignorance and inadequacy, and of the defensive intolerance, superiority, and slightly prudish judgementalism that often characterize an attitude to the rest of the world—and to a society which is felt to be so woefully wanting.

Dorothea's response to Casaubon's proposal is, we are told, that of one whose soul is possessed by the fact that a fuller life was opening before her. "She was a neophyte, about to enter on a higher grade of initiation" (ibid., p. 67). Infused with adolescent, idealistic fervour, Dorothea seeks to render her life complete by union to one whose mind, as she subsequently discovers, reflects "in a vague labyrinthine extension every quality she herself brought" (ibid., p. 46). She is impressed "by the scope of his great work, also of attractively labyrinthine extension" (ibid., p. 46). She has, in other words, fallen victim to her own projections, to the idealization of a much older and, as she believes, a wiser man. She was "altogether captivated" by one who, to her mind, "would reconcile complete knowledge with devoted piety. Here was a modern Augustine who united the glories of doctor and saint" (ibid., p. 47). (One cannot but remember that Dorothea is an orphan, in the care of her well-meaning, but gushing and bombastic uncle—not a figure who could easily lend himself as an object of paternal admiration and respect for one such as Dorothea.)

Early on, Dorothea, like Casaubon, suffers from the delusion that to know about things, accumulating sufficient "learning" or information, would provide "the Key to all Mythologies"—a key that would bring about a solution to life (again expressing the adolescent delusion that there could be such a thing). This is a flight, in other words, into certainty at the expense of a sense of reality. As Bion put it, she "could not see the wisdom for the knowledge" (unpublished). Dorothea's slow and painful disillusionment challenges to the uttermost her capacity to learn from experience. It initiates a state of mind in which, as admiration for erudition yields to appreciation of wisdom, she can begin to envisage a very different kind of relationship, which also brings together "the sensual and the tender".

In the course of the novel, Dorothea loses her infantile dreams and is stripped of her projective fantasies. In the ghastly loneliness of her honeymoon in Rome she discovers the difference between a narcissistic orientation to the world: "an udder to feed our supreme selves", and an attitude which can recognize "an equivalent centre of self whence the lights and shadows must always fall with a certain difference" (Eliot, 1872, p. 243). George Eliot's descriptions of such fundamentally diverse mental attitudes could be said to define what Klein was later to theorize as the distinction between the paranoid–schizoid and the depressive positions. These descriptions also define the developmental process in adolescence as being from a primarily self-regarding and self-interested state of mind in the early pubertal and immediately post-pubertal years to a later capacity, if things go well, to accommodate others and to have some sensitivity and regard for their very otherness.

Working through oedipal anxiety is intrinsic to gaining an ability to tolerate the loss of a sense of one's own centrality in the world, and to being able to appreciate the gains that ensue from simply taking one's place among others. Dorothea suffers the loneliness of disillusionment and separation, and begins to recognize the significance of separateness. With Casaubon's sudden death, she relinquishes, naïvely and perhaps too readily, her omnipotent adolescent ideals for the more painful reality of frustration, disappointment, and a circumscribed life, which is now blighted by the dead hand of her late husband. His pathological jealousy has forbidden his young widow further marriage, thus destroying any possibility of a future family or personal sexual fulfilment. (Those sympathetic to Casaubon might well point here to an oedipal clue to his profound inability internally to develop, and to his massive intellectual defences against emotional engagement.)

The real test of the quality and strength of Dorothea's internal object comes, as it does for Jane Austen's Emma, with the agonizing "recognition" that the external person is different from the person she has trusted him to be. With Emma, this conviction rests on a certainty that the loved one is lost to someone else, that Mr Knightly has not forever kept *her* at the centre of his being—for Emma, the profoundest narcissistic wound. With Dorothea, the threatened loss is of the one as she had felt him to be: '"Nothing could have changed me" [she says to Ladislaw, the man she has realized she really loves], but her heart was swelling, and it was difficult to go on; she made a great effort over herself to say in a low tremulous voice, "but thinking that you were different—not so good as I had believed you to be"' (*ibid.*, p. 867).

The long night of agony that Dorothea spends on her bedroom floor, wracked with inescapable anguish as "the limit of her existence was reached", crystallizes a process that, over time, has been working within her. She had, earlier in the day, come upon Will Ladislaw in an apparently compromising situation. She had spent the day resisting her real feelings, busying herself with good works and social calls. Only now, in her own room, was she able to admit to herself the depth of her love. Now, she recognized the intensity of her shattered faith, and the loss of the belief that had sustained her since the days in Rome. Now, "with a full consciousness which had never awakened before, she stretched out her arms towards him and cried with bitter tears that their nearness was but a parting vision: [now] she discovered her passion to herself in the unshrinking utterance of despair" (*ibid.*, p. 844). Her experience was of a formless object—a "changed belief exhausted of hope, a detected illusion" (*ibid.*, p. 845). The fire of her anger flamed out from the midst of scorn and indignation, "of fitful returns of spurning reproach" (*ibid.*, p. 845) and of jealous offended pride—and finally, she sobbed herself to sleep.

In the narrative of Dorothea's dark night of the soul we have a compelling account of the capacity of the internal object to survive the fallibility of the external, and of the process by which that occurs. Dorothea does not, George Eliot tells us, sit "in the narrow cell of her calamity, in the besotted misery of a consciousness that only sees another's lot as an accident of its own" (*ibid.*, p. 845). She does not, in other words, sink into self-regarding melancholia. She forces herself to *think*, not only of her own misery, but also of the meaning of others' lives. She gives her attention to what is apart from herself—"all this vivid sympathetic experience returned to her now as a power: it asserted itself as *acquired knowledge* asserts itself and will not let us see as we saw in the day of our ignorance" (*ibid.*, p. 846, my italics). Dorothea draws on her own irremediable grief as a source of strength to others. She draws on capabilities that she has "acquired" over time, as she begins to learn from her own *real* experience, relinquishing the scholarly "under-labourer", or "too good-to-be-true" versions of herself.

The inner reality and meaning of this momentous expression of the thrust towards development is beautifully described in external terms—a kind of "objective correlative" for internal processes:

> She opened her curtains and looked out towards the bit of road that lay in view, and fields beyond, outside the entrance-gates. On the road there was a man with a bundle on his back and a woman carrying her baby; in the field she could see figures moving, perhaps the shepherd with his dog. Far off in the bending sky was the pearly light; and she felt the largeness of the world and the manifold wakings of men to labour and endurance. She was a part of that involuntary, palpitating life, and could neither look out on it from her luxurious shelter as a mere spectator, nor hide her eyes in selfish complaining. [Eliot, 1872, p. 846]

This is not only a movingly understated description of the generosity of a mature mind; it is also a marvellous evocation of introjective identification having been taking place over time. In the face of Dorothea's conviction that the external object has been lost, the internal object holds. It does not vanish or collapse because the external representation, originally the mother (or the mother's breast) has left the field of present perception. It holds, moreover, in such a way that Dorothea can bear, in her desolate state, to look out and see precisely what she feels so excluded from—a man with a bundle on his back and a woman carrying her baby. This is supremely delicately expressed. We do not know, for sure, that this is a young family being registered by Dorothea, but we cannot but surmise.

Dorothea's sources of nourishment are mysterious. Her strength does seem to lie in some kind of deep-seated belief in a good object (perhaps gleaned from the experience of the presence and early loss of her mother), variously expressed in George Eliot's language of morality—a language that strains between the "right and wrong" polarity of mora*lism,* and the profoundly mixed achievement of an ethical stance in relation to what a person can reasonably aspire to. In this last crisis, Dorothea "yearned towards the perfect Right, that it might make a throne within her, and rule her errant will" (*ibid.*, p. 846). The response to her tormented cry of, "What should I do—how should I act now?" (*ibid.*, p. 846) comes from within—she again finds herself looking outside the "entrance-gates" of her own mind to the existence of others' lives, "whence the lights and shadows must always fall with a certain difference".

It has often been observed that her marriage to Will Ladislaw (the ardent young radical who evokes, both physically and morally, the idealism of a latter-day Shelley) was a disappointing conclusion to this extraordinary description of Dorothea's capacity to grow through experience, to re-encounter and work through the basic oedipal issues that repeatedly assail the young person. Dorothea's struggle with that most central of adolescent tasks, finding and establishing an intimate partner, the task of becoming one of a couple, is not matched by an equivalent sense of such a process in Ladislaw. It has been suggested, however (Irma Brenman-Pick, personal communication), that Ladislaw contains the partially unresolved part of Dorothea, and that an aspect of the emotional bond in this and other marriages is with a part of oneself that remains projected.

George Eliot does not, in fact, require us to think of this marriage as a perfect statement of appropriate union. Referring to Dorothea's two marriages, she writes:

> Certainly, those determining acts of her life were not ideally beautiful. They were the mixed result of a young and noble impulse struggling amidst the conditions of an imperfect social state, in which great feelings will often take the aspect of error, and great faith the aspect of illusion. For there is no creature whose inward being is so strong that it is not greatly determined by what lies outside it. [Eliot, 1872, p. 896]

The dimensions of the internal voyage towards maturity, and towards some adult capacities, are, as so often in the nineteenth-century novel, much more extensive and momentous than any confidence suggested in the married states in which they eventuate—though these, it is emphasized, are but a beginning, possibly a "great beginning" (*ibid.*, p. 890). This final restatement of one of the book's central themes—the relationship between character and environment—does not have to reconcile us to the actual marriage. Rather, it points to marriage as a symbolic statement that Dorothea now has the internal capacity for love and for intimacy. It may also point to an alternative possibility, that marriage is not so much an idealized state as one made up of two people who are now on a developmental journey *together*, constantly re-negotiating the ideal and the real in relation to each other, and embarking on the shared struggle to realize a "good enough" marriage of which the future is unknown. None the less, it is one in which the reader has a certain confidence that each partner will continue growing, both independently, and together. Despite the narrative disparity between Dorothea's development and Ladislaw's, the final pages make it clear that if they are to be a couple, idealization and denigration must not come into it. The reader's desire for perfect resolution has also to be challenged.

The finalé makes clear that

> the developmental process lies not in "historic acts" but in the coming-to-have-a-truer vision-of-the-world and of the self-in-the-world, aided, indeed initiated, by a capacity to learn from experience instead of adapting to the structures of social conformity. It involves seeing self and life as they are—stripped of grandiosity, of emotional*ism*, of self-righteousness, and of the impulse, subjectively, to defend against psychic pain by being someone one isn't. [Waddell, 1991, p. 159]

A further way of designating the psychic shifts that take place during this adolescent process is in the description of how the force of projective mechanisms slowly yields to greater introjective capacities, of a more receptive and positive kind. An aspect of George Eliot's genius, as of Jane Austen's, is her ability to draw attention to the significance of the tiniest details of behaviour and intent as they precisely chart these shifts in a character, over time. With Dorothea, the tendency toward the introjective becomes steadily stronger. George Eliot describes the process as being like "the subtle muscular movements which are not taken account of in consciousness, though they bring about the end that we fix our mind on and desire"; "those invisible thoroughfares . . . that delicate poise and transition which determine the growth of happy or unhappy consciousness" (Eliot, 1872, p.194). So, in the course of *Middlemarch*, Dorothea, battered and disillusioned as "the new real future replaces the imaginary" (ibid., p. 226), changes through learning that life must be undergone and that such undergoing, as it presents itself at each significant epoch of her late adolescent struggle, involves constant challenges to the sense of her known self. Theses are repeatedly marked and tested by the central oedipal challenges, those of "rivalry and relinquishment", in relation to other characters in the novel, and in relation to internal aspects of herself. "That new real future which was replacing the imaginary drew its material from the endless minutiae, by which her view of Mr Casaubon and her wifely relation, now that she was married to him, was gradually changing with the secret motion of a watch-hand from what it had been in her maiden dream" (ibid., p. 226).

That "gradual change" is, we might infer, an aspect of the kind of working through which is involved in the adolescent process—a working through of infantile omnipotence, splitting and projection. Dorothea develops a capacity that seems to be rooted in the internal object being able to sustain the failure, absence, or fallibility of the external. It becomes clear that, in psychic reality, the internal readiness for "marriage"—that is, for true emotional and sexual commitment—is based on the capacity to survive loss and disillusionment, to mourn what has had to be given up. For this can engender belief in an internal, intimate couple that may then find expression in an external partnership, one that can carry the implication of regeneration and renewal.

"Marriage", as a symbol of the capacity for intimacy and of this very notion of regeneration and renewal, is a hallmark of classic literature. To be able, in the fullest and deepest sense, to be a couple (only conventionally marked by marriage) constitutes a profoundly optimistic statement of psychic continuity. Perhaps the clearest expression of this psychic continuity is to be found in Shakespeare's comedies. Suzanne Langer (1953) describes the essence of comedy as embodying in symbolic form our sense of happiness, in feeling that we can meet and master the changes and chances of life as it confronts us. In just such a way Shakespeare's great Festive Comedies may be taken as descriptions of the happy outcome (despite the tyrannical overtones of many of the beginnings, and melancholic undertones that so often pervade) of the developmental process and of adolescence in particular. For the comic plots, with their improbabilities, coincidences, sudden reversals, disguisings and unmaskings, cross-dressings and bisexual possibilities, present us with what Rosalind, in *As You Like It*, calls the "full stream of the world". It is the full stream of a particular kind of world, where the characters, to varying degrees, engage with different aspects of themselves. They have to, if the final marriages, which are really to do with renewal rather than mere convention, are to take place.

I can only touch on the world of the comedies here. They present an altogether more ebullient, experimental, and mythic version of things than the novels I have described. In the wholly symbolic worlds of Illyria, the Forest of Arden, the Duke's Oak in a wood near Athens, or, indeed, of Prospero's island, marriage carries with it the resolution of the internal adolescent conflict between conformity and individuality, between received identity and the capacity to be oneself; and, quite explicitly, the sense of the characters partly working through their respective oedipal crises. Many of the comedies begin in an atmosphere of patriarchal authority and denial. These are situations that must be confronted and resolved by the characters in the course of the plays, as they struggle to shed versions of pseudo-maturity imposed from without, and to engage with the creative, imaginative symbolic possibilities within. The comedies are, in other words, profoundly to do with separation and individuation, and with the onward march of the generations that each have to find their own distinctive way of proceeding.

What characterizes the final marriages in many of the comedies is the dramatic evidence that they are the outcome of significant experiments with bisexual aspects of the self. One might even say that the great comic heroines, Viola in *Twelfth Night*, for example, or Rosalind in *As You Like It*, are constituted as heroines through their very capacities also to be Cesario and Ganymede. They have the ability to combine in themselves essential elements, both male and female, that they engage with, or that finally come together in a potentially creative union. Identity becomes a matter not of imitation, or superficial identification with external conventional mores, nor of projective identification with roles and characteristics, but one of examination of inner meanings and of potential integration, such that authentic, creative processes may occur. These processes could be re-described, psychoanalytically, in terms of a renegotiation of the oedipal situation in adolescence.

I will now turn to such a renegotiation in a particularly troubled young man's late adolescence, in an attempt further to explore the issues under consideration in the context of a lengthy analysis. The young man (I shall call him Tom) was the child of a young mother and her lover—someone whom she regarded as the love of her life. Tom spent his first few years alone with his mother. He idealized her and clearly believed himself to be idealized too. My own sense, over time in the transference, was that this relationship may have been far less ideal than he felt it to be; that his mother may have been quite depressed, and at times rather remote from her much loved baby—the fruit of a passionate, failed relationship. At other times, she may have been over-involved, intrusive, and perhaps demanded idealization as a means of keeping her from the break-downs that she suffered with the births of each of her subsequent children.

This young woman, perhaps for reasons of economic depen-dency, perhaps wanting to provide her son with a family, married when Tom was four. It seemed clear that she did not love her husband. Tom felt utterly betrayed. She became a weak and fickle tormentor in his mind—a whore who had deceived and abandoned him, despite secretly still loving him best of all but being "too cowardly" to show it. He railed at her for her callow infidelity. A profound split emerged in Tom's adolescent years, between women as the fountain of all beauty and truth on the one hand and, on the other, of women as degraded and contemptible individuals. This posed enormous obstacles to the possibility of ongoing relation-ships with any young woman he felt drawn to. It seemed as though the feeding and loving mother could not, in any sense, be allowed also to be the sexual mother—in this case, his hated stepfather's partner.

It is a common defensive belief that all parental sexual activity ceases with a child's own conception (to be confounded by a sibling presence, or confirmed by an absence). In his earliest years, Tom ambivalently enjoyed only the very sporadic presence of his natural father and had, until the age of four, basked in the delusory sense that he was his mother's sole possession, and she his. It seemed that his primary sense of betrayal when his mother had married linked to his later masturbatory fantasies, and, for periods, his transference passions. These focused on me (his analyst), and on women gener-ally as degenerate, sadistic creatures, exacting cruel and perverse punishment on him, as the guilty and abject child/victim. Tom's predicament epitomized a much under-recognized problem for stepchildren—the abhorrent necessity of having to confront continuing parental sexuality. This can be especially difficult for the child who, whatever the profound feelings of guilt and loss endured in the course of the parents' separation, has none the less briefly relished a sense of triumph. The triumph, especially in the case of the son of a separated or single mother, is cataclysmically shattered when a new relationship begins. The normal processes of rivalry and relinquishment are disrupted, even fractured, by new and unwelcome psychosexual possibilities. These erect potential roadblocks to the child's development and require greater attention than can usually be accorded in the new and exciting setting of fresh, intimate and erotic parental adventures.

As the analysis unfolded it seemed fairly clear that in Tom's early years he had no sense of an external or internal parental union that was secure enough to withstand the ordinary and necessary struggles of the oedipal situation. The first dream Tom brought to analysis constituted a powerful statement of his psychic experience of lacking containment in early infancy, whatever his consciously idealized version of events suggested to the contrary. It also expressed his fear that he would repeat this experience in analysis. He dreamt that:

> He was trying to play tennis on an indoor court of which one of the walls was missing. Each time he threw the ball up to serve, it bounced back prematurely from an unnaturally low ceiling, making it impossible for him to set the ball in play.

Tom's dream graphically described his psychic predicament. Something fundamental was missing—both, we may infer, from his own experience of being contained by a primary maternal object and from the setting of his life without a father. The *potentially* bounded space of his mother's mind was felt to be lacking a crucial dimension, the missing wall indicating a central component missing in her inner structure. She seemed to have oscillated between depression and idealization, which was directed towards her lover and baby, in comparison with her disappointing marriage. With no solid, dyadic experience of being mentally and emotionally held, Tom had been incapable of achieving the kind of equilibrium essential to coping with the sudden eruption into his life of a new rival. Then, and always, he experienced his rival as the "incarnation of malignant misunderstanding" (Britton, 1992, p. 41).

This "malignant" union with what, in different states of mind, Tom took to be both his unwilling and yet also his wantonly too willing mother, seemed to have created a combined figure that personified "contradiction, meaninglessness, and chaos" (ibid., p. 41). This figure had set him on the path of academic failure, mental confusion, victimhood, and, ultimately, sexual perversity. The potentially fateful consequences of lacking the wherewithal to deal with this oedipal reverse were sealed by the further tragic loss of his mother's mind. With the births of his many younger siblings his mother suffered successive psychotic breakdowns, from which she never wholly recovered. Tom laid the full intolerable weight and responsibility for the rage, pain, hurt, and desperation of these terrible experiences of abandonment, birth, and breakdown at his stepfather's door. Tom had been stuck in an oedipal crisis, and unable to move towards a genuine sense of himself; rather than a collection of posturing, projective "cardboard cut-out figures", "an unconfident social wreck", as he said much later when he felt he was finally "no longer always trying to be in someone else's head in order to look at myself".

This last insight came towards the end of his long analysis. Previously, he had sometimes been able to touch on a more solid experience of his own identity, and move slowly towards a loving relationship, providing the basis for establishing the kind of family he felt he had never had. This profound wish carried with it both reparative components and some founded on a determination *not* to repeat. His genuine desires had long been terribly hampered by aspects of his own pathology, and by blocks to his capacity to integrate his profoundly split, indeed "fractured" (O'Shaughnessy, 1989, p. 142) experiences of the parental couple, motherhood, and womanhood.

Throughout his adolescence, for example, Tom was infatuated with a young woman. As far as I could understand, he experienced her as being very similar, both in looks and in character, to his beautiful, depressed, and quixotic pre-psychotic mother. For years this girl preoccupied Tom in fantasies, dreams, and daydreams. His idealized union with her occupied a "reservation" type place in his mind, preserved, in Freud's terms, as "an island of activity . . . separated from the mainstream of the individual's life" (Britton, 1992, p. 34). Tom similarly experienced the breakdown of much less significant relationships as death dealing in their psychic impact. He felt the young woman's eventual, and never fully explained, abandonment of him as irreparable in its replication of his original loss. Perversity, which is often the main incumbent of the "reservation" was, in Tom's case, not reliably held in this especially protected and defended setting. It was increasingly "on the loose", actively disrupting his life, first with genital exposure, then with sex chat lines, and, finally, with sado-masochistic activities with prostitutes. His perverse inclinations also continuously sabotaged the possibility of an honest, intimate relationship with one who became his regular girlfriend—a young woman of enormous devotion and loyalty, despite all the difficulties (for the main, kept secret from her).

A third mode of relating to women first made its appearance in the consulting room, and was soon enacted in an infatuation with a fellow student. The desire for physical contact with me (presented as a child-like longing for me to touch or to hold his head or hand) had become an insistent theme in the analytic relationship. It was expressed in the form of a pseudo-intimate liaison with a young woman (by all accounts a disturbed and vulnerable "waif"), again conjuring up an image of his "child" mother. The relationship seemed to be entirely based on skin-to-skin contact—mainly stroking—and obsessional surface-to-surface touch. The two-dimensionality of this mode of relating evoked an infantile quality of the sort Esther Bick (1968) describes as defensive, a primitive kind that lacked any sense of mutual interiority. Projective and introjective processes were absent. Something structurally fundamental was missing, precisely as the "tennis court" dream represented.

Tom's traumatic early circumstances seemed to have induced both a denial of, and a rivalry with, the parental relationship. This rivalry later became a constant feature in the analysis, both in the transference and in his frequent and vivid dreams. Such transference and dream manifestations in some respects marked a significant step forward, despite their being, at times, accompanied by an intensification of perverse acting-out. Although I was initially

rendered wholly despondent by this evidence of continuing pathology, I began to view it as being, at least in part, closely bound up
with a step forward in his ambivalent struggle towards progress—
of a *reculer pour mieux sauter* kind (Quinodoz, 2002)—and as a recognition of the pain of oedipal feelings. The feelings, previously so
rigidly defended against, were now arousing renewed and intense
resistance—so intense that the pain found expression either in the
exacerbation of perverse fantasies, or in the symbolic content of the
dream itself.

Two of Tom's dreams, a year apart from one another, draw
together the central threads of the foregoing discussion. The threads
link the oedipal situation with the depressive position, as this
particular troubled adolescent struggles against irremediable disappointment, falters, and again struggles on towards an internal
capacity for a genuine relationship, which for the moment is only
glimpsed, very partial, and constantly wavering under the impact
of ever-revived crises of separation. These two dreams focus on the
fragility of the analytic gains, and the threatening imminence of
losses, as idealization vies with the insecurely introjected analytic
function of containment that had, for periods, enabled his slow
steps towards psychic change.

After some significant indications of a growing capacity for
introjective identification with a creative internal parental couple,
Tom's development had again become stuck, and seemed to be
foundering on the rocks of grievance and perversity. His abiding,
suffocating rage about his birth parents never properly having
been "together" and his stepfather's "intrusion" into his life had
only partially diminished in the course of analysis. In Tom's mind,
his stepfather had wrought havoc, inflicting on him his many
unwanted siblings and causing his mother's "madness". He experienced this stepfather as someone who forever set him apart from
the "Garden of Eden" of each of his natural parent's idealized relationship with himself, "the fruit of their mutual love". In his mind,
he, Tom, had been the "main event" of their brief relationship with
one another. The fact that he, as psychic "linch-pin", could not
sustain them was a reality against which he had, thereafter, both
fought (omnipotently) and given in to (submissively). It was
certainly something that he had never managed psychically to
accommodate.

His mother originated from an island in southern Europe, across the water from the mainland of another country, which was his stepfather's place of origin. For many years, Tom had idealized his early time with his mother in their "island home" together, speaking their "mother tongue". He had utterly denigrated his stepfather as a bully and a tyrant, coming from a hostile and persecuting "foreign" culture. In important ways Tom had always been his mother's "island" boy. His lyrical reminiscences of these early years reminded me of Yeats's *Lake Isle of Innisfree*. Judith Edwards (2003) beautifully describes the psychically unworked-through experience of this "lake-isle", in terms of early escapist fantasies. These are dramatically, though not definitively, expressed in a dream, which took place a year or so before the termination of Tom's analysis.

During the analysis, much work had been done, with many false dawns, on relinquishing the fantasy of establishing a relationship that might realize Tom's idealized exclusivity of a one-to-one baby–mother duo. Tom could not bear to allow the object, whether in the analytic relationship or in life, its own separateness and freedom. The dream offered evidence that some such sustained capacity might be possible, that a shift *could* take place from the idealized, defensive adherence to an exclusive, external love object, and towards some recognition of a more inclusive, creative inner world. Occasionally, in the transference, I had glimpsed a burgeoning capacity to escape the thrall of the persecutory stepfather and embrace, instead, the more ambivalent and, in significant ways, painful possibility of a link to a father figure of a very different kind. There were also signs of Tom being able to retrieve some of his more extreme projections and to live in a less fractured state. The dream represented such changes. However, the dream imagery itself, and the nature of its articulation, offered powerful evidence of the continuing centrality of an oedipal impasse in which the baby's experience is one of exaggerated awe, wonder, and idealization, instead of a more measured, respectful stance in the face an older generation's learning that needs to be absorbed and moved on from if true oedipal differentiation is to occur.

Haltingly, yet with unusual articulation, Tom recounted his dream:

I was a member of crew on a ship in the Mediterranean. The sun was shining and the wind fresh. Unexpectedly, for it was not charted on any map, an island appeared midway between my mother's island home and my stepfather's place of origin on the mainland opposite. It was a stunning island, unimaginably beautiful, awe-inspiring in fact. There were sheer cliffs and the light was rare and lovely. The land was blue, green, grey. I suddenly found myself *on* the island, in the company of a middle-aged couple who lived there. The man was honourable and his wife, too, seemed imbued with the wisdom of the ages. The couple seemed to encompass between them some kind of real experience of life. They lived a very simple existence. They explained to me something of their way of being. It was very basic and mainly to do with the natural elements. What struck me, initially, was the extraordinary nature of the different views of both the mainland and the island that I could experience from this unfamiliar perspective. In each case the view of the land that the new island afforded was much more particular and detailed than anything I had been able to see before. Despite the enormous distance, I could still clearly discern, on each shore, streets, hills, and even houses and people. This enabled me to think about the respective cultures of these two different countries and to bring them into some kind of reconciliation in my mind. The man and his wife showed me books of pictures of the island, ancient books—the topography in different states of weather and season. In some pictures there were snow and dangerous polar bears. There were also beautiful plates showing the natural history of the island. It was as if the wise couple's memories of the island brought together some kind of pre-history of the place that combined aspects of both cultures. After showing me these amazing books of some kind of integrated past, the couple moved outside the house and we began exploring the actual terrain. They pointed out to me the lovely hills, cliffs, wild expanses, mountain ranges, gullies, whirlpools—all the wonderful, natural beauties of the surroundings.

Having described the dream in such unwontedly and exaggeratedly lyrical terms, Tom's tone and interest suddenly switched away from the poetry of the wondrous isle and its inhabitants, to a totally different feeling; a compelling attraction to a fantasy encounter with a man who was about to hurt him sexually. The island-world suddenly slipped away and he found himself fighting with, and giving in to, the desire for a painful and abusive sexual enactment. Within a few moments, the dream/island site of creative possibility was obscured by a cloud of perversion, as if to recreate the sensual simplification of pseudo-integration—vulgar, concrete, and devoid of any trace of the sympathetic imagination and oedi-pal resolution that the dream revealed his inner self was capable of, if only fleetingly.

It was as if the creative, and as yet unrealized, possibility of getting to know a more integrated self which could cope with being the young outsider of a "grown-up", established relationship, had been briefly glimpsed in this experience of a benign "combined object". However, the degree of idealization of the whole situation perhaps inevitably invited some kind of catastrophic counter-force. In the session itself, this new perspective on things was instantly hi-jacked by an unwelcome bit of self-knowledge—the recognition of a "somebody else" in himself, experienced as invasive and abusive. In a trice, the possibility of integration had become so frightening and challenging that Tom had reverted to the perverse, masochistic pleasures in which he had long sought refuge from the split world of his childhood experience. The fear of recognizing and granting that there could be some relationship in his life that might reduce the vast distance between his "island-mother"-self and his "main-land stepfather"-self, relentlessly drew Tom towards a persecutory figure. The figure threatens any attempt on Tom's part to reconcile the painfully polarized aspects of his inner world, militates against any properly loving relationship in his external world, and against any concrete creativity of a kind to which Tom had so often aspired.

This dream has a mythic quality that brings into relation the oedipal experience both of separation and of potential integration. The aesthetic dimension is particularly significant. It impacts on the patient's sensibility of this idealized island-world, and on his use of perversity as a refuge from the overwhelming nature of the percep-tion of new possibilities within, as well as from the inherent insta-bility of such an island "psychic retreat" as a basis for any genuine development.

The island as a "psychic retreat", of the kind described by Judith Edwards (drawing on Steiner, 1993), makes its first appearance in this dream. Even more striking was one that occurred almost a year later when Tom, with considerable trepidation and ambivalence, was contemplating the end of his analysis. He described the follow-ing dream, interpolating associations as he went along:

> I was driving across an elevated structure—a bit like a motorway only somehow the structure was much more arched and less substantial. I

was with an older woman [probably a bit like you] and I knew that I was entering a foreign country. It was Canada [which I immediately associate with my mother]. As we descended from the arc of the structure the landscape opened out before us. At the centre was a vast lake, in the middle of which was an island that seemed like some kind of quintessence of Canada itself. It was extraordinarily beautiful. I was enthralled and over-awed with the wonder of it. Somehow it represented a sort of condensation of the features of the rest of the country. [It epitomized my memories of being in my first, and in a sense, only home.] Next we seemed to be on the island and my woman companion was saying goodbye as she went off in another direction. This seemed acceptable at first but then I became terrified of being alone. Soon afterwards I encountered an older man who seemed to be pointing the way out to me. It felt like it was the right direction but I didn't know whether I could go that way and I felt completely panicked and just stood still.

Tom said that there seemed to be much more to that part of the dream—that is, more about the exquisite loveliness and idyllic charms of the island/world in the middle of the lake. However, as in the post-dream fantasy of the previous year, he suddenly found himself in a quite different emotional space—this time in the dream itself:

Suddenly, I was inside a building—a vast interior of which the external features of the architecture, that is, the street-facing façade, now presented themselves as somehow inside, so that I was viewing the outside as if from within. I felt frightened, even desperate. I now seemed to be being pursued by some kind of malign force or forces that were out to get me. I found myself frantically flapping my arms and hands in an effort to rise above the ground and to fly out of reach of my persecutors. I was aware that I was facing two doors. One seemed to be the right door and the other the wrong one. I was utterly perplexed. Which door was the safe one to go through? I felt that if I was mistaken, forces of destruction and persecution would be awaiting me on the far side.

This dream seemed to speak directly to Tom's predicament as he approached the end of a long analytic relationship, and to how he conducted his life outside. With his (analyst) female companion, he was coming down to earth. And yet the approach was across a structure which felt insubstantial and somewhat artificially elevated (the insecure support as he nears the end of treatment). The dream seems to describe some kind of experience of being "on the way down" towards an ordinary landscape in which men and women, and generations, take their place in the onward flow of things. The difficult "journey" is arrested by the sudden sighting of the island in the middle of the lake, another island of extraordinary magnificence and compelling attraction—the "Lake Isle of Innisfree". The island is again described in lyrical terms, as if to represent, in its location and geography, the gem (nipple) in the middle of the lake (breast)—the exclusively erotic and idealized focus of the whole landscape—that of life or of the analytic experience. It was the epitome of everything most desirable and gratifying. Yet, in so being, it occluded the real with the ideal. The next events in the dream suggest the impossibility for Tom of allowing his travelling (analytic) companion to depart. In his anxiety, he suffers paralysing indecision about an unknown male figure that points out the way to him. Faced with a benign paternal object, he freezes.

In the light of the dream material that follows, we might surmise that, fearful about the impending loss of his analyst, Tom became unable to relinquish what now represented itself as an enthralling island–breast, which he felt was only available to him when he was physically *with* his actual analytic companion. Overwhelmed in the face of imminent separation, he loses contact with the kind of combined, albeit idealized, object that had featured so prominently in his dream a year previously. He cannot allow these "older" figures to be together. One takes the place of the other and he cannot accept help or move on. His predicament is represented by what happens next in the dream. Suddenly, everything turns inside out. The external features of the building's architecture are to be found inside instead. In this inside-out world, Tom frantically resorts to "flying", flapping, and fiddling (masturbatory practices well-known from previous dreams), in a desperate effort to "rise above" the anxieties associated with the ordinary landscape experiences of finding his own way in life—to him, still "a foreign country". The dream-lake, drawn on to defend against the pain of relinquishment, offered no substantial protection in his plight and his (moral) universe is turned inside-out in his panic and isolation.

In this second part of the dream, persecutory forces are actively assailing him and his masturbatory fantasies are failing him.

Caught up, now, in a world of extreme splitting and projection, Tom becomes confused and cannot tell right from wrong. The choice of the two doors would seem to represent some kind of extreme polarity between good and bad with a complete confusion, in the dream-terms, as to which would release more persecutory forces and which would offer him succour and relief. The anxiety which propelled him from the "good" back to the "idealized" object (as we can see in each of the two island-dreams, a year apart) was now further propelling him into the topsy-turvy world of his defensive, amoral universe of fear and indecision.

The inability to know which door to choose seemed to describe the predicament that the baby finds himself in, when he cannot replace the lost, idealized, wondrous breast/nipple/island with any kind of ordinary experience that feels supportable and liveable. It suggests, moreover, the oedipal dilemma in which one choice has to be made over another—a choice fraught with longing, guilt, persecution, and loss—a choice forever to be made, unmade, and again remade. Under the pressure of the fear of separation, now felt as abandonment, the island of the previous year dramatically changes in character within the dream itself, not as a conscious after-flight, as before. That earlier island had been one where, despite the excessive lyricism and idealization, the qualities of an experienced, thoughtful and wise combined object could nevertheless be recognized, engaged with and learned from. In fear, however, that he would not be able to "bear" the "polar" opposites in himself that were now being brought into relation with one another, Tom had previously escaped into his familiar, lurid, and exciting world of sexual fantasy. Yet the dream language and content did, none the less, betoken the fact that something *was* coming together within him, and that that "something" was becoming available in the realization of burgeoning creative possibilities in Tom's personality. In the course of the year he had begun his own writing—some poetry and a television drama.

The second dream describes how fragile these therapeutic gains were. The good breast can again be swiftly traduced and turned into an idealized version of itself, leaving Tom with little sense of inner resources of his own, and unable to make use of the directions he could be given by a helpful, "grown-up", paternal aspect of himself. He wants to be inside and outside at the same time and is left confused as to which is which. He is defenceless and persecuted as a consequence—in the grip of frantic masturbatory excitement. With a more securely internalized capacity for containment, he might have been able to hold on to those links of relatedness, which had begun to feature so clearly the previous year. He might also have been able to resist the more paranoid–schizoid forces expressed in the later dream, forces which drove him to seek union with an idealized/perfect breast and in so doing undermined his capacity for relinquishment, for ambivalence, and for the courage to find his own way. Tom was communicating the intensity of his destructive and negative feelings, and engaging fully in their exploration—a *sine qua non* of oedipal resolution. And so his struggles continued. Now, however, in the shadow of his final analytic separation, the resurfacing of some of the more extreme aspects of his pathology did not feel as negative and destructive as they might at first appear. They seemed to indicate less a paranoid–schizoid regression to the familiar territorial retreats of earlier days than evidence of the process Quinodoz (2002) describes as representing a more depressive capacity to acknowledge the ongoing necessity to work and re-work the damaging consequences of so severe an oedipal *impasse*.

The profoundly contrasting experiences of these two late adolescents, Dorothea and Tom, throw into sharp relief the starkly different processes and outcomes of their respective oedipal struggles in terms of establishing internal capacities for "marriage". In each case, external circumstances have a defining impact. Tracing of the interplay of inner and outer forces of the particular "web" of life in the "Middlemarch" we each inhabit is an explicit and central concern for George Eliot, as for the analyst. Despite the early loss of her parents and the social limitations of her existence, Dorothea's "noble nature" is able, ultimately, to look beyond the mental "park palings" of her restricted world, to tolerate being at the lonely point of the triangle and, as a consequence, to establish a lasting, loving relationship. Internally these constitute "historic acts"—though not ones that the "world" would particularly recognize or celebrate. They are "historic" in that they determine a person's capacity to grow. They are rooted in that person's past and determine his or her legacy to future generations. Their strength and calibre are repeatedly tried and tested in the crucible of the oedipal situation.

Dorothea's story has the breadth and universality of great literature. Tom's profound difficulties bound him within a very different narrative—one which throws into question how far someone with a so fatally idealized and denigrated internal mother can get towards anything resembling what is being called an oedipal resolution. With such a seductive relationship with his early mother—which he endlessly recreated in the idealized, eroticized transference—what hope did he have of genuine relinquishment? What chance did he have of getting off this island retreat if everything away from it was experienced as so persecuting, unsafe, and terrible? When his mother lost her mind Tom lost the opportunity to struggle with disillusionment and ambivalence. He clung, instead, to a past ideal in his fantasies, while in his actions he punished and besmirched his object and himself. Consequently, his capacity to find and sustain a relationship of genuine love and intimacy was seriously impaired.

Late adolescence is the time when the re-engagement with the oedipal situation during the preceding few years can begin to bear fruit. In many cases this adolescent process takes much longer—it may extend into the twenties, or even to the thirties and beyond. But the links between adolescent development, oedipal resolution, and the internal capacity to be a couple are at their closest and most developmentally significant at this time. As already stated, the traditional emblem for the finding of a life-long partner is marriage, which, as George Eliot says in the finale to *Middlemarch*, "has been the bourne of so many narratives, is still a great beginning" (Eliot, 1872, p. 890).

Acknowledgements

With thanks to James Fisher and to Kate Barrows for conversation and reflection on the text.

Note

1. I have explored these issues at greater length in Waddell, M. (1998). Late adolescence: fictional lives. In: *Inside Lives: Psychoanalysis and the Growth of the Personality*. London: Karnac (2002).

CHAPTER FIVE

Shadows of the parental couple: oedipal themes in Bergman's *Fanny and Alexander*

Viveka Nyberg

Introduction

I ngmar Bergman's creativity spans dozens of films and half a century. *Fanny and Alexander*, filmed in 1982, is widely regarded as a crowning masterwork of world cinema. Few film-makers have drawn so unashamedly on their personal experience to feed their creative work and *Fanny and Alexander* is among Bergman's most autobiographical films. The film is generally seen as depicting a more benign, less angst-ridden projection of Bergman's psychic world than some of his earlier work (Horrox, 1988; Törnqvist, 1995).

Fanny and Alexander is an immensely rich and complex film, multi-layered and allusive, profound in its exploration of character, an enduring work of art. This chapter limits its study to one aspect of the film—the oedipal themes that Bergman explores in the course of the narrative. The film charts the psychic development of Alexander, its central character, in his struggle with his oedipal demons. The spectator follows Alexander through a mythic journey of hate and love where he fears that he has, in turn, killed off both father and stepfather as rivals for his mother's affection. In the course of the story Alexander is forced to confront their ghosts and to arrive at some kind of resolution.

The chapter also explores three important couples in the film, to see how Bergman's screen characters enact the process of passing unresolved oedipal phantasies and anxieties down the generational line. I will suggest that Bergman's portrayal of Alexander is of a boy re-enacting his parents' unresolved oedipal feelings in his struggle to find a "third position", from which he may find greater freedom to witness rather than repeat the pattern (Britton, 1989, 1998). In the course of the film the audience may gain, through Alexander's experience, a deeper understanding of the state of the couple relationship when the containment of the couple is failing.

Finally, this chapter refers to some of Bergman's published auto-biographical material and considers what Alexander's character may tell us about Bergman's personal history. Throughout the film Alexander's journey is conducted alongside his younger sister, Fanny, whose presence is neither accidental nor superfluous. This chapter, none the less, reflects primarily on the character of Alexander, who can be seen, in a sense, to represent Bergman himself.

Fanny and Alexander

At the start of *Fanny and Alexander* Bergman introduces us to nine-year-old Alexander, wandering through his grandmother's apartment, which is set in a wealthy university town in turn-of-the-century Sweden. The Ekdahl household is preparing its sumptuous Christmas celebrations, a situation that introduces us to each of the offspring of Alexander's grandmother, Helena. She is the matriarchal dowager who acts as a firm but accepting pillar in the lives of her extended family. Bergman portrays her as a well-known actress, who retains her poise and grace and enjoys a comfortable, bourgeois lifestyle. The intensity of the celebrations suggests to us that this grandiose, idealized display is concealing darker tensions and emotions below the surface. Helena has three sons—Oscar, Carl, and Gustav. Each is married, and the first act of the film introduces us to their partners.

Oscar is married to Emilie; these are Fanny and Alexander's parents. They are actors, and patrons of an amateur theatre company sponsored financially by Helena. Oscar is portrayed as a weak, sentimental character, a second-rate actor who has a poor grasp of the boundaries between performance and reality. This is underlined by the way in which he appears in the film, declaiming speeches and rehearsing his theatrical role rather than confronting the real world. Oscar takes refuge in the "little world" of the imagination, which he counter-poses to the "big world" beyond the theatre. The audience is left in no doubt as to which of these worlds he prefers. Oscar's character resembles Britton's (1989) description of the hysteric, who does not have the internal space to imagine, but instead mounts the stage and plays the part that he is unable to conceive in his imagination. In this sense, Oscar is the constant performer in the play, but is unable to step out of this role in order to adopt the role of the observer.

The audience is left unsure whether his wife Emilie is emotionally more available, or whether she simply performs her allotted role with greater skill and conviction. Emilie is portrayed as beautiful and aloof in equal measure. Her relationship with the children seems functional but distant, as if her mind is ruled by other preoccupations. She seems to have more awareness of her aching emptiness than her husband does. The audience learns from Helena that Oscar is impotent, and that he has been unable to satisfy his wife sexually since Fanny's birth. Helena expresses admiration for the discretion with which her daughter-in-law conducts her extramarital affairs, implicitly condoning this behaviour while underlining her son's impotence. The marriage can perhaps be described as dominated by narcissistic object relating (Ruszczynski, 1995). Ruszczynski describes how such a couple can be characterized by a distancing coldness on the one hand, or a confused togetherness on the other, and that many couples oscillate unpredictably between the two positions. Oscar and Emilie maintain a respectable façade. Perhaps the "confused togetherness" is expressed in the intensity with which they play out their marital roles with public empathy and respect, while concealing the emotional vacuum at the heart of the relationship. As viewers, we may speculate that Oscar's and Emilie's sexual relationship ended at Fanny's birth, when the arrival of their daughter heightened Oscar's unresolved oedipal anxieties. The combination of a sexually impotent father and a mother who is open to extra-marital affairs perhaps makes Emilie appear all the more exciting and available as an object for Alexander's oedipal longings.

Oscar's mother Helena is characterized as a powerful woman. Although her three sons have reached midlife, they are dependent on her social and financial support. She is the strong, pivotal force that seems to hold the family together. The audience is led to believe that she has survived and prospered because of her acute observation of other people. At one point she notes, "we play our roles, some with negligence, others with duty". Later she says, "one role follows the other, the thing is not to shrink away". Clearly, Helena takes pains to measure up to her own criteria. She exudes an air of sardonic distance and good-humoured indulgence toward her sons, who remain, in a sense, infantalized. It is perhaps significant that Bergman has drawn Helena's character in the film as a widow. The absence of a potent husband and father puts the relationship between mother and sons into sharper relief. This seems to enhance the audience's observation of the family dynamic, and aid its understanding of how unresolved oedipal phantasies and anxieties are unconsciously passed down and re-enacted over the generations. For example, we learn that Helena herself has taken lovers and that her husband was distant and unresponsive.

We are introduced to Jacobi, a Jewish family friend who is also Helena's lover. We sense an erotic attraction between them, although Jacobi is evidently not required to fulfil the role of *pater familias*. It is Helena who sets the terms and Jacobi who carries out her commands, an arrangement that appears mutually satisfactory. They seem to relate to each other through a shared ironic, sceptical distance towards the world, rather than through any passionate bond. Their secret embraces seem to underline the fact that Helena does not have a "real" husband, but a lover who sneaks in under cover of dark.

It seems that Helena's grown sons display, in different ways, unresolved oedipal feelings. They find it hard to separate from mother and to move forward in a purposeful way. Oscar has married a woman not unlike his mother. His impotence, at one level, may represent a self-inflicted punishment for his unresolved guilty oedipal feelings towards his glamorous and exciting mother. Oscar's mother was open to extra-marital relationships because his father was so remote. The absence, through death, of the father has metaphorically handed the staff of authority to the mother. This pattern is replicated in the relationship of Alexander's parents. On the surface, Alexander seems to value and admire his father. This is evident in the way he watches the father's rehearsals, identifying with Oscar's devotion to the art of imagining. However, the father is also his rival for mother's affection, and the nursery stands adjacent to the parents' bedroom. Through the interconnecting doors, Alexander can overhear their conversations, and sense the frozen absence of parental intercourse. The audience learns that Alexander is fearful at night and sometimes sneaks into the same bed as Maj, the pretty, young nursemaid. Maj plays the role of a willing "ersatz" mother who provides a sexually arousing relationship. Alexander can enact with Maj what he might rather do with his mother. Alexander is pictured as someone consumed by his own oedipal longings, and surrounded by others' eroticized fantasies and frustrations.

Oscar's younger brother, Carl, is married to Lydia. Bergman presents their relationship as an archetypal, anti-libidinal union. Carl is an infantile drunkard, a third-rate academic gradually losing his tenuous grip on life. He rages with self-hatred, drowning in his own bile, and yet he is humiliatingly dependent on his wife, who paradoxically abases herself to him. As if to underscore Carl's self-loathing, he delights in farting contests with his brother's children. Together Lydia and Carl seem trapped in a repetitive pattern of Carl's abusive cruelty, countered by Lydia's pitying forgiveness, which, in turn, transforms Carl's fury into impotent bombast. Their couple relationship is imprinted by the kind of "projective gridlock" identified by Morgan (1995). She describes "a particular kind of couple relationship in which the couple have a problem feeling psychically separate and different from each other, and hence create between them a relationship in which they feel locked together in a defensive collusion within which there is only very limited growth" (Morgan, 1995, p. 33). Carl is always threatening to leave the "mediocrity" of his "barren" wife, but we know these are empty words. Without his wife Carl would have to own his projections and confront the reality of his own barrenness and mediocrity. The more Carl's abuse escalates, the more Lydia pleads in servility. As he goads her, her abasement seems to confirm his lack of worth and potency. This paradoxically gives Lydia the upper hand, as her pity nullifies Carl's spiteful rage. Theirs is a symbiotic relationship where the couple is chained together by their mutual fears about their capacity to survive independently. The more benign aspect of their dependence is manifested in moments of sentimental remorse and reconciliation. When Lydia, at Carl's request, sings a German Lieder on Christmas Eve, Carl wipes a tear from his eye and, for a moment, the audience glimpses the desperate pact that binds them.

The youngest brother is Gustav. Bergman portrays him as a rakish but loveable "billy-goat", driven primarily by his insatiable sexual appetite. On Christmas Eve, he joyfully makes love to Maj, the new maid, only to follow up the next morning by mounting his long-suffering but complicit wife. Like a small child, he considers erotic pleasure as his birthright, whatever the consequences. His wife Alma tolerates and even encourages his escapades, perhaps because she is bored with her husband's voracious demands. Alma gives Maj, her husband's latest conquest, a suggestive dress as a Christmas present. This threesome could be seen as a harmless *menage à trois*, were it not for the tragedy of their daughter Petra.

Petra is alone in the extended household in recognizing the pain caused by her father's adulterous affairs. She refuses to join her mother in condoning Gustav's dalliances. Petra's response is to withdraw into a state of mute accusation. She silently presents her father with the breakfast tray after he has spent the night with the maid, who is of similar age to Petra. There seems to be no space in father's mind to notice his daughter's longing for his affection. While the women around her appear glamorous and attractive, Petra seems drab and unfeminine, devoid of her father's confirmation of her womanliness. Although Petra features only briefly in the film, this does not reflect her relative importance to the narrative. The fact that her father has seduced a string of women of her own age, but seems blind to Petra's existence, appears brutal and heartless, undermining Gustav's notion of himself as a loveable rogue.

In one scene, Gustav promises Maj to set her up in a coffee-shop in return for her favours. Maj gently teases him, assuming that his promises are simply part of the seduction process. Gustav's narcissism is deeply offended and he withdraws in a short-lived tantrum. In his unthinking grandiosity, Gustav is convinced that he is doing right by everyone, and his response to Maj's challenge is infantile rage. Similarly, when Helena questions his relationship with the pregnant Maj, Gustav reacts with petulant fury.

In his paper "Love, Oedipus and the couple", Kernberg (1995) suggests that the Don Juan syndrome does not have a single aetiology, but exists along a continuum. "The promiscuous, narcissistic personality is a much more severe type of Don Juan than the infantile, dependent, rebellious, but effeminate type . . ." (Kernberg, 1995, p. 51). It would seem that Bergman's Gustav resembles the infantile and rebellious Don Juan described by Kernberg, governed by a mild masochistic or hysteric pathology. Gustav seems unable to tolerate feelings of oedipal exclusion, and perhaps his re-enactment of threesome relationships is an attempt to re-instate early phantasies that deny the reality of his exclusion from the parental couple's sexual relationship. The loss of the illusion of possessive exclusivity may be one of the most difficult developmental hurdles to be negotiated throughout life (Johns, 1996).

Perhaps this is best illustrated elsewhere by his brother Carl when, in a drunken moment, he tells his wife: "First I am a prince, the heir to the kingdom. Suddenly, before I know it, I am deposed". This seems to convey the sentiment of someone who has lost his position as mother's "little prince" prematurely, as if Carl has never recovered from being usurped from mother's affection. Perhaps this illustrates the dilemma of someone who is unable to make a demand for the whole kingdom, and is unable to identify with the potent father and husband. Boswell writes in her paper "The Oedipus complex": "Together with the awareness of exclusion goes the experience of finding out, of learning. This process of change and growth always involves pain, but it also opens up the potential for warmer and more generous relationships" (Boswell, 2001, p. 79). Bergman allows us, through his portrayal of the three brothers, to witness their respective strategies for avoiding the pain of exclusion and, as a consequence, the interruption in the process of psychic growth and development.

As the Christmas Eve celebrations draw to a close Helena and her lover Jacobi sit quietly for a moment in the drawing-room. Elsewhere, in the nursery, the children are too excited to sleep. Alexander plays with his Christmas gift, a "magic lantern", a paraffin-fuelled slide-projector. The story he projects on the wall for the other children is about a girl whose mother is dead. While the father is carousing with loose companions, the ghost of the dead mother re-appears. This story is in effect a mirror reversal of the film's narrative and suggests that the hateful feelings can also be directed towards the mother.

The second act of the film begins with a scene in which Alexander's father, Oscar, rehearses the role of The Ghost in Shakespeare's *Hamlet*. Alexander sits in the auditorium, watching his father, enraptured by the drama. The murdered Ghost pleads with Hamlet to avenge the crime and save the royal family from incestuous ruin. During this rehearsal Oscar is suddenly struck down by fatal illness. Later, as Oscar lies on his deathbed, Alexander seems terrified, trying to hide beneath the bed. Oscar reassures Alexander that he must not be afraid, that death is nothing to fear. It seems characteristic of Oscar's priorities that his final words are instructions to his wife to take over the directorship of the theatre to ensure that "all must continue as usual".

In his autobiography, *The Magic Lantern*, Bergman frequently returns to a notion that fear itself creates what is most feared, an idea powerfully illustrated in Sophocles' *Oedipus Rex*. In the myth the Oracle has predicted that Oedipus will kill his father and marry his mother. Oedipus then tries to escape from the curse, and he leaves his country and the couple he knows as his parents. By so doing, he eventually ends up re-enacting his worst fear, by unknowingly killing his father and marrying his mother. Bergman's use of The Ghost's speech in *Hamlet* as Oscar's finale is, of course, significant. Perhaps Alexander identifies with Hamlet's agony at being torn between wanting to avenge his father's murderer while also wanting his father, the rival, to be dead so he can have sole access to the mother. The fact of Oscar's death may, in Alexander's psychic world, translate into a phantasy where the thing he both most feared and desired has in fact occurred as a result of his oedipal longings for his mother. Perhaps, like Hamlet, Alexander unconsciously fears that he has been cruelly punished for his desires.

In the third act Bergman transports us to the theatre one year later. Emilie has apparently tired of the world of theatre. In a speech to the actors, she conveys her sense of her life as full of self-deception: "I only bother about myself, not reality". The reason for her change of heart is explained by the arrival of Mr Edvard

Vergérus, the local Bishop, at her side. We learn that the Bishop has been her spiritual support during the past year, and that their friendship has grown into an attachment.

Bergman offers us a glimpse of how the Bishop will influence Alexander's life. Emilie has received a letter from Alexander's headmaster saying that her son has spread a story that she has sold him to a travelling circus. She is devastated by what she regards as Alexander's deception and turns to the Bishop for help. The Bishop humiliates Alexander by enforcing a reluctant confession. Those who are familiar with Bergman's autobiography will know that he is drawing our attention to a parallel experience of his own. As a small boy Bergman told a similar story at school, and was similarly punished and humiliated by his own father. In the film, the real father of Bergman's memory appears as the evil stepfather, a sadistic imposter stripped of the status of the real father. Moreover, Alexander's mother has transferred her affections to the rival. The rival is not, like Oscar, just an impotent cipher, but is a potent threat, and plans to possess the mother more effectively than his predecessor. Through the phantasy of being sold to a travelling theatre Bergman points to Alexander's sense of abandonment by his rejecting mother.

When Emilie and the Bishop announce to the children their plan to marry, the ghost of Alexander's father re-appears, smiling ironically, while Alexander mutters curses to himself. The Bishop takes the family to see the residence where his own mother and relatives live. He describes his home as imbued by an atmosphere of purity and austerity. The audience can perhaps recognize elements of Bergman's own father, also a priest, in the portrayal of Vergérus. The Bishop demands that all three should come to his house without any possessions, clothes, jewels, or toys. They are to leave their old habits and thoughts behind. He says, "You are to come to your new life as though newly born". Emilie seems attracted to the absolute austerity of the Bishop's life, stating; "my life has been empty and superficial, thoughtless, and comfortable. I have always longed for the life you live". Despite his severe demands, the Bishop offers Emilie enhanced social standing and appears as an imposing, potent figure. In some ways, he represents a narcissistic mirror image of Emilie's own self-idealization and vanity. He lays a claim to maleness that no one else in the film is permitted to do.

It seems that Emilie is searching for someone who will challenge her morality and perhaps also punish her. The audience may speculate whether Emilie feels guilt towards her dead husband because of her past infidelities. We may also wonder whether Emilie harbours her own unresolved oedipal feelings towards Alexander, whether her aloofness towards him may be a defence against her own eroticized desires—a sentiment touched on in Bergman's autobiography.

We witness the wedding of Emilie and the Bishop. After the ceremony, Helena stands pensively at the window watching the children follow their parents to their new home, stripped of all their possessions. Helena notes, with sadness, that she suspects they will have Emilie back quite soon. At this point in the film Bergman turns the children's lives into a nightmare drawn from a fairy tale. The Bishop's residence is cold and damp and the food is uneatable. The children are clothed in coarse tunics and the windows in the nursery are locked. Alexander detests his stepfather and senses that the feeling is mutual.

On the very first evening Emilie seems to grasp that her marriage is a horrific mistake, but she pleads with the children not to lose heart. When she kisses Alexander goodnight he turns away, as if anticipating his mother's treachery in sleeping with the Bishop. She chides him by saying: "Don't act Hamlet, my son. I'm not Queen Gertrude, your kind stepfather is no king of Denmark, and this is not Elsinore Castle, even if it does look gloomy". With this comment, Bergman explicitly reminds us of the oedipal themes of Shakespeare's play. The film hints at Emilie's growing awareness that, for Alexander, the struggle to possess her represents part of his psychic reality. Unlike the young Hamlet, Alexander is still a child who cannot compete head to head with the Bishop.

The film returns briefly to the idyllic world of the Ekdahl household. Save for Emilie and the children, the extended family is together again, this time in Helena's beautiful summerhouse. Maj, the maid, is visibly pregnant, expecting Gustav's child. There is, however, a mood of melancholy and sadness. Helena and Maj are preoccupied about the welfare of Emilie and the children. Emilie, who is now expecting the Bishop's child, surprises Helena with a secret visit. She blames her loneliness and poor judgement in marrying Edvard Vergérus. She explains to Helena how she had thirsted for a more truthful life, one of demands, purity, and joy in the performance of duty. Instead she lives in fear of her husband's tyrannical rages. She has asked for a divorce but he refuses to consent. Emilie is consumed with anxiety. In particular, she worries about Alexander, whom she describes as being mad with jealousy. She adds that he doesn't realize the jealousy is mutual and that the Bishop merely awaits the right opportunity to crush Alexander. We are struck by the change in Emilie, who seems, for the first time, ready to recognize the depth of her children's suffering. As Emilie realizes that she cannot attain truth via her husband's miserable piety, she paradoxically discovers in her own suffering the strength to face her real situation.

Meanwhile, at the Bishop's residence, Fanny and Alexander are locked in the nursery, praying that their stepfather will die. They repeat, like a mantra, "Die, you Devil". Before Emilie's return, the Bishop viciously beats Alexander, again for imagining a story. This time, Alexander accuses his stepfather of murdering his first wife and their two children, refusing to believe that they had drowned accidentally. Again, Bergman's relationship with his father seems to converge with Alexander's experience of his stepfather, as Bergman describes a similar scene in his autobiography. When Alexander finally confesses that he lied, his stepfather praises him for having won a great victory over himself. The Bishop claims that his love for Alexander compels him to chasten the boy, even if it hurts himself. After the beating, Alexander is forced to beg forgiveness and to kiss the Bishop's hand. None the less, there is, in Alexander's resistance, a glimpse of his utter determination to survive and prevail. Each battle with the Bishop seems to reinforce his sense of defiance and his refusal to be crushed. Perhaps Alexander's refusal to differentiate between lies and truth becomes his saviour. Through his imagination he can distance himself and use his phantasy as a way of playing with his hatred and fear. Perhaps Bergman is intimating that the powers of the imagination became his own escape from similar conflicts. The spectator of the film watches a creation that derives from Bergman's own phantasies and internal child's reality. In his autobiography Bergman describes himself as adept at creating an outer persona to protect his true self. Lying offered him a kind of protection and, like Alexander, Bergman at times found it hard to distinguish between fantasy and reality.

When Emilie returns she finds Alexander huddled on the attic floor, with weals on his buttocks from the Bishop's beating. Later in the evening, as Emilie confronts her husband, she seems to recognize that their life together is unsustainable and that she must leave him. He threatens to take away her children if she decides to abandon him. From now on the children are locked in their rooms, attended by the Bishop's mother and sister. His jealous oedipal rage is now directed towards both Emilie and Alexander. Since he recognizes that he has lost Emilie's affection, he punishes both mother and son for his expulsion from the marital bed.

The final act depicts Alexander's journey from a state of impotent rage to a more integrated state, where he begins to own his sexuality and masculinity. Helena, ever a controlling force in the film, enlists Jacobi to rescue the children from the Bishop's residence. Bergman achieves this by confronting, or perhaps reminding, the audience with the fact that the film is, after all, a story where anything can happen. The escape is performed as if by magic. Fanny and Alexander appear to be in two different rooms at the same time. Whether this fortuitous magic emanates from the author, from Jacobi, or from some other source, is left to our imagination. This device enables Jacobi to smuggle the children out of the house in a giant chest. As in a fairy tale, the Bishop is tricked into signing over the contents of the chest, which Jacobi contracts to purchase.

Jacobi takes the children not to Helena, but to his own house. He lives in a labyrinthine cavern crammed with antiques, a mythical maze of strange objects and monstrous puppet figures. The children are introduced to Jacobi's nephews, Aron and Ismael. This haunting "Jewish" environment represents a world of otherness, set apart from the "Swedish" world encountered elsewhere in the film. It is in this other space that Alexander's emotional journey can reach its climax. Jacobi, as a kind of ringmaster/magician, is central to Bergman's tale. Not only does he redeem the children from the Bishop's lair, but he also offers some kind of framework for the comprehension of their, up till now, senseless and terrifying experiences. Jacobi tells Alexander an ancient Hebrew story about a young boy on a pilgrimage to an unknown land. In this story, the boy's emotional pain and tears become the rain that feeds the world. Jacobi implies that Alexander's torment may not have been in vain, and that it might ultimately be transformed into a creative force.

When Alexander awakes in the night and goes to relieve himself, his father's ghost appears to him once again. This time, Alexander speaks to the dead father, berating him for being useless, in life as in death. "Since you can't help us, you might as well think of yourself and clear off to Heaven, or wherever you're going." He adds that his father should "Tell God to kill the Bishop". His father replies, helplessly: "You must be gentle with people". Alexander has recognized that the father cannot protect him and that he must find his own efficacy. Oscar was, in effect, a "ghost" father during life, and ironically became a more persistent presence after death. The audience is, perhaps, left with the feeling that Oscar's worst crime was failing to save his son from the mother, by acting as a potent husband. By his acceptance of a pretend marriage, he left the field open for Alexander's overwhelming oedipal imagery. Alexander now seems able to let go of the useless, idealized father. Through his rage, Alexander seems to differentiate himself from the dead father and in so doing, like the boy in Jacobi's story, he begins to tap the resources of his own internal well.

His next meeting in the course of this magical night is with Ismael. Bergman portrays Ismael as androgynous, a symbolic union of male and female sexuality. Ismael is locked in his room because he is seen to possess monstrous, unspoken, "awkward talents", which perhaps include pederasty or cannibalism. Ismael requests that Alexander spends half an hour with him in his locked cell. Alexander willingly consents to enter Ismael's embrace. Ismael perhaps represents a universal darkness in all of us, secrets that must be locked away in the pre-conscious, in a constant tension between expression and suppression. Ismael's awkward talent is, in part, an ability to go in and out of the other, rather like a ghost. Through merging with Alexander he is able to know Alexander's pain. This is illustrated in the moment when Alexander writes his name on a piece of paper and finds that he has written Ismael's name instead. Ismael becomes the medium by which Alexander can confront the destructiveness of his phantasies. Through Ismael he experiences a vision of his stepfather engulfed in flames. Ismael seems to open Alexander's eyes and force him to face the consequences of his own hatred. In so doing, it is as if an internal boil has been lanced. Alexander now seems able to own the nascent, cursing, homicidal monster lodged in his own soul. Conversely, he can also own his love and passion. In this scene Bergman seems to invert the narrative. Alexander and his sister, having escaped from the horrors of the Bishop's home, have stepped into a different space, where perversity appears as normality. Now that he has allowed himself to cast off the ghost of the dead father, it appears that Alexander's oedipal rage holds diminished sway.

At the Bishop's residence, Emilie doubles the dose of bromide in her husband's broth, so that she can escape her confinement. She successfully slips out of the house but, as if by magic, that very night the Bishop's aunt accidentally upsets a candle, so that the Bishop is burnt to death, exactly as Alexander had imagined.

Like the beginning of the film, its epilogue reveals an elaborate party for the Ekdahl clan. The family gathers to celebrate a double christening. Emilie has given birth to a baby daughter, as has Maj, the maid. Gustav is in expansive mood, extolling the apparent resolution to the children's ordeal and the birth of the two babies:

> We might just as well ignore the big things. We must live in the little, the little world. We should be content with that and cultivate it and make the best of it. Suddenly death strikes, suddenly the abyss opens, the storm howls and disaster is upon us—all that we *know*. But let's not think of all that unpleasantness . . . it is necessary, and not the least shameful, to take pleasure in the little world, good food, gentle smiles, fruit-trees in bloom, waltzes.

It is as if Bergman allows the audience to relax for a moment, to catch its breath, before the threat of death and the "abyss" descends again. Yet, Gustav's attempt to banish these demons paradoxically reminds us of their continued threat. The family shares the happy occasion—with the exception of Alexander, who seems detached. He eats his cake in a sloppy, ungainly manner, more an awkward adolescent than the obedient child we met at the start of the film. Emilie projects a sweet, idealized picture of motherhood, but the audience is deprived of any reconciliation between Emilie and her son. It seems that Alexander's sense of oedipal betrayal remains very much alive. Despite Gustav's attempt to restore family harmony, it is evident that Alexander stubbornly resists inclusion in this order. We sense that his journey has taken him beyond the reach of Gustav's platitudes.

At the very end of the film the rug is pulled, almost literally, from under our feet, as another ghost trips up Alexander. This time it is the dead stepfather. The Bishop reminds him that "You can't escape me". Although the audience is caught off-guard by the Bishop's re-appearance, Alexander seems unperturbed by the threat. Rather than seeking solace from his mother, in the final scene Alexander calmly rests his head in his grandmother's lap.

As with the oedipus complex, there is neither a happy, nor an unhappy ending to the film. Alexander has, in the course of the narrative, confronted his rivalry with both his father and stepfather and he has, in some sense, seen off both their ghosts. It is arguable that, in the course of the film, Alexander has been struggling with the generational impact of unresolved oedipal feelings. The matriarchal grandmother has been unable to allow her sons, including Alexander's father, to separate and individuate from her. Consequently, Alexander's parents have not succeeded in sufficiently containing their sexual and relational difficulties that have, in turn, inflamed Alexander's imagination. In the scene where, like Hamlet, he finally addresses his father's ghost, Alexander appears to have made an internal move from subject to object. It is as if Jacobi's story has enabled Alexander to make sense of his own pain and suffering. He is able to confront his father as a real, rather than an idealized object. Once the observer position exists in Alexander's mind he is able to move towards a position where he can also be observed. The creation of the space to be an individual is a process that involves some recognition of the primary couple (Britton, 1989). The audience witnesses this in the encounter with Ismael, where Alexander can tolerate Ismael having access to his darkest phantasies. By confronting the impotence of his father and the aggression of his stepfather, Alexander, to some extent, can recognize aspects of the reality of the parental relationship. Britton suggests that recognition of the parental relationship creates a boundary for the internal world, making possible what he calls "triangular space":

> If the link between the parents perceived in love and hate can be tolerated in the child's mind, it provides him with a prototype for

an object relationship of a third kind in which he is a witness and not a participant. A third position then comes into existence from which object relationships can be observed. Given this, we can also envisage being observed. This provides us with a capacity for seeing ourselves in interaction with others and for entertaining another point of view whilst retaining our own, for reflecting on ourselves whilst being ourselves. [Britton, 1989, p. 86]

The process of moving towards a third position seems to change Alexander's relationship with his mother. Near the end of the film Alexander is clearly part of the family again, sitting close to the dinner table while at the same time observing his mother out of the corner of his eye. This reflective distance is underlined in the final scene, where Alexander takes refuge in his grandmother's lap, rather than his mother's. Perhaps Alexander is now better equipped to handle his own sexual excitement. He instinctively seems to know that his grandmother's lap acts as a safeguard against his longings for his mother. Perhaps Bergman suggests that any resolution of Alexander's oedipal struggles will be temporary and incomplete and that demons will always remain.

Bergman published his autobiography, *The Magic Lantern*, in 1988—five years after the release of *Fanny and Alexander*. In the book, Bergman recalls an event that took place in his late forties. He was working in Stockholm's Royal Dramatic Theatre when his mother telephoned with news that his father had been taken to hospital for emergency surgery. She asked Bergman to pay him a visit. Bergman replied that they had nothing to say to each other, and he felt nothing but indifference towards his father. His mother became tearful, pleading with Bergman to do this for her sake. Bergman asked his mother to excuse him from this persistent emotional blackmail, and claimed that her tears had never made an impression on him. He then slammed the receiver down. Later that evening Bergman received a phone call from reception saying that a "Mrs Bergman" had arrived to speak to him. By this stage Bergman had been married several times, so there were a number of candidates for the role of "Mrs Bergman". He asked which "damned Mrs Bergman" was demanding his attention (Bergman, 1988, p. 5). The receptionist explained that "Mrs Bergman" was in fact his mother and that she asked to see him immediately. When they met, his mother was furious with rage and struck him force-fully as he reached to embrace her. They eventually reconciled and Bergman promised to visit his father. This was his last meeting with his mother, because she died unexpectedly a few days later. As if we were observing a family scene through a keyhole, this episode dramatizes the fraught triangular relationship between Bergman and his elderly parents.

Bergman was born in 1918. He was an ailing second son, who was predicted not to survive childhood. His maternal grandmother, as on other occasions thereafter, came to his rescue by taking him to her country house where she found him a wet nurse. Bergman discovered that illness was something his mother, as a qualified nurse, found interesting, and that it commanded her attention and tenderness. Bergman portrays the relationship with his mother as both highly charged and lacking in constancy. He describes how he passionately adored her, but the intensity of his devotion and his sudden rages irritated her. She would dismiss him in cold, ironic tones and Bergman would cry tears of rage and disappointment.

Bergman discovered an additional way to command his mother's attention. Since his mother's chosen weapon was indif-ference, Bergman mirrored her response. "I also learnt to subdue my passions, and started on a peculiar game, the primary ingredi-ents of which were arrogance and a cool friendliness" (Bergman, 1988, p. 4). Bergman identifies his greatest problem as never being given an opportunity to reveal his game-playing, never being allowed to be enveloped in a love that, after all, was reciproca-ted. When he discussed this dynamic with his mother in her old age, she told him that a famous pediatrician had warned her to reject what she described as her son's "sickly approaches" because "indulgence" would damage him for life.

Bergman's father was a priest and based the children's upbring-ing on turn-of-the-century Christian conceptions of sin, confession, punishment, forgiveness, and grace. In his autobiography Bergman remembers his common early experiences of humiliation by his father. For example, when he wet himself he would be dressed in a red skirt for everyone's amusement. Punishment was seen as some-thing self-evident and it could be either swift and brutal or complex and sophisticated. Bergman describes how the immediate conse-quence of confession was to be frozen out. Later, the parties were summoned to his father's room, where interrogation was renewed. After that, the carpet- beater was brought out and Bergman himself had to declare how many blows he deserved. After the punishment, he was expected to kiss his father's hand and ask for forgiveness. Like Alexander's mother, Bergman's mother also enjoyed discreet extra-marital affairs, but religious piety and custom prevented any separation from his father.

Bergman's autobiography appears savagely truthful. He shame-lessly reveals unflattering aspects of his private life to the reader, with no attempt to justify or excuse himself. He resists offering the reader redeeming traits, as if this might constitute an artistic short-cut to bypass the truth. He reveals an obsessive, almost indiscriminate sexuality, which rendered him relentlessly faithless. For a large part of his life he was unable to trust others. He also describes his voracious emotional neediness, his anxious fears and, above all, his bad conscience. He exposes his psychosomatic symptoms and his diarrhoea. He professes his tempestuous and compulsive need to remain creative.

Perhaps it is this unblinking self-knowledge, this inability to deny his own experience, however painful, that allows Bergman to unveil the subjective world of his creations, his characters. While they are not identical, the film narrative reveals aspects of Bergman in a similar way as dream material reveals aspects of the patient's inner world. In some sense, the three Ekdahl brothers represent different aspects of Bergman himself. Oscar apparently uses "the arts" to cope with the insufferable reality of the "bigger world". Gustav's compulsive erotic adventures echo Bergman's own temp-estuous love affairs, described in his autobiography. Carl's bitter despair and self-loathing were constant companions throughout Bergman's life and work (Törnqvist, 1995). Jacobi, as the children's ultimate saviour, perhaps represents the magician in Bergman, who mediates and transforms experiences, who translates chaotic, prim-itive nightmares into some kind of resolution, through complex, metaphorical and artistic expression.

Freud first referred to the myth of Oedipus in a letter to Fliess in October 1897. He described how, in the course of self-analysis, he discovered that falling in love with the mother and jealousy of the father seemed to represent a "universal event of childhood" (Freud, 1897, p. 265). Freud pointed to the character of Hamlet, and pondered his apparent reluctance to avenge the murder of his father by killing his uncle. Freud suggested that Hamlet's hesitation derives from his unconscious sense of guilt, arising from his illicit passion for his mother. Freud notes that Hamlet brings down a punishment on himself, suffering the same fate as his father— poisoning by the same rival. Freud had already, at this point, made a link between the oedipus complex and unconscious guilt, and this idea was to become a cornerstone in his future thinking (Freud, 1923, 1924, 1930).

In his autobiography Bergman emphasizes his attempts to evade and deny guilty feelings, which have haunted him through- out his life in the form of a constant bad conscience. The centrality of unconscious guilt is ever-present in Bergman's films. Through the actions and reflections of his complex characters Bergman illus- trates how this experience moulds and determines interpersonal relationships.

Britton, in his paper "Subjectivity, objectivity and triangular space" (1998b) suggests that, for some patients, the oedipal situa- tion is dreaded, not just because it brings with it unwanted and painful feelings, but because it is felt to be a catastrophe. These are patients who have encountered, in phantasy or in fact, the primal scene without having established a secure base with a maternal object. The consequence of this is that the belief in the good mater- nal object has been retained by splitting off the experience of misun- derstanding and attributing it to a third person. This third person is the father of the primitive oedipal situation who becomes the embodiment of "malignant understanding" (Britton's italics). Then the phantasized union of the parents is experienced as a monstrous event, which personifies meaninglessness and chaos. From Berg- man's autobiographical account of his early upbringing we recog- nize the history of a little boy who did not experience the union of his parents as benign and containing. It is fair to speculate, noting Bergman's early illnesses, that there may have been an early failure of containment in his relationship with his mother. His own subjec- tive experience certainly seems to have been that he pined for his mother's affection, but was met by her coolness and calculated distance. Perhaps his hateful feelings towards his father, who executed premeditated beatings, heightened his oedipal envy and rage and intensified his feelings of guilt. Like his fictional character,

Alexander, perhaps Bergman was left with the psychic inheritance of the apparent lack of oedipal resolution.

Summary

This chapter has attempted to explore some of the oedipal themes in *Fanny and Alexander*. It has done so by following Alexander's mythical journey through his own fictional drama, where he confronts within himself heightened oedipal anxieties and longings. The central couples in the film indicate the power of unresolved oedipal feelings, which may be passed on, and re-enacted, across generations. Alexander's difficulties can be understood, at least in part, as a response to a breakdown of containment in the parental relationship. Britton's notion of a "third position" helps us better to understand Alexander's attempts to find a standpoint from which he can make sense of his experiences. Finally, the chapter has explored some of the oedipal issues in the film, in relation to Bergman's personal history.

Fanny and Alexander is a magnificent, multi-faceted work of art, which cannot be reduced to any one theme within its complex narrative. What makes the film so remarkable is Bergman's consummate artistry in exploring these, and other powerful issues, with immense richness, subtlety, and ambiguity, while at the same time engaging his audience. Bergman resists any attempt to sweeten the burden of the human condition by suggesting that Alexander can somehow achieve a final resolution of his pain. We know that the Bishop's Ghost is correct in warning: "You can't escape me". Like the rest of us, Bergman's Alexander is left at the end of the film to continue his struggle with the intractable difficulty of his personal history.

CHAPTER SIX

"It seemed to have to do with something else . . ."

Henry James' *What Maisie Knew* and Bion's theory of thinking*

Sasha Brookes

> "Earth Water Fire and Air
> Met together in a garden fair,
> Put in a basket bound with skin,
> If you answer this riddle you'll never begin"
>
> Robin Williamson

During Henry James' development as a novelist, his attention increasingly focused on the minds of his characters, and with the nature of their thinking and the "knowledge" upon which it was based. He became more and more interested in how his people variously know and do not know themselves, each other, and the experiences with which their creator presented them. *What Maisie Knew* was published in 1897, at the beginning of the "third period" of his work, during which he was the most preoccupied with the life or death of minds either nourished by, or starved of, knowledge of themselves, and of the world outside them.

---

*This chapter has formerly been published in the *International Journal of Psycho-Analysis*, 83(2): 2002

In 1896, he wrote in his journal: "It is now indeed that I may do the work of my life. . . . I have only to face my problems . . .". These problems were not to be named. "But all that is of the ineffable", he wrote next. The "problems" which, when faced, would yield "the work of his life" are only to be known, either by author or reader, by a process of imaginative acquaintance with "the work" itself.

The title *What Maisie Knew* places knowing as a process squarely before the mind's eye of the reader. It conjures up "the ineffable" by means of the empty, unspecified "what" that challenges the reader's attention and directs it towards something which cannot be named in advance or in the abstract. The story of what Maisie knew is the story of Maisie's problems and how she faced them—of the growing relationship between herself and her external realities; and the closely related growth of her internal world of thoughts and feelings: her knowledge.

What Maisie Knew was being conceived at the same historical moment—at the approach of the twentieth century—as *The Interpretation of Dreams*. Here Freud, in making his understanding of the strange tragedy of Oedipus central to psychoanalysis, did name the problem that must be faced on the road to knowledge. His reading of Sophocles' drama depended upon his most radical postulate: the existence of a dynamic unconscious aspect of the mind. He argued that the tragedy draws everyone deeply into its far-fetched plot because

> there must be a voice within us ready to recognise the compelling force of destiny in the *Oedipus* . . . his destiny moves us only because it might have been ours—because the oracle laid the same curse upon us before our birth as upon him. [Freud, 1900a, p. 262]

With the new advantage of psychoanalytic knowledge, Freud showed that we can become conscious of, and stand outside, our identification with Oedipus. We can seek an answer to the principle riddle of our lives, finding our guesses confirmed by stray facts and memories of our histories that now make sense to us. This kind of understanding deeply impressed Little Hans (Freud, 1909b), and proves its usefulness every day in psychotherapy or in self-analysis, the source from which Freud derived it. Dora, however, would have none of it (Freud, 1905e).

Freud used the oedipal tragedy's emotional effect on its audience to support his hypotheses; first, that we have deep feelings of which we are unconscious, and second, that these feelings give us a sense of recognition of the truth of psychoanalytic insight. This kind of knowledge, which we draw from our unconscious processes of mind, presents itself in feeling and not in words. Freud evidently thought it carries its own conviction, and is to be trusted. He was presumably referring to it when he later said that a man who doubts his own love may, or indeed must, doubt every lesser thing (Freud, 1909d).

With hindsight, it now seems that Freud was speaking of two different kinds of knowing, and did not pause in his argument to make an explicit distinction between them. Winter (1999) quotes the historian of education Fritz Ringer, who noted that the German academic tradition of Freud's time distinguished between interpretative understanding, *verstehen*, and another kind of understanding, *erleben*, which is not under conscious control, and involves a reader in reproducing within herself "the inner states which gave rise to the text" (Winter, 1999, p. 45). Both are necessary, as is continual interaction between them in order to understand experience, whether of art or life. "If you (only) answer this riddle, you'll never begin."

At the beginning of the next millennium, and after many years of learning about phenomena that we know we will never predict or measure, we now recognize, without alarm, that Freud's view of knowledge, both hermeneutic and deductive, is self-enclosed. It addresses the problem of human thought, and does not reach outside its own subject matter; our minds and their way of discovering their unconscious knowledge through the telling of a story— from *erleben* to *verstehen*.

In this chapter I will refer to a work of art that is contemporary with the birth of psychoanalysis and created without access to psychoanalytic thought, in order to support Freud's contention that the oedipal situation is the problem that must be faced on the road to knowledge. This is the ineffable problem that James did not try to articulate, but that he set himself to express and explore in his novel. I also wish to suggest that present-day psychoanalytic theory allows us to add significantly to the understanding of humanity Freud gained from his particular guess at the Sphinx's riddle. Since he wrote, with the help of his discoveries, other thinkers have been concentrating on what we take with us, inside ourselves, when we go to meet the Sphinx. Henry James' story of Maisie's journey towards knowing foreshadows, in my view, the post-Kleinian model of the mind developed by Bion and his successors. Like Sophocles' play, James' novel holds more meaning within it than its creator was aware of, or could have been aware of at the time of its writing.

In particular, James continually presents his characters with the choice Wilfred Bion tells us people are constantly facing: the choice between suffering and evading, knowing and not knowing about our experience of life (Bion, 1967). Both Freud and Klein recognized that human children confronted with the riddle of life have a powerful wish to know the facts and find an answer (Freud, 1905d; Klein, 1928). Both also described some of the ingenious ways we find to ignore the facts and falsify the answer. Bion (1967) recognized our lifelong struggle between the wish to know, and the wish not to.

In this connection Freud noted some odd deductions made by children from their observations aimed at finding out where babies come from, but did not recognize the extent of defensive refusal to know in early sexual theories. Chasseguet-Smirgel (1985), referring to McDougall (1986) points out that Little Hans' theory of his mother's widdler protected him from knowledge of the oedipal situation as Klein defined it. He "defend(ed) himself against reality by repudiating it . . ." as Klein observes in another context. She continues, speaking of development in general, "the criterion of all later capacity for adaptation to reality, is the degree in which (children) are able to tolerate the deprivations that result from the Oedipus situation" (Klein, 1927a, p. 128).

Had Hans acknowledged his mother's female genital, he would have been confronted with the knowledge that his parents' genitals were complementary, and, hence, with the primal scene (Britton, 1998a). He suppressed the facts which would have brought the painful truth home to him and, as a consequence, found himself imprisoned in the house by a phobia, in an inner unknown state of fear and guilt about his oedipal wishes. Knowing the truth about his parents' relationship and his exclusion from it was painful, and involved giving up the phantasy of overcoming his father and taking his place. But it allowed Hans to know himself as a child conceived by a mother and father together, and from this standpoint of reality to continue his exploration of both his inner and his outer worlds.

Ronald Britton (1998a) has stated unequivocally what the end of Hans' story implies. It is only from the "third position" in the oedipal triangle, which Hans was able to occupy at the end of his analysis, that we are able to begin knowing. Gathering both kinds of knowledge—objective knowledge of reality, which differs from cherished phantasies, and also empathic knowledge of experience, which requires a capacity to recognize the separateness of loved and desired others—depends on the capacity to take the third position. The process of development confronts everyone with the difference between phantasy and reality, and with the separateness of others. But there are tremendous differences between, for example, the characters in *What Maisie Knew* in the degree to which they can embrace this knowledge, make it part of themselves and build on it. Many of them find it unbearable and unthinkable, and turn away from it. The differences between James' characters can be better understood, in my view, by considering which of them is able to take the third position.

Maisie is the one who has the capacity and makes the choice to know "most" as James says. What does she learn and where does it leave her? And where did she get her capacity to know, which her parents seem to lack completely? I shall draw together Bion's empathic and empirical understanding with James' intuitive and expressive creation of sixty years earlier, to show how they "give a sense of truth" by "combining different . . . views of the same object" (Britton, 1998, p. 34). In this case, these are different views of the process of knowing or not knowing one's experience.

The reader of *What Maisie Knew* shares with Maisie her emergence into consciousness. As far as I am aware, this is unique in James' fiction. He wrote about other children, and occasionally looked back at the childhood of characters we read about as adults, but only in Maisie's case did he evoke the first awakening shock when something longed for is missing. For Maisie, it is fat. Her calves were too thin, as her father's friends told her; they pinched her legs "until she shrieked—her shriek was much admired—and reproached them with being toothpicks" (James, 1966, p. 22).

We find Maisie with her nurse in Kensington Gardens, trying to get to grips with this. James never specifies her age nor tells his readers how much time is passing in the course of the story, but here she sounds as if she is four or five. We have been told, in a dry preamble, that her very tall, good-looking, fashionable parents have just divorced with as much publicity as possible, each accusing the other of being the worst, and battling over their child in a passion of hatred that was actually the only passion of their lives. At first the court inclined to her father, not so much because he was any better than her mother, but because the disgrace of a woman was more appalling. Then it became clear that Beale Farange, Maisie's father, had spent a considerable sum given to him earlier by his wife for Maisie's maintenance, on the understanding that he would not take divorce proceedings. He could neither raise this money nor "render the least account" of it, and his lawyers proposed a compromise that gave custody of the child to each parent in turn. Maisie is at her father's when we meet her, looked after by Moddle, whose only demand was that Maisie not play too far, and who was always on the bench when Maisie returned to it. Maisie has just left behind the time when she had only that desire to meet. James gives a minute account of her first collision with ineluctable reality which corresponds exactly to the paradigm proposed by Bion in his paper "A theory of thinking" (1962a).

Bion's hypothesis is that the process of thinking comes into being, given good enough conditions, in order to deal with thoughts. Thoughts arise only from an absence of what is desired: when the breast is present there need be no thought. A hungry baby is filled with the thought that she is dying, and cries to rid herself of unthinkable fear and horror.

Sometimes, in good conditions, a mother has an unconscious capacity to register and recognize her hungry child's experience, and can think about it and name it. Consciously, the mother thinks that the baby is hungry and prepares to feed it, while unconsciously she accepts the ejected thoughts that her infant could not bear, and uses her own thinking capacity (called alpha function by Bion) to give them meaning. When this happens the baby is able to take back into herself a meaningful experience ("the baby sounds really upset"). When it fails to happen, because a parent either cannot recognize or cannot tolerate the baby's experience, instead of missing an absent breast the baby feels assaulted by overwhelming emptiness and meaninglessness: an abyss, a void, chaos.

In Bion's view, when a meaningful emotional interchange between the inner worlds of mother and infant accompanies physical feeding, it provides for the growth of a mind, just as milk provides for the growth of a body. Following Klein's (1952b) model, Bion specified clearly the intrapsychic processes involved in the interchange. A baby must project its passionate feelings, having as yet no capacity to tolerate them, and when things are going well the projections can be unconsciously known and accepted by the parent. In the best case, the parent has sympathy with what the infant is experiencing, and is also able to think that it isn't the end of the world, though the baby may feel it is. After a sojourn, as Bion says, in the maternal unconscious, the infant can receive her feelings back, with the sense that they have been thinkable to the parent, though they were not so to herself. From many such unconscious experiences by an infant of unconscious "maternal reverie" grows an experience of mind, as a place where feelings become meaningful through the mental capacity Bion called alpha function.

Precisely this happens between Moddle and Maisie. Maisie looks anxiously at other children's legs and asks Moddle if they, too, are toothpicks? "Moddle was terribly truthful; she always said: 'Oh my dear, you'll not find such another pair as your own.' It seemed to have to do with something else that Moddle often said: 'You feel the strain—that's where it is; and you'll feel it still worse, you know'" (James, 1966, p. 22).

Maisie delivers her painful bewilderment to her nurse's mind, and Moddle does not deny or palliate Maisie's experience. She accepts the truth of it, and goes on to give it meaning by linking it with the events of Maisie's life. Maisie feels the strain of her broken home and warring parents and it shows in her legs, and as she grows older and knows more of her difficulties, she will feel them more acutely. Maisie takes in from Moddle a dim but real sense that her toothpick legs can be accepted; and more, that their meaning can be thought about. At this stage of her life, no one else connected with her is able to know or think about her feelings at all. Henry James provides Maisie, in her relationship with Moddle, with the experience of maternal reverie, within which she can start to grow her own mind.

He tells us that, during her time at the Kensington Gardens, Maisie was unable to think about many of the experiences she had:

> It was only after some time that she was able to attach . . . the mean-ing for which these things had waited . . . she found in her mind a collection of images and echoes to which meanings were attach-able—images and echoes kept for her in the childish dusk, the dim closet, the high drawers, like games she wasn't yet big enough to play. The great strain meanwhile was that of carrying by the right end the things her father said about her mother—things mostly indeed that Moddle, on a glimpse of them, as if they had been complicated toys or difficult books, took out of her hands and put away in the closet. [James, 1966, p. 23]

Moddle seems to have shown Maisie that there were things that a child of her age could not and should not think about yet, and Maisie, who experienced them, kept them in her mental closet. When the time came for Maisie to go to her mother's house,

> The ingenious Moddle had . . . written on a paper in very big easy words ever so many pleasures she would enjoy at the other house. These promises ranged from "a mother's fond love" to "a nice poached egg for your tea" . . . so that it was a real support to Maisie, at the supreme hour, to feel how . . . the paper was thrust away in her pocket and there clenched in her fist. [James, 1966, p. 23]

The relationship between Moddle and Maisie has a profounder meaning and even more resonance and beauty when it is seen in the light of the "container–contained" relationship, one of Bion's most important contributions to psychoanalytic theory (Bion, 1967). The container–contained relationship happens when one puts unthinkable experience in the closet of a thinking mind, which gives back the sense that somewhere the experience *is* thinkable: the mind's alpha-function has "attached" meaning to it. James also used the metaphor of a container in his description of the mental cupboard in which Moddle put the experiences that Maisie was unable to make sense of. When the time came for them to separate, Moddle created a symbolic container in the unknown "other house" for Maisie to keep in her mind. She undertook that it would offer holding and nourishment to the lonely and frightened child, and, in the piece of paper, provided a physical token of her own function of containment for Maisie to take with her. Maisie's father, however, gave her a message to take to her mother that must have been a very great strain to carry by the right end: that her mother was "a nasty horrid pig".

It is quite difficult even for an adult reader, distant by more than a century from this message, to think about it, but consideration suggests that its form is more appalling than its content. Its language makes clear that instead of parents, Maisie had two infuriated children of her own age who evidently had no closets to put their fury in, and no one to help them create any. The two opposite experiences, of containment and the absence of it, seem at this point in the story to come to Maisie with equal intensity. Moddle happened to be there when Maisie's father gave Maisie his message, and was shocked out of her accustomed position of social inferiority and silence into saying directly: "You ought to be perfectly ashamed of yourself!" Maisie remembered her "sudden disrespect and crimson face" more vividly at the time than the words of Beale's message, although when her mother later asked her for them she was able faithfully to repeat them. However, Maisie kept Moddle's outrage on her behalf in her closet, and must have contributed to her later revelation that "everything was bad because she had been employed to make it so".

By the time she went to the other house, Maisie had evidently taken in and made part of herself Moddle's belief in a container; a place where thoughts (originally arising from the absence or loss of something) could be kept, in the hope that thinking and linking ("it seemed to have to do with something else . . .") would give experience a meaning. She had also participated many times in the opposite process; the destruction of meaning through links being broken. James presents a clear instance of this opposite process in relation to Maisie's legs, which had also given rise to her first experience of thinking. It is no accident that her father's friends attacked her in the place where she felt the strain—where her suffering was manifest. Unable to bear her vulnerability, they pinched her calves until she shrieked and admired her vocalizations as a diverting performance.

James presents the creation and destruction of emotional meaning close together in relation to the same legs, and again the profundity of his vision is made more evident in relation to Bion's concepts of K and −K (Bion, 1967). K signifies the desire for knowledge; knowledge which, Bion believed, must continually be created in every mind, by linking feeling with thinking and the inner world with the outer. In reading Maisie's story, we discover some of the rewards of this process of creating knowledge but, as Moddle knew, it involves meeting painful truth and recalcitrant reality. When this feels intolerable, the alternative is to destroy meaning by destroying the links between inner emotional reality and outer reality, as do the "gentlemen" who divert themselves by making Maisie shriek. The consequences of much destruction of meaning by −K also become clear in the progress of James' narrative.

Maisie's revelation—"that everything was bad because she had been employed to make it so"—came to her through her first encounter with romance. Her new governess, Miss Overmore, "by a mere roll of those fine eyes which Maisie already admired" conveyed to Maisie that there was an alternative to an endless tit-for-tat. This somehow caused a tremendous reverberation in the container, the closet of memory instituted by Moddle;

> It was literally a moral revolution and accomplished in the depths of her nature. The stiff dolls on the dusky shelves began to move their arms and legs; old forms and phases began to have a sense that frightened her. She had a new feeling, a feeling of danger; on which a new remedy rose to meet it, the idea of an inner self or, in other words, of concealment. [James, 1966, p. 25]

Maisie's admiration for Miss Overmore's fine eyes seems to have brought her to an encounter with the oedipal situation, and this encounter breathed life into Maisie's potential for thinking and learning from experience. Her mother had told Maisie to tell her father that he "lies and knows he lies". Maisie, in the established mode of family communication, had vivaciously asked Miss Overmore, "*Does* he know he lies?" The governess conveyed to Maisie an unspoken message; "how can I say Yes after your papa has been so kind to me?" (James, 1966, p. 27). Just as Miss Overmore—though employed by Maisie's mother Ida Farange—declined to insult Beale, Maisie saw she could stop taking her parents' messages. "Her parted lips locked themselves with the determination to be employed no longer. She would . . . repeat nothing".

Maisie's revelation was of a couple with a relationship of kindness, which she saw shining in contrast to the parental couple whose retaliatory messages of hate she had been carrying. This vision led to "a moral revolution . . . accomplished in the depths of her nature". How can it have done so?

Maisie was able to commit experience too difficult for her to Moddle's maternal reverie, whence it returned as thinkable. Together, they created mental space for the storage of experience too hard for the child to think about, and found ways to build "a guard within" Maisie, to help her at times of crisis (Rilke, 1987). They shared the belief that experience can be faced and considered; in Bion's terms, they had a container–contained relationship. The "moral revolution" accomplished in the depths of Maisie's nature can be seen as the container–contained relationship coming to life inside her inner world, where she conceives of herself as storing or concealing harmful messages in her closet, so that they do no further harm. By her silence, she determines to protect her vision of a couple with a relationship of kindness. The vision even sustains her through Ida dashing her from the top of the stairs almost to the bottom because she will no longer be a go-between. It is illuminating to consider further the sources and implications of the revolution in Maisie's internal world, in the light of psychoanalytic theory in general, and in particular Bion's theory of the development of thinking.

There is a striking difference in Maisie's position in relation to the two couples in her life at this moment. She is now perhaps eight or nine. She has been employed by the retaliatory couple as a medium to link them together with insults and outrages, and up until now there has been no reason to feel herself separate from them and their relationship. They do not conceive of her as a separate person, although they conceived her. She sees the "kind" couple, however, in a relationship that excludes her; at this point, they do not seem to need her to link them together. Maisie thus finds herself in the third position.

There must be a crucial distinction, which James' language here helps to clarify, between the third position and the ignominious and agonizing position of oedipal defeat. Evidently this defeat cannot be bypassed by anyone, and perhaps experiencing it was what made four-year-old Maisie's feelings about her legs so poignant.

However, she does not remain confined in the oedipal triangle where the only possibilities are defeat and triumph, which must alternate, and where blindness, rather than seeing and knowing, is chosen. In her moral revolution "she had a new feeling: a feeling of danger" born of the realization that she was being used by her parents to hurt each other. Then, "a new remedy rose to meet it, the idea of an inner self". It seems that Maisie was able to bear the moment of frightening vision because in extremity she found her "inner self" rose to meet her; she was not simply cast into the outer darkness of the excluded (or exploited) third. Readers may be reminded of Moddle's paper of consolations, which Maisie had thrust into her pocket and there clenched in her fist, giving her something unseen, inside, to help her; a symbol of the "guard within".

Maisie's mind-changing vision appeared in her inner world to herself alone. Only after making clear with what a "prodigious spirit" she interpreted and understood it does James show her trying to fit it to the real relations of her visionary "kind" couple in the outer world. There, things were more complicated, and an adult reader can have an advantage over Maisie, who wonderingly remembered Beale's words to the "almost too pretty" young governess; "I've only to look at you to see that you're a person I can appeal to for help to save my daughter". Adult readers see Beale's predatory pounce out of the groves of Kensington Gardens, and hear his words as wolfishly unctuous and false. His character for his daughter, however, was still too difficult a book for her age, and she kept it to read later. Reading James' novel "later" in the light of Bion's theory of functions (Bion, 1962b), it is possible to compare Maisie's relations to her parental couple and to the new couple formed by her father and her governess to see that her function was essentially the same for both.

Bion's model of the mind (1962, 1967) gives the need for meaning equal weight as a dynamic mental force with the forces of love and hate. He tried to avoid coining omniscient-sounding abstract nouns to denote mental processes that are unconscious and fundamentally mysterious to us, and instead used letters of the alphabet as signifiers. One effect of this choice is to present with striking clarity his view that each mental force can at any given time be working either creatively (signified as +) or destructively (−). Everyone, for

instance, is always engaged either in creating or in destroying meaning, and the distastefully moralistic and hypocritical flavour of
Beale's opening line convinces us immediately of his bad faith (−K).

Beale's statement also illustrates Bion's theory that the dynamics
L, H, and K are always performing a relating function (Bion, 1967).
In one sentence, Beale stages a paranoid–schizoid alliance with
Miss Overmore, in which they appear idealized as "goodie" res-
cuers opposed to the wicked Ida. No thinking or understanding
will take place in this black and white drama. They need something
to bring them together, however, in the absence of L, H, or K, and
Beale instantaneously recruits Maisie to serve as a pretext. Readers
are already well aware of her function for Beale and Ida, of linking
them together in an addictive and destructive relationship that, I
think, gives us a suggestive glimpse of −L (Bion, 1967). Now Maisie
is to be employed as a link again, and at first sight, it seems her
function for the new couple might be different and perhaps better.

Henry James dearly loved to contemplate the overdetermined
entanglements of human affairs, presumably valuing awareness of
the complexity of experience as Keats did in writing about "negative capability", and as Bion did in writing about learning from
experience. Maisie's linking function for the second couple emerges
from the detail of the narrative as both better, and no better (from
the point of view of her own welfare), than her function for the first.

As far as she can, Miss Overmore loves Maisie and appreciates
what she later called her "plain, dull charm of character", her perse-
vering struggle to know her experience and to learn from it. As
Miss Overmore's relationship with Maisie develops, it raises for the
reader the question of what it is for the adults in the story to be
parental, of what it is to know the child who does so much knowing. Maisie's natural parents are quite incapable of knowing about
anyone else, trapped as they are in their narcissistic echo chambers.
But that by no means makes them insignificant for Maisie. James
makes knowing them and accepting them Maisie's deepest and
hardest developmental task. Miss Overmore can occasionally know
and love Maisie, but she is not able to think about anything from
Maisie's point of view, or give up any pursuit of her own for
Maisie's benefit.

James makes clear that, when Miss Overmore appeared at
Beale's house, though delighted to see her, she had not come

because of Maisie. A poor girl with beauty and high spirits, she had come to take her chance with Beale, as an alternative to the social extinction of being a governess. By the time that Beale unceremoniously married her and she became "Mrs Beale", the plot had also thickened at the other house, and Ida had found Mrs Wix as a cheap governess for Maisie. Mrs Wix had had little education, and with her one dress, her thick glasses and her greasy button of hair, seemed grotesquely unattractive. Beauty is both important and skin-deep in Maisie's story. Her parents, Mrs Beale, and Sir Claude (who becomes Maisie's stepfather) are all lovely to look at. Mrs Wix, however, "touched the little girl in a spot that had never even yet been reached. . . . What Maisie felt was that she had been, with passion and anguish, a mother . . . this was something Miss Overmore was not, something (strangely, confusingly) that mamma was even less" (James, 1966, p. 30).

Mrs Wix's passion and anguish partly relate to the death of her own child but, as she will show, she is richly capable of feeling for Maisie. Being a mother, for James, is evidently not simply a matter of biological parenthood, but has to do with Bion's K; with knowing empathically and containing the feelings of a child. Mrs Beale later remarked that Mrs Wix was "as ignorant as a fish" of conventional learning. However, Mrs Wix had not only "moral sense" but could also think realistically about basic truths, like generational difference, which were denied by Maisie's other "parents".

Ida next married Sir Claude, "ever so much younger" than herself and with whom, as Maisie learned from Mrs Wix, she was deeply in love. Soon Mrs Wix and Maisie were also in love with the charming Sir Claude, "a family man" who loved Maisie and presently arrived at Beale's to see her and, inevitably, to be charmed by Mrs Beale. Maisie, as she says, had now "brought together" a third couple. Sir Claude is yet a brighter figure of romance for her than Mrs Beale, and he is also able, in a big-brotherly style, to be a parent to Maisie. Maisie knows this third couple are her dearest and best hope, though she also knows that Mrs Wix is always there intensely waiting.

In the course of the narrative, every encounter between Maisie and her natural parents consists of the opposite of their knowing her—of their trying either to drag something out of her or to push something into her. When there is no psychic container, feelings must be ejected; and other people are dragged in to fill up the empty spaces. James makes it plain that Beale and Ida connected themselves to others by means of projective identification (Klein, 1946), and he vividly shows us the consequences, as both come to feel progressively more empty and impoverished. They experience this concretely as material poverty. Beale is last seen as the paid companion of a rich Countess, whose whiskery hideousness frightens Maisie. Ida, in finally resigning as Maisie's mother, struggles to pay Maisie off with a ten-pound note and cannot quite bring herself to do it.

Maisie accepts some of their projections. "Better to reign in Hell than serve in Heaven" might have been their joint motto, and when they cannot make others be what they want, they angrily spoil every relationship, becoming more despairing and destructive as the story goes on. This deterioration shows itself to Maisie in various ways; for instance Ida's make-up becomes ever thicker and more dramatic as, presumably, she feels emotionally more unreal; "her huge painted eyes . . . were like Japanese lanterns swung under festal arches". Both parents severally break their ties with Maisie, putting it to her that they are being rejected and deserted by their child. Maisie accepts this from them both, partly because she knows them and what they would be bound to say, and partly because there is an element of truth in it. She knows that Beale and Ida cannot be parents to her, and she must cling to the third couple she has linked together, the couple she loves best and with whom she has most chance of relationship. This couple are betraying her natural parents, but this cannot be any concern of Maisie's. The betrayal seems inevitable, however, in the context of a post-Kleinian reading of James. As Beale and Ida are unable to occupy the third position, they must recurrently move from oedipal triumph, via betrayal, to oedipal defeat.

Unlike Beale and Ida, Sir Claude and Mrs Beale do not only use Maisie to embody aspects of their inner worlds. However, Mrs Beale is unable to keep Maisie in mind, and James poignantly demonstrates this through Maisie's shocking lack of routine education. Miss Overmore began as her governess, but as soon as she took up with Maisie's papa, had no more time to teach her. Mrs Wix tried, though handicapped by her own little learning, and with constant lapses into romancing about Sir Claude and Henrietta

Matilda, her lost daughter, who had been run over by a hansom-cab. For long stretches of time at her father's, however, Maisie was completely lonely and neglected, although she had somehow managed to learn the piano and a little French. As part of a projected regime for Maisie to attend lectures (that had the advantage of being free) in "Glower Street", Mrs Beale once came rushing in late for a lecture that was, in any case, unintelligible.

Sir Claude had more capacity to think about and remember his stepdaughter, though his tender name for her, "Maisie-boy", shows he did not think of her as a daughter, or, evidently, of himself as a father. He erratically and impractically provided for Maisie and Mrs Wix, whose meals at Ida's had become scanty and unpredictable "jam-suppers", so that they were glad of his gift of an enormous iced cake. Maisie's families were now falling apart. Her stepparents had an adulterous relationship, and her natural parents were growing increasingly absent and scandalous. Finally there was a crisis, and Maisie found herself fleeing to France with Sir Claude and the Mrs Wix, who had been her only resource in Mrs Beale's absence.

In Boulogne, entrancing in its foreignness—its seascapes and golden Virgin, coffee, and buttered rolls—Maisie came to make another link in her mind equal in importance to her earlier moral revolution. James articulates it simply. "What helped the child was that she knew what she wanted. All her learning and learning had made her at last learn that" (James, 1966, p. 244). The flight to France had been the project of a fourth couple, Sir Claude and Mrs Wix, also linked together by Maisie. Mrs Wix had inspired Sir Claude to take Maisie (and herself as female attendant and governess) away from Beale and Ida, who had now effectively abandoned her, and to try to make a decent life for them all. Although this would fulfil part of Mrs Wix's fond dream, there is also a sacrifice for her to make, for she cannot have Sir Claude as partner, and instead will be a motherly servant to him and Maisie. In the scene at Boulogne, however, the cast of four, including Sir Claude and Mrs Beale (who soon appears), Maisie and Mrs Wix, reveal and discover vital aspects of their inner selves.

Mrs Beale has always known what she wants, and now it is a "family" in the south of France, where living is cheap and she, Maisie, and Sir Claude can be together in a way that will nominally save appearances. If Mrs Wix will come too, so much the better; and Mrs Beale potently "makes love" to her and tries to seduce her out of her "moral sense". A psychoanalytic reading gives a deeper meaning than the conventional to this attribute of Mrs Wix's. She insists that an unmarried couple cannot be Maisie's parents, but her honesty and conviction seem to reach beyond this legal impediment, which the couple are sure they can remove in time.

Readers of the intense dénouement of the narrative share Maisie's feelings in a way that, so far, they have not. We have previously felt for her, as she was pinched and neglected, grabbed to Ida's bosom and squashed against her jewellery, or sent flying out of it again with such force that she had to be caught by bystanders. Now we feel with her, as she feels "at the bottom of a hole". We feel her "faintest purest coldest conviction" that her beloved Sir Claude, the parent who loved her best, is lying to her, feel that "little by little it gave her a settled terror". Maisie knew all her fear and grief and held it within herself, and as a result "she knew what she wanted".

This form of words is important, as it indicates again the internal container–contained relationship. There are two "shes" in the sentence, and though they are both Maisie, they are different aspects of her. The one who knows is the guard within, aware of what Maisie wanted as an emotional being and human child, and prepared to stand up for her right to it. This assertion on Maisie's part is not entirely new in the narrative. Before their flight, Maisie and Sir Claude had accidentally encountered Ida and her current lover (in the park again). Ida had sent Maisie to walk with the Captain (her new lover), while she and her husband confronted each other. The Captain had completely espoused Ida's cause, and told Maisie emotionally, "your mother's an angel. . . . Look here, she's *true!*". Maisie was deeply touched by this invocation of idealized womanhood, and sobbing "oh mother, mother", urged the Captain to say he loved Ida, and asked him not to stop loving her.

By the time Ida came to take her leave of her daughter, the Captain had become to her "the biggest cad in London". Maisie had accepted Ida's story that she was a noble, shattered victim of circumstances, who now must "try South Africa" or expire. However, she protested against and resisted Ida's attack on the ideal couple, in which she had momentarily been enshrined. Knowing the difference between good and bad begins in splitting and idealization and draws from unconscious origins the inspiration to find truth and beauty in "real life"—as Maisie does, with grief and pain, at the end of her story.

What Maisie found she wanted was that she and Sir Claude should fly together. If he would sacrifice Mrs Beale, she would sacrifice Mrs Wix. Sir Claude almost shared her exhilarating, momentary hope that they could escape together to Paris, but he hesitated and they missed the train. With her back to him to protect him from her feelings, Maisie swallowed her tears of disappointment, clasping the volumes of the *bibliothèque rose* he had bought her. When she turned back to him, her terror had gone with her tears. She was beginning to know that they could not be a father–daughter couple, as Sir Claude would not leave Mrs Beale. Maisie was faced with a grown-up rival who had risked her reputation for Sir Claude; a partner of his own generation who offered a sexual relationship.

There certainly was a way for Maisie to join this couple, and both Sir Claude and Mrs Beale told her directly that she was essential to it. "You've done us the most tremendous good, and you'll do it still and always, don't you see? We can't let you go—you're everything" (James, 1966, p. 229). Maisie could have her old job back and continue her linking function for her parental couple, and with it, the split experience of powerlessness and omnipotence which had characterized her strange childhood.

Maisie's moment in the third position, however—knowing that she wants the man she loves and is too young to have him—seems to have done for her what it had done for Little Hans at an earlier age. She knows she is still a child. Mrs Wix's "moral sense" that she should not have parents living in sin seems superficial compared to the sense they perhaps shared, that she should not always and forever be "doing the most tremendous good" to her parental couple. She should be having lessons and reading the "Malheurs de Sophie", and Mrs Wix, in her own more obvious way, refuses to be a party to the sacrifice of Maisie's childhood.

It seems that at this dénouement Sir Claude began to understand what Maisie knew. "I haven't known what to call it . . . but . . . it's the most beautiful thing I've ever met—it's . . . sacred" (James, 1966, p. 242). Maisie, in order to be the child she was, must tear herself away from the beloved but delusive adults that she had hoped would be her family. As Sir Claude sees, Maisie can be herself—a child—but they are unable to be their age: parental adults. Maisie's revelation could, prosaically, be called being in touch with reality, or learning from experience, but Sir Claude's allusion to the beautiful and the sacred reminds us that the creative life of the mind starts with acknowledging reality. Moddle had tenderly acknowledged Maisie's legs; "Oh my dear, you'll not find such another pair as your own". Sir Claude now lovingly acknowledged that he lacked Maisie's power to know what was good for her. He could only do what Mrs Beale wanted.

Bion's K is not quantifiable. "Memory should not be called knowledge", as Keats wrote (Gittings, 1987, p. 66). K is the linking function whereby the mind ingests experience and is nourished by it. −K starves or poisons the mind by denying or distorting reality, such as the truth of generational difference. Maisie knew that she must not poison her precious, "sacred" faculty of knowing by returning to a pseudo-family, where she took responsibility for the adults instead of their taking it for her.

The novel ends at this moral and emotional height, but it is characteristic of James that he does not lose touch with the vital question of what Maisie and Mrs Wix were going to live on. Readers have long known that "the child was provided for, thanks to a crafty godmother . . . who had left her something in such a manner that the parents could appropriate only the income" (James, 1966, p. 20). Maisie's thanks are also due to her stepfather, the one parent who has at last come to know her, and to a variety of unidealized mothers—Ida, without whom she would not have been born; Moddle, without whom she would have known nothing; her crafty godmother; Miss Overmore with her fine eyes; and Mrs Wix, who is able to be true to her principles. At the last, Maisie is neither omnipotent nor helpless, but realistically dependent.

CHAPTER SEVEN

The painful truth

Monica Lanman

My theme in this chapter is the developmental challenge we all face in relinquishing a primary phantasy of omnipotent and exclusive possession of the other, in favour of tolerating diverse and sometimes, conflicting relationships "beyond the pair". I have sought to illustrate the inevitable pain involved in this process, and some of the ways we try to avoid it. The paper approaches this subject from several different angles, which I hope will prove convergent. I start from Freud's "Parricide" paper (1928b) and briefly touch on his literary examples. I refer to a contemporary children's story and then, using more recent psychoanalytic thinking about Oedipus, I discuss some examples of how this challenge can affect adult couple relationships.

The metaphor that psychoanalysis derives from Sophocles' *Oedipus Rex* is used to describe a set of dilemmas that are key to the construction of our internal world. It refers to our earliest experience of a threesome, with a primary carer and the rivals for her attention. Themes of rivalry and jealousy, and of the longing for exclusivity, in tension with the longing for individual freedom from the constraints imposed by others, are the drivers for very many of our stories, plays, contemporary films, and television dramas about relationships. Threesomes are pervasive and cause trouble. As Freud puts it in his paper on Dostoevsky (1928b), "It can scarcely be owing to chance that three of the masterpieces of the literature of all time—the *Oedipus Rex* of Sophocles, Shakespeare's *Hamlet* and Dostoevsky's *The Brothers Karamazov* should all deal with the same subject, parricide. In all three, moreover, the motive for the deed, sexual rivalry for a woman, is laid bare" (*ibid.*, p. 188).

Each of these tales derives its disturbing power partly from the fact that the father is actually murdered, but also from the anguished sense of complicity on the part of those who either did the deed in less than full awareness of what they were doing (Oedipus), or were not directly responsible for the murder in question (Hamlet, and three of the four Karamazov brothers). This latter was also the case for Dostoevsky himself, whose own violent father was murdered by a stranger. Freud discusses evidence for Dostoevsky's unconscious sense of guilt for the crime he didn't actually commit: his epilepsy (which Freud suggests was hysterical), his novels about criminals, and his acceptance of what was, in reality, unjust banishment to Siberia by the Tsar, among other aspects. Freud also touches on some of the manifestations of pain and guilt related to oedipal phantasies, whether conscious or unconscious, enacted or not, in the three works of literature that he refers to.

In recent years, Steiner has significantly extended our awareness of the evasion of truth in the Oedipus story. He discusses Sophocles' *Oedipus* plays in terms of a movement from denial to omnipotence in the face of unbearable truth:

> When he is forced to face reality and can maintain the cover-up no longer, Oedipus does so with great courage. It is not easy for him, and we see him vacillating and struggling with his ambivalence, but this only makes his final achievement the more impressive. I will argue that this movement towards truth is tragically reversed in *Oedipus at Colon* . . . I believe that this reversal actually begins in the first play at the point when Oedipus blinds himself . . . (at) the climax of *Oedipus the King* . . . it seems to me that Sophocles recognizes that the truth, when it is fully revealed, is too terrible to be endured and that through his self-mutilation Oedipus is already in retreat from it. [Steiner, 1993, p. 122]

Let us consider the effect of guilt about their father's murder on the three Karamazov brothers and the illegitimate fourth. The actual murderer—the illegitimate, epileptic Smerdyakov—kills himself. Ivan develops "delirium tremens". Mitya manages to make a tenuous relationship with a woman, despite his imprisonment for the murder. Finally Alyosha, who seems the least caught up in hatred of the father, remains single but manages to be the kindest to others, including to a band of boys in need of guidance. Interestingly, he bears the name of Dostoevsky's own son, who died of epilepsy in his third year. It is as if he is to represent the possibility of innocence or redemption. In fact, I think Alyosha reaches something of a depressive resolution of the oedipal issue, which he works through in his relationship with his substitute father, the Elder Zossima. He idealizes this substitute father, and then goes through a crisis of anxiety when he dies. A much greater crisis for Alyosha follows over the discovery that, after death, Zossima is not immune from putrefaction as a true saint should be. This is a huge test of Alyosha's capacity to cope with a degree of disillusionment in relation to this "father", and he is nearly overwhelmed with rage and self-loathing at this point. He throws himself at a prostitute, the same one who is already involved with his father and his brother, and who is eager to prove that she can seduce even him into the rivalrous entanglement. But somehow he and she discover a redeeming, loving recognition of each other in the midst of this storm of destructiveness, and Alyosha goes on to provide some sort of calm, moral centre, in the midst of the subsequent horror.

For Hamlet, the two fathers he does eventually kill are his potential father-in-law and his stepfather, not his own natural father. However, long before these deaths occur, his moroseness at his mother's hasty re-marriage after his father's death, and his anguish at the news of his father's murder, are extreme, and suffused with guilt. He contemplates suicide and, significantly for our purpose here, he destroys Ophelia for offering him a loving partnership of his own; "Get thee to a nunnery: why wouldst thou be a breeder of sinners? I am myself indifferent honest; but yet I could accuse me of such things that it were better my mother had not borne me". Some of the best-known lines in English literature derive from this oedipal melancholy of his "To be or not to be . . ." or:

> It goes so heavily with my disposition that this goodly frame, the
> earth, seems to me a sterile promontory; this most excellent canopy,

the air, look you, this brave o'erhanging firmament, this majestical roof fretted with golden fire, why, it appears no other thing to me but a foul and pestilent congregation of vapours. What a piece of work is man . . .

In the end, of course, Hamlet dies in the process of killing the man who murdered his father and married his mother, the man in whom he surely unconsciously recognizes his own guilt. The audience is offered no relief from this finale of destruction, apart from Horatio's loving valediction,

> Now, cracks a noble heart. Goodnight, sweet prince,
> And flights of angels sing thee to thy rest!
>
> [*Hamlet*, 5.ii.]

In his Dostoevsky paper, Freud was concerned with the possibility of the "dissolution" of the oedipus complex in boys through relinquishment of rivalry. He saw the creation of the superego as driven by guilt about parricidal phantasies, derived from the wish to become like, and indeed to replace, the father. He also discusses the alternative "feminine position" for boys of masochistic submission to the father, both positions entailing fear of castration. Since then, psychoanalytic thinking has widened and deepened our understanding of oedipal issues to include more complex and shifting identifications and longings shared by both sexes, and more primitive anxieties about intrusion, abandonment, and annihilation, in what has become known as the "early oedipal situation" (Klein, 1945). In *The Oedipus Complex Today* (Steiner, 1989), the different contributors each emphasize the connection between working through the oedipus complex, the toleration of ambivalence in working through the depressive position, and the capacity for tolerating connections between different mental elements (thinking). Britton and Feldman (1989) both point out that the casualty, if this development goes wrong, may not only be the relationship between persons, but the psychic capacity to make emotional connections and allow ideas to interact with each other in the process of thinking.

Oedipal issues in this sense suffuse and underpin all our relating, both in phantasy and in external reality. I was struck recently by a contemporary children's story, fast acquiring an adult following, which incorporates some of this from a child's perspective. In Philip Pullman's *Northern Lights*, one of his strikingly creative ideas is the "alethiometer" or "truth measure". This device requires its reader to make its hands point to three symbols, and then "hold in their mind" the many different levels of meaning each symbol has "without fretting at it or pushing for an answer". A free pointer then travels round the dial until it settles somewhere and its "reader" senses the answer. Not everyone can do it, but the child heroine of the story finds that she usually can. She describes the search for meaning involved in "reading" the instrument:

> "And how do you know where these meanings are?"
>
> "I kind of see 'em. Or feel 'em rather, like climbing down a ladder at night, you put your foot down and there's another rung. Well, I put my mind down and there's another meaning, and I kind of sense what it is. Then I put 'em all together. There's a trick in it, like focusing your eyes."

There is one terrible occasion, however, when what the instrument is trying to tell her is unbearable, and she backs away in incomprehension.

> "Yes, I see what it says. . . . [that both her parents want something she's got] . . . for this experiment, whatever it is." She stopped there, to take a deep breath. Something was troubling her, and she didn't know what it was. She was sure that this *something* that was so important was the alethiometer itself, because after all, [her mother] *had* wanted it, and what else could it be? And yet it wasn't, because the alethiometer had a different way of referring to itself, and this wasn't it. "I suppose it's the alethiometer," she said unhappily. "It's what I thought all along. I've got to take it to [her father] before she gets it. If *she* gets it, we'll all die" . . . she felt so tired, so bone-deep weary and sad that to die would have been a relief. [Pullman, 1995, p. 360].

(And later, as the crisis unfolded):

> Now Lyra's head was full of a roar, as if she were trying to stifle some knowledge from her own consciousness. . . . and then she suddenly collapsed, and a fierce cry of despair enveloped her. . . . She had just realized what she had done. [*ibid.*, p. 380]

She had allowed herself to be a pawn in the perverse destructive purpose of her father by bringing her childhood love, Roger, to her father for him to sacrifice. Here it is as if the Oedipus myth is reversed, and it is the father demanding possession of the daughter. We might imagine that this represents both a child's way of construing the inter-generational transgression, partly as a result of projection, but it also draws on the all-too-frequent reality of parental misuse and exploitation of their power for the perverse enactment of their own unresolved oedipal conflicts.

Northern Lights can be read at many levels; children's adventure story, science fiction, allegory about the evils of organized religion and other institutions of power—but arguably one of the sources of its strength is the feeling that it is earthed in a psychologically truthful account of a child growing up. In the story, the child Lyra is by herself, with some supporters here and there, but essentially alone in taking on her remote, neglectful father (originally going to rescue him), and her seductive witch of a mother. The separated parents turn out to be involved sexually with each other, and also in parallel ways in activities that lead to the evil destruction of children's spirits. Gradually things get more complicated, and we are led far beyond the simple world of child heroes and monstrous parents of some children's stories (for example Roald Dahl's *Matilda*) into Lyra's struggle with betrayal, disillusion, denial, and ambivalence, in herself as well as in others. Although the obvious configuration in the book is one of parents' attack on children, which might be seen at least in part as the child's own projected attack on the parents, nevertheless we also see Lyra's growing awareness of her complicity, and some of the complex reasons for it.

In an essay on the book, Margaret and Michael Rustin (2003) comment in detail on many of its themes from the point of view of child development. They compare the reading of the alethiometer to "the discipline necessary in psychoanalytic dream interpretation", and to "reading itself". I think it bears comparison beyond this to the process of thinking itself, dependent as that is on a capacity for triangulation, developed through the painful negotiation of oedipal issues.

As Britton so succinctly puts it:

The closure of the oedipal triangle by the recognition of the link joining the parents provides a limiting boundary for the internal world. It creates what I call a "triangular space"—i.e. a space bounded by the three persons of the oedipal situation and all their potential relationships. It includes, therefore, the possibility of being a participant in a relationship and observed by a third person as well as being an observer of a relationship between two people. [Britton, 1989, p. 86]

Or, as Feldman (1989, p. 127) states; "I have also tried to show the link between the way in which the oedipal situation is construed internally and the patient's capacity to think, as any real understanding is dependent on the identification with a couple capable of a creative intercourse". Feldman, too, is referring to the situation in which the subject is able to tolerate the idea of a parental intercourse from which s/he is excluded; a world in which shifting identifications are possible, because the individual is able to step outside the boundary of the original all-encompassing pair to acknowledge a wider reality. This is only possible if the loss of the exclusivity of the original mother–infant pair is tolerable, rather than being experienced as catastrophic (Bion, 1959; Klein, 1928).

Pullman's alethiometer is a metaphor for bringing together the different things one knows and allowing them to lead to a new thought, a synthesis, and a better grasp of the truth. Often, of course, one is inhibited in this process because it requires relinquishment of familiar (safer) constructions in favour of pictures that disturb, and may be threatening or painful. The psychic work required to deal with the oedipal situation provides a prototype for this movement. Indeed, its status in psychoanalysis is as more than a prototype, more than a metaphor, but actually as the key developmental experience, suffused with unavoidable pain and grief. Lyra's anguish when she has to face an aspect of the truth about her relationship to her father, as above, has a universal resonance.

Fisher (1993) discusses the influence of contemporary thinking about the oedipus complex on couple psychotherapy. He examines the development of Freud's ideas, from the primacy of the castration complex to the centrality of ambivalence in the resolution of the oedipus complex for both sexes, and the:

painfully tragic erotic attachment that reaches across a chasm, a chasm created by the inexorable difference between the generations, by the reality of the difference between the experience of being the parent and the experience of being the child. In this sense, questions about the universality of the oedipal conflict are misconstrued. Nothing could be more universal than the difference between the generations. Mother's own sexual feelings are aroused in what she must finally acknowledge as an impossible link. Of course, it is not literally impossible, as Oedipus and Jocasta knew. But to cross that line is to *pervert*, not to erase, the reality of the difference between the generations. The core of the oedipal, and we should hasten to add, of the Jocastan tragedy is that feelings do cross that divide. In addition, they lead to a dilemma from which there is no painless escape, except by self-crippling illusions or an attack on the psychic apparatus itself and its capabilities. [Fisher, 1993, p. 150]

Fisher asks "how does one come to tolerate the intolerable?" (*ibid.*, p. 151). His answer, echoing Britton's, is through the early experience of adequate maternal containment of infantile anxieties. He discusses this in relation to Bion's ideas, and to those of Winnicott, who contrasts the "good-enough" mother with the mother who engenders a false-self relationship with her baby. "Good enough" includes the capacity to tolerate hate between herself and her baby. In other words, what is needed, if development is to be facilitated, if we are to become able to face the truth, is some combination of innate capacity and adequately containing early experience. The latter requires a "parent" who can themselves bear to know painful truths about differentiation and separateness, and who can mediate them for the infant by providing what Winnicott called manageable "doses". Subsequent relationships, psychotherapy or analysis may eventually compensate in some degree for the lack of a sufficiency of these early experiences.

The idea around which I have built this chapter is that an inevitably painful transition from an illusion of duality to negotiating the reality of a world beyond the pair is fundamental to human development re-encountered repeatedly. Defences against our knowledge of this, with its implications of rivalry, potential exclusion, and pain, and its echoes of our early oedipal experience, pervade our lives and colour our attempts to participate in a new pairing as adults. As I indicated earlier, Shakespeare's Hamlet, traumatized by the enactment of his phantasies by those around him, could not manage this transition to a same-generational relationship but was driven to destroy it, and Ophelia with it.

So what happens when we focus our attention on adult couples, and their relationship as the embodiment of their individual oedipal experiences? There are several dimensions to consider. First, it is a central tenet of psychoanalytic work with couples that two individuals who make up a semi-permanent coupling tend to have done so at least partly because they share an unconscious internal configuration. Arguably, this is based on similar or complementary oedipal derivatives. In consultations with couples we discover repeatedly that the partners' significant emotional histories contain striking parallels or "matching" experiences, as for John and Sally in the example below. A recent study (Lanman, Grier, & Evans, 2003) showed that psychoanalytic couple therapists independently agree on key modes of unconscious functioning shared between the partners in a couple, using a measure based on the Kleinian spectrum of paranoid–schizoid to depressive psychological constellations.

Two partners tend to re-enact unresolved aspects of these internal object relations in their relationship with each other and (when in therapy), in their separate or joint relationship with their therapist/s. They also tend to enact them in relation to any children they have. Where this is problematic, we may find the partners using the children as weapons against each other, or being over-involved, or hating and neglecting them.

It is curious mathematics, but in psychological terms, the capacity to be part of a developmental and creative couple relationship in adulthood involves tolerance of threesomes. It involves a capacity to tolerate difference, otherness, and three-dimensionality in the sense that each partner has an independent relationship to other things; whether people, work, interests, ideas, or history. Each partner may have an individual therapist, previous partners or spouses, and, with them, children. The present partnership offers the chance of reworking and rebalancing the original tensions between the bliss (and terror) of the all-encompassing dyad, and the stimulus (and fear) of exploring what lies outside it. For many couples, this balance continues to be very hard to find, even before the arrival of their own children. Attempted exclusion may be directed at potential or actual children, or at other relationships that either partner has with work or friends. Alternative cosy dualities may be set up with a child, or through having an affair, in an attempt to exclude the partner from a new pairing.

Adult coupling can all too easily become a collusive "us against the world", or, on the other hand, a perpetual polarization, or even fight, in the face of these pressures. A more developmental partnership needs to be built on the ability sufficiently to separate from our dyadic origin (psychologically speaking), to tolerate being excluded, and to discover the rewards of diversifying. Only then will there be room in the relationship for two people to genuinely co-exist, and consequently for children to be appropriately valued and cared for, with a flexibility that tolerates shifting patterns of inclusion and exclusion.

In psychoanalytic couple psychotherapy, it is both the patient–therapist relationship and the actualization of the internal couple relationship between a real-life adult couple that are studied. The structure of the therapy brings both therapist and patients up against an actual three-cornered reality in the consulting room, or even a four-cornered one, since we sometimes work in pairs. While this generates a challenging amount of data, it does provide an opportunity to study the movement in the "drama" from several different perspectives. Something like Lyra's alethiometer is needed, where the different protagonists, the different levels of meaning, and the different locations (internal or external) can be held in mind until some pattern is perceived. The pattern will be rooted in some version of the developmental challenge, the conflict between safety and increasing exposure to difference and change. Often the unconscious resistance to change is huge, and the process of change, if it is possible at all, may involve negotiating a degree of breakdown on the way.

These issues tend to spill out beyond the consulting room, and are reflected in different aspects of our engagement with adult couples. The contemporary oedipal lens is helpful in understanding the core dilemma as it is expressed both within psychotherapy sessions and in the wider context of the work. I will draw my clinical illustrations[1] from three points on this spectrum; one the inter-agency negotiations over a "case", one arising within supervision of a couple psychotherapy, and one directly from therapeutic encounters with couples. All of these situations involve the movement between pairing and relating beyond the pair that is so fundamental to a lively and creative engagement with the world. So often this movement feels like a wrenching of oneself away from something safer, and putting that at risk in pursuit of something more truthful but much harder to bear.

The inter-agency example involved a couple who referred themselves for couple therapy at the suggestion of their daughter's psychiatrist. The grown-up daughter was struggling to deal with memories of "inappropriate touching" by her father in her childhood, and was refusing contact with her parents. It appeared that the parents were being asked to jump through certain hoops in order to qualify to meet her. Although there was no actual contract between the daughter's doctor and the parents' therapist, after the parents' therapy had finished the daughter's psychiatrist wanted information about "reform" in their attitudes to the daughter.

She first tried to do this by suggesting to the parents that they ask their therapist for a report. I was brought in by their therapist at this stage, as clinical manager, to provide an independent, "institutional" view, because he felt like refusing to respond at all to this intrusive request, coming as it did through his patients but on behalf of someone else. However, he was concerned that there might be repercussions for our Institute if he simply refused.

Initially, I too felt incensed, feeling tempted to support an outright refusal. However, I also felt torn between the conflicting needs. How could I support my colleague in protecting the couple's privacy without jeopardizing their chances of getting to meet their daughter? There were three sets of pairs, perhaps four, for whom relating beyond the pair seemed to be required, but was being experienced as a threat. There was the daughter and her psychiatrist, who were in a sense demanding reassurance about the threat felt to be posed to the daughter's development by the parents. This one did not pull at me so much, perhaps because they were in another agency and the daughter was, after all, an adult now. In addition, it was not her treatment that was threatened with intrusion. It seemed that the nature of the pairing between the daughter and her psychiatrist involved an enactment of a wish to reverse the original child's vulnerability by intruding on the parents' space: getting into their bedroom, as it were. It was as if the "child's" vulnerability was being prolonged in a frozen way, within a dyadic retreat, while the parents were to be intruded on instead. At the same time the idea of questioning the parents' therapist suggested a phantasy that the original missing protection for the child could be provided by therapists interacting on behalf of the family, sparing the daughter the need to ask the questions through direct interaction with her own parents.

Undeniably, I felt more identified with the patients of my own institution, wishing to protect and stand up for their "pairing" with their therapist. At the same time I feared that their parent–child relating with their daughter might be sabotaged if we were provocative (or, from another point of view, too protective) in our response. Finally (the fourth pairing), there was my relationship with my colleague, my respect for his work, and my reluctance to take issue with him.

This I felt I had to do, however. I was the one supposed to balance all these conflicting needs, uncomfortable though it felt to put the link with a different agency above my link with my colleague. I thought that the way through must lie in a kind of sorting out of the "generations". Although some might find this an alien metaphor, I felt that in these circumstances the next step would be for the therapists to deal with each other, just as parents need at times to talk to each other to resolve their differences, rather than using their children (or in this case any of the patients) as go-betweens. Rather than prolong a process of messages being passed by the couple, therefore, I invited the daughter's psychiatrist to contact us direct so that we could discuss her request and explain our position. She responded by sending us a detailed list of questions. This provided the opportunity for the professionals to sort something out between them, although it still felt to us like a request for inappropriate and intrusive interference with the parents' therapy. But at least the parents were less likely to be blamed for whatever we did. I knew I might be leading the daughter's psychiatrist on to expect answers to her questions, and so, if I didn't deliver what she wanted, I might still be failing to make anything better. This was what my colleague predicted. In fact, when I wrote explaining our position as best I could, I received a reply that acknowledged our different approaches, and seemed to accept the limits we felt we had to put on our communication.

I suggest that what we see here is a particularly vivid example of something about which many of us in the "helping professions" can feel in conflict and become confused. Political correctness, freedom of information, and confidentiality can all seem to collide in apparently arbitrary ways. Counsellors in some settings feel they should never discuss their clients with referring GPs; patients sometimes argue that professionals involved with them can only communicate with each other provided the patient sees all correspondence; legal rights of access to records mean that professionals restrict what they put into "official" records. Among all of this, I believe that unresolved oedipal anxieties can have a powerful influence. Hard thinking is necessary to work out which communications belong "between the parents" (or professionals), when it is appropriate and important to protect a dyadic communication between parent and child (or therapist and patient), and when it may be necessary to break into this for some overriding reason. This thinking should not be simply a matter of rules and procedures, but must take into account the underlying anxieties and phantasies. None of us can avoid being pushed and pulled by the temptations to intrude, to exclude, or to retain privileged access for ourselves. But we need to recognize these things, and do what we can to process them, rather than imagining that imposed rules can substitute for awareness, or can prevent us from succumbing unawares and acting out. As Feldman writes, in relation to fathers:

> There is thus no way the father can behave that will not stimulate the child's aggressive and/or sexual phantasies. What the child needs of him is some awareness of these impulses, with a sufficiently firm base within himself (part of which involves experiencing himself as a member of a mature couple), so that the child's impulses and phantasies (and his own) have neither to be denied nor acted out. [Feldman, 1989, pp. 105–106]

In the case I have sketched here, my role pushed me to act as "outsider"; as a kind of "grand-parent", managing a boundary between the two professionals, one of whom wished for inappropriate access to the other, while the other, in reaction, wished to refuse any contact. Having written this last phrase, it strikes me again how precisely the interaction between the professionals reflected the relationship between the parents and the child in the patient family, as these played out over time (the father was said to have gained inappropriate access to the daughter and the daughter was now refusing contact with her parents). However, the point I want to emphasize is that the process of resolving such situations is never easy or free of conflicting pressures.

My second illustration is located in the process of supervision of couple psychotherapy. Again, this is one specific location from which the issues can, I think, be generalized to a wide variety of supervisory situations, including supervison of individual therapy and even self-supervision. The "supervisor" represents the view from outside, the third point in the triangle. So, when supervising couple psychotherapy I often find myself drawing attention to the role of the partner who is not being focused on, or to the avoided topic or affect; in other words to that which is being experienced as lying outside the current pairing. From the perspective of psychoanalytic couple therapy, it is important to consider this "excluded" aspect, which may be located in one partner more than the other, as part of the interlinked couple functioning, carrying meaning for both partners.

The example I have in mind involved the presentation in supervision of a couple where one partner's difficulties were more visible than the other's, a not unusual situation. The therapist often found himself caught up in work focused on the wife, whose extreme touchiness over her husband's provocations led to frequent rows. The wife demanded that the husband should avoid challenging her in particular areas where he knew she reacted badly, and the husband resented the expectation that he should take such care to look after her. She did indeed seem particularly vulnerable, and this was linked to particularly difficult childhood experiences to do with rowing parents and a somewhat "suffocating" mother. In fact, the husband had proposed in a previous session that it would be better if his wife did some work with the therapist without him present at all, and perhaps he should withdraw for a while. The therapist realized that this suggestion fitted in rather too comfortably with, and highlighted his own concentration on, the wife. For me as the supervisor it was tempting to join my supervisee in his view, and I felt quite uncomfortable to have to offer an alternative that made him feel he had missed taking a "couple view". However, as an outsider I was able to notice that, in the session we were considering, there was a parallel version of the "wife's problem" in the husband's material. He, like the wife, had designated a "no-go" area in himself, when he asserted that under no circumstances was he prepared to discuss his attitude to money.

We began to wonder if the therapist had been complying with an implicit injunction to avoid focusing on the husband's version of the difficulties. In fact, the problems were much more shared than either partner could easily acknowledge. It was as if the idea that both partners in the couple might feel deprived and in need of special consideration and care was unbearable to both. They had developed a split view; in which both were complicit, and into which they tried to hijack the therapist. In this view they enacted a picture of one needy one, and one who was supposed to care for them (the therapist being asked to replace the husband), rather than the couple's having to grapple with competing feelings of need, which would require more flexibility and shifting identifications if some needs were to be taken care of for each. They tried to cling to the dyad to ward off the triangle.

Related ideas about supervision as a triangular relationship are explored in depth by Mattinson (1975) and by Hughes and Pengelly (1997). They emphasize the essential point that one cannot avoid being caught up in these enactments, indeed that is a necessary part of the process of reaching understanding. At any one time, either supervisor or supervisee is likely to be more involved with one aspect than another. It is the potential for movement that matters, as opposed to clinging to an idealized "deadly equal" triangle where everything must be even-handed all the time.

The task of holding the peacefulness of agreement together with the often uncomfortable, but developmentally important other point of view, without simply shifting to an alternative seemingly cosy duality, is often vividly highlighted in work with couples. One couple I saw were childless at the point when they sought help, seemingly struggling to maintain a particular kind of defence against separateness in an attempt to ward off the feared dangers of being two different people, each with their own relationship to the world outside. They had developed a relationship of the kind Fisher describes as a "false self couple", in which the husband, Alex, required that the wife, Sarah, should comply with his views on all aspects of behaviour. She should not wear such flamboyant clothes, she should not argue so assertively in company. She should share his tastes. She, an intelligent, attractive, young woman, was doing her best to fit in, convinced that she could make the relationship work if only she tried harder, and was frightened by his every frown. Both of them felt completely victimized by this unbearable situation, and yet unable to leave it. As Fisher succinctly puts it, "the failure to master these (oedipal) anxieties is experienced as a desperate lack of a sense of psychological or emotional space— space to think, to be different and separate, space in which to enter or leave a relationship" (Fisher, 1993, p. 145).

Sarah was Italian, and naturally expressive. Her mother seemed always to have lived in the shadow of her father, having had a breakdown in the process. When she met Alex, she was unconventional and colourful, perhaps in an extreme, and defensively "individual" way. She was drawn to his apparent solidity and strength, and seemed to have set about submitting herself to him as her mother had done to her father.

Alex, on the other hand, was British, and had endured a traumatic separation from his mother when he was sent to live with a restrictive aunt and uncle, aged six, because his parents went abroad. He had a sense of a lost golden age, and felt he had spent the rest of his childhood trying to fit in with tough paternal expectations when he did visit his parents. His mother had seemed grief-stricken and helpless about him ever since. Alex was drawn to Sarah's freedom and exuberance, but then found himself trying to suppress it in just the way his own had been cut off. He, like her, seemed to be enacting a phantasy of a parental couple relationship where the woman submitted to the man, despite great cost to both. Genuine separateness and individuation seemed highly threatening to each of these two, and their joint solution was to attempt to obliterate it.

As the picture unfolded, I felt myself to be witnessing something awful. It seemed extraordinary that Alex had brought Sarah to therapy to get her to behave better. Then I realized that Sarah had the same aim in mind. The fact that serious psychological abuse was going on, with an abuser and a complicit victim, seemed painful truth enough. However, this situation protected both of them from something worse, namely the threat of separation. It felt to them as though the acknowledgement of difference between them could only leave each of them in an intolerably lonely place, and would lead inevitably to actual separation. It seemed to me as if what threatened was a repetition of the premature wrenching away of an infant who was not yet viable from a mother who had not been able to provide a sufficiently solid experience of dyadic security to enable her infant to face the world beyond her. The response, enacted in this marriage, had been to turn to an omnipotent phantasy that there need not be any looking beyond.

Alex felt terribly misunderstood, claiming that he wanted nothing more than that Sarah should stand up against his pressure, "in a loving way". Sarah felt that this was an impossible task, but she could sense Alex's vulnerability, and wanted to make him feel loved. Each of them longed for unconditional love, which for the two of them meant two diametrically opposite things. If Sarah loved Alex she would want to do the "little things" he liked. If Alex loved Sarah he would appreciate her ways more and not try to change them. Their joint solution seemed to have been to sacrifice one for the sake of the other, but without success because neither was happy. Psychic separation was being confused with abandonment. Unsurprisingly, therefore, actual separation also seemed unthinkable to both of them, and the ultimate proof of failure and of being unloved.

As the therapy proceeded, Sarah was able to explore some of her anxieties about the possible breakdown of the relationship, and found she could begin to distinguish the dilemma facing her in the marriage from others she had lumped together with it in her mind. She clearly felt that to stand up to Alex would inevitably lead to leaving him, or being left by him. On top of that, she assumed that she would necessarily have to leave London, her job, her friends, and even the country if she left Alex. She came to feel that she did have some room to make choices about these things, and could think more flexibly than she had allowed herself to do. She vividly described her expectation that marriage would open things up, and how instead she felt it had narrowed things down for her. Alex, on the other hand, found it harder to think flexibly. He seemed caught in a more rigid version of the shared phantasy, which might mean that change, if it came, would be more catastrophic for him.

Alex and Sarah were in trouble as a couple without children, but frequently it is the arrival of children that triggers the breakdown of a precarious balance. Neither partner can maintain even the illusion of having the other's undivided attention. Alternative calls on each of them are unlikely to be symmetrical, and fluctuating inequalities threaten the previous security. Each has to become the parent who in their own early life may have been hated, despised, feared, or who may never have adequately engaged with them. They find themselves in bed with the representative of the other parent, who may have been over-seductive, or experienced as unbearably rejecting.

For John and Sally, their relationship appeared to have provided a refuge from the painfulness of their early experiences, until children arrived. In the early days of the marriage the relationship worked, albeit with Sally being more of the "responsible adult" and John playing more of the adolescent. They had fun together, and each could feel put first by the other. However, trouble came with the arrival of their first child. John felt terribly displaced and rejected, not only by Sally, but also by the baby while Sally was feeding her. He felt could not give his daughter anything. Sally felt she had to become increasingly competent, juggling work and baby. Their relationship deteriorated, and this was when they sought help.

Sally was the eldest child in her original family, the children being born at short intervals after each other, with an often absent father. Sally dealt with the painful fact of her father's rejection, and having to share her mother with the other babies, by identifying with her mother, to the extent that she became a fellow-carer for the others. Characteristically she looks on the bright side, tries to be positive, proactive, and efficient, and her siblings still lean on her. In the couple therapy, she tended to appear competent and cheerful, although in a way that could have a relentless quality, suggesting its defensiveness.

Sessions were often dominated by "the problem of John's moods". I could easily be drawn into attending more to John, with Sally's help, because John was the more obviously troubled. Only as this structure was repeatedly interpreted (which required me to notice it in a different way) did Sally become aware of the way she edited out and projected her own distress and rage about being ignored or taken for granted again, as if she had no needs of her own. In the course of the therapy, she became more aware of, and able to be articulate about, how upset and angry she was when this happened.

John was also the oldest in his family. His younger sister was quite ill as a baby, and continues to this day to be fussed over and put first. John coped by fitting in, being the good one, and not daring to protest lest things got worse. From when John was eight until he was around eleven, the family had to cope with the mother's absences due to recurrent bouts of hospitalization for depression. It seems that, in his family, feelings about this were never discussed. This was not unlike what happened in Sally's family, although she had dealt with it differently. As an adult, John (unlike Sally) did palpably get into bad moods and feel terrible, but tended to have no idea why this had happened, or what his feelings were about. Usually, he could not allow anyone to explore them with him. This seemed at times despairing, and at other times more as if there was an active refusal to allow contact, a perpetuation of the bad experience of being excluded, while at the same time provoking an excluded feeling in whoever was trying to help. This could be understood as being part evacuation, part communication, depending on the capacity of the other to process the experience of how very vulnerable to rejection (by his mother, by his wife-become-mother, and then by me as I stepped back to consider Sally's side of things) he felt.

This couple's shared early experience was of not being sufficiently understood or thought about, and each in their different ways defended against knowingly feeling the pain of this exclusion. The original exclusions for these two were multiple. There was the child's exclusion from the procreative parental relationship, and, on top of that, rejection by each parent in favour of work or illness or other children. Sibling rivalries, as they so often do, carried a part of the underlying oedipal rivalries. Over the months of couple therapy, the couple became more able to see and think about how they provoked each other, the different forms in which each enacted, or hid, or got rid of anger and distress, and why. Eventually they decided to embark on having a second child. Very tellingly, they initially presented this in terms of *"then we'll have one each so no one will be left out"*.

In the course of the pregnancy, John increased the tension by giving up his job, declaring that he could no longer stand the stresses of his managerial post. He decided to take time to write, as he had long wanted to. So he was at home, but not available, and taking over the dining room with his papers, giving rise to nagging from Sally who would come home from her part-time job to find nothing helpful to the household had been done. There seemed something regressive about this, as if John was reasserting his need to be looked after, and to be more in the home, although doing it in a way that made it a bad experience for him. Neither partner felt looked after. At the same time, John decided the family should move house. This seemed to embody an attempt to make room for the baby, and to acquire enough room to establish a semi-child-free area for the couple. However, he became more and more gloomy, as though trying to extend further beyond the safe pair while at the same time protecting it was all too much for him. He had difficulty joining Sally in any excited anticipation of the baby. Sally, meantime, despite the anxiety all this stirred up in her, continued to cling to her determination to cope. Both seemed to be making increasingly painful efforts to manage having their "safe haven" re-invaded, just when they had begun to re-establish it after the first child's arrival.

Then the boy baby arrived and John seemed to come apart. The baby, by crying all the time and always being in their new adult sitting room or bedroom, had robbed him of the newfound space to be with Sally alone. He hated Sally for having done this to him. He overemphasized his link with his daughter by comparison with both son and wife. Sally was in despair, but continued to manage more or less single-handedly with both children. The baby was brought to the sessions at this time. For me, it was acutely painful to witness this little creature, held on his mother's knee, having his father glare at him and say how much he hated him. I felt as if I could glimpse Laius wanting to expose baby Oedipus on the mountainside.

Which pairing was the most in jeopardy at this point: the mother–baby link, the husband–wife link, or the therapist–patient link in relation to John (and of course the one to Sally also)? Each seemed so completely threatened by the others. Somehow, I had to hold together in my mind the intensely powerful and appealing call of the baby's extreme vulnerability, and the needs of the nursing mother–baby pair, with the plight of the father, also my patient. I had previously experienced the way that John would state things in extreme terms, perhaps partly to provoke from me the condemnation and rejection he unconsciously felt towards himself. In addition, at this point his recurring ambivalence towards the therapy itself crystallized into hostility once more. He thought it was a waste of time or worse, because everything was worse, and that the therapy was responsible. I was the parent bound to fail each of them again. I felt under great pressure to join the couple in their sense that our (and their) staying together in this situation was unbearable, even dangerous. John missed a few sessions, and Sally clung to coming to the therapy and to the chance of a pairing with me. She was being, in a sense, the good girl, and projecting into John the messy, destructive rage and near breakdown induced by the situation. She also clung to feeding the baby day and night on demand, finding it a temporary refuge from her despair over being abandoned by her partner. This meant that, to get any sleep at all, John slept in a separate room, increasing the sense of mutual abandonment. The different pairings were experienced as mutually exclusive, and so the oedipal configuration was reinforced.

The difficulties had been more obviously enacted by John up to that point. However, when the time came for Sally to wean her son, she in turn became quite depressed, confirming the lack of a viable "triangular" psychic space internally, within which movement from one pairing to the other felt possible. Instead, it felt catastrophic. Moreover, because John's internal world matched hers in this respect, he felt unable to intervene effectively, but instead felt angrily powerless.

For both partners in this relationship, the oedipal configuration contained several elements. They shared an early experience of mothers who seemed to have turned away prematurely from a primary preoccupation with them in favour of one or more siblings. They also shared an experience of abandonment by the parent of the opposite sex. Therefore, for each of them, the necessary support for negotiating the development from dyad to creative triangle was significantly depleted. Excessively painful truths had been prematurely forced on them. They created a kind of refuge from all this in their relationship and even imagined that having "one child each" could reinforce the refuge. However, when that illusion came under pressure from reality, the old hatreds resurfaced and had to be wrestled with all over again.

What determines the extent to which this painful knowledge can be assimilated, metabolized, grown through? This chapter is not about the process or outcome of therapies, but of course the answer lies partly in the nature of the therapeutic engagement the couple enters, and whether they can stick with it for long enough. Some couples feel unable to engage. Some withdraw, either altogether, or perhaps one or other into individual therapy, sometimes dissolving their relationship in the process. Some find themselves able to become very committed to the therapeutic work over considerable periods of time. Change sometimes means one or other having something of a breakdown in the process of acquiring a new way of understanding things. It seems likely that these outcomes depend at least partly on the original containment or lack of it that each experienced as an infant, which determined their capacity to negotiate oedipal experiences, and eventually to bear the pain involved in psychic growth and development. The painfulness of this developmental process means that we all of us, in a part of ourselves, are repeatedly tempted to turn away from it.

Note

1. I should say at this point that I have disguised my examples, both through the alteration of certain facts and identifying details, and through compositing more than one case within each example. There is no completely satisfactory way of dealing with these issues, but I have tried to preserve the integrity of the experiences I describe while safeguarding the privacy of those involved.

CHAPTER EIGHT

The oedipus complex as observed in work with couples and their children

Lisa Miller

Working with children and their families offers an unpar-
alleled opportunity to observe the oedipus complex in
action. Whereas work with adults always involves looking back to childhood development, combined with direct experience in the transference and deductions from past and current
behaviour, work with children gives a taste of the thing in itself in
a different way. The child's struggle with the oedipal configuration
of emotions depends, for its success, on how substantially its
parents have navigated the same journey. Infant observation shows
how early the process begins, and observing young children shows
how it goes on. However, clinical practice is interesting in so far as
we can take a view of difficulties that are actually preventing
emotional growth and causing something disturbed and aberrant to
develop instead.

Sarah

The first case, which impressed itself on my mind as demonstrating
this, took place years ago and I have briefly alluded to it elsewhere.

A couple came to see me under the auspices of the Tavistock Under Five's Counselling service. This was, and still is, a service offering brief work—up to five sessions—to parents or a parent anxious about their baby or small child. Mr and Mrs S, a young married couple, brought their daughter Sarah to me. Mrs S had made the appointment by telephone, and the intake secretary had noted that the caller was agitated and upset, and could hardly restrain herself from revealing all the details on the telephone. The secretary relayed the salient fact that she had been told the parents had quarrelled violently over the child's problem. Sarah was fifteen months old and the central trouble, which the parents identified when they arrived, was that Sarah completely refused to be weaned. To begin with, I thought that reluctance to wean at this age sounded a minor trouble, but I changed my mind when I heard that Sarah had almost never been separated from her mother, day or night. I had ample chance to see this little girl's intolerance of separation and loss. Not only did she cling to her mother, but she wanted the breast every ten minutes or so. Sarah was too anxious to play and was completely silent.

Her parents, especially her mother, were notably anxious; the story they told was revealing. Mr S was clearly someone who wanted to be understanding, and said he had expected his wife to be entirely taken up with the baby for a while; but now, he said with a touch of infuriated pride, "I'd like my wife back!" They described how Mrs S and Sarah had found it heard to establish breast-feeding, but how they had been greatly helped by a Breast Feeding League. This group was still most important in Mrs S's life. The prevailing orthodoxy was the maxim "wait till the baby is ready to wean itself". However, that day seemed unlikely to arrive at the current rate. With a certain relish, of which she was perhaps unaware, Mrs S detailed the advice she had been given to help move Sarah out of their bed and promote the weaning process, as well as how hopeless it all was. Indeed, I felt hopeless myself, as one after another grandmothers, aunts, neighbours, health visitor, and GP were set up and shot down. All of them had (in my view) been offering excellent advice.

What had brought them here at this time? It seemed that Mr S was finally jibbing. The quarrel alluded to in the original telephone call had been the result of his irritation. The quarrel had got out of hand rather quickly; they "never normally disagreed" but had come to blows, and Mrs S, especially, was shaken to the depths. She explained to me how much she had wanted Mr S to be a "hands-on father" because her own father had combined being away a lot with being heavy-handed in reproach and discipline. She wanted something quite different and felt that, until now, she had found it.

For almost three sessions, spaced out at intervals of two or three weeks, I looked set to join the parade of useless advisers. The only difference, I hope, was that I was not giving advice. I was, however, treated as though I were, and sensible ideas (put Sarah in a cot) were pronounced yet again to have been tried and found wanting. Then, towards the end of the third session, Mr S snapped. He unexpectedly lost his temper with me and plainly outlined his opinion of me, which was low. Inwardly, I felt he had a point. How was it that I lacked any technical equipment, any psychoanalytic apparatus, to deal with this situation, where a toddler was getting away with murder, and (judging from her unhappy bearing) suffering the consequences? Mrs S seemed surprised and somewhat energized by her husband's vigorous outburst, and found herself substantially agreeing with him. To my astonishment, they returned three weeks later for the next planned meeting with an account of progress. Sarah was in her room, in her bed at night, and breast-feeding had diminished to an unremarkable level. In this and the final session I saw emerge a small girl who began to take a lively interest in the toys I provided and, more striking still, began to talk.

Discussion

From the point of view of her oedipal development, what did we see happen? The picture first presented was of a mother and baby glued together so that it was impossible to insert anything between them. It was hardly even a one-to-one relationship when it was at its extreme; the two of them were one. A state of mind dominated that saw the idea of separation as cruel. This had, I think, been manifest all Sarah's life. Mr and Mrs S had also been operating as one. Sarah had two mothers rather than a mother and father; her actual mother, and a second one, who deferred to the first, imitated her, felt she was sure to be right, and echoed her narcissistically. At the same time, something potentially destructive was going on. The more I heard about the Breast Feeding League the more convinced I was that for Mrs S it had become, at an unconscious level, a League Against Fathers. Unconsciously, both Mr and Mrs S subscribed to the theory that it was a brutal act for someone to step in and point out that time was passing, that Sarah needed to be up on her own two feet, and must be helped to do it.

In short, they had been holding out against the paternal function, against the idea that there was two of anything. For even in the earliest stages of a baby's development there needs to be the growing intimation that there is a division between mother and infant, that something comes to part them. At first, we see this in the baby's need to apprehend small comings and goings, in order to develop the concept of a mind of its own, a place where thoughts, memories, and a sense of self can live. We see babies in the first year of life relating one-to-one with father, mother, or childminder and we think of them as part of a dyad. This is not incorrect, but in order to conceptualize two, there has to be a notion of three in the background: first one person, then a gap between them, then the second person. The development of the concept of the gap is closely linked to the baby's growing awareness that, when she is absent, the mother exists elsewhere and indeed with somebody else. Here, we have the oedipal configuration, which all three members of the S family resisted.

They were resisting the idea of being three. The hurdle they were falling at is the classical hurdle of the depressive position, so closely linked to oedipal growth. Mrs S did not want a husband like her notion of her father. However, she had recreated the world she knew; an unacknowledged presence, like her absent father, ruled her actions and kept her under its thumb. Mrs S projected this tyrant into Sarah. It was Sarah's anger that, without realizing it, both parents feared and dreaded as a fresh version of the primitive superego that Mrs S's thunderous father had embodied. Both parents subscribed to the phantasy that unconsciously told them the heavens would open if anyone said "no" to Sarah. To begin with, the needs of a tiny infant are imperative, but within weeks, the urgency lessens. Mr and Mrs S had, no doubt, also gained satisfaction from projecting their own infantile omnipotence into Sarah and seeing it gratified, thus seeing early need prolonged beyond its life-span. This gratification involved them in another layer of phantasy: the attack on the good, potent father. Instead of fresh ideas entering and becoming real in action, every single useful notion was nipped in the bud. Castration abounded.

I sensed this in the "anti-father" quality of Mrs S's version of her breast-feeding group. For her, at an unconscious level, it signified having joined up with a gang of harpies devoted to denying the paternal principle, and keeping forever at bay the idea of the combined object. Mrs S allowed only similarities, only narcissistic unions of a rather primitive sort, within reach of her mind, and she had found a partner who, for a time, would comply and connive.

However, it did not last forever. The corner had, of course, been turned before I ever saw them. Mr S had finally felt driven to protest, and a mixture of fuels presumably fired his exasperation. On the one hand, he was right. It was not good for Sarah and not good for them to be behaving in this way. On the other hand, he had gone along with what Mrs S so feared, and yielded to the impulse to bully, thus failing to contain the implicit sadism. Mrs S was terrified. However, in their encounter with me some measure of containment must have taken place, perhaps at just the right time. Mr S burst forth with his attack on me—attack no doubt full of reproach towards the feeble good father of their combined, unconscious phantasy. It is plain that they both felt let down. Repeatedly, people had tried to insert the reality principle into their family life. The outward form was that of sensible advice, yet the inner meaning was more than that. What other people, and I, tried to say was developmentally vital. The message was the essential oedipal one: you are not two, you are three. That is to say, the internal family consists of a combined object—a couple—in relation to their creation, a child. The parents are, of necessity, older than the child. The child is, by definition, a dependent being. The grown-ups are responsible for looking after the infant not only physically, but also psychically.

This involves them in adult action. The step into the depressive position is taken by their accepting responsibility for the child's anger and distress, out of concern and a realistic estimate of the child's stage of emotional development. It involves seeing the truth, seeing things as they are. In this case, the truth of the matter was that two otherwise resourceful and ordinary people were being ruled by the whim of a baby. It seems, by their later account, that after the outburst in my room, the parents had been able to connect with each other like two reasonably thoughtful adults working together in the interest of the child. They described how they had discussed implementing again some of the measures suggested before, and finding to their relief that, this time round, they started gradually to work. The parents had discovered independence. Just as the infant, at the first encounter with depressive anxiety, emerges with appetite for the benefits of a separate existence, the couple saw again something they both must have tangled with in infancy. This was to face the difficulty of experiencing one's own feelings and thus to be granted a greater conviction of one's own capacities.

Mr and Mrs S were able to see that they both felt cross with Sarah. This went with a measure of daring to provoke Sarah's rage. In the event, Sarah's rage was a paper tiger. Sarah, it seems, was rather glad to be relieved of her burden of projections and complied with her parents' requests once they had made up their combined mind. I was interested to see that weaning indeed promotes development, as Melanie Klein points out. Sarah had been freed from the prohibition enjoined upon her by a narcissistic organization. This organization had threatened that any move towards her separate existence would bring catastrophe, and of course, this is a phenomenon that we see in a far more established and recalcitrant form in the clinical population of older children. The pleasure that Sarah now took in living her own life was evident. Independence for the parental couple, space to lead their own lives, had led to independence for her, which she demonstrated in her eager play. The rapid development of her speech followed the unconscious acknowledgement of her separateness. This is not a mere separateness from her mother, but involves the unconscious idea that her parents can get together without her and conceive good ideas. Talking always involves some acceptance of separateness. Whereas much, and much that is powerful, can be conveyed wordlessly, only words will do for some things. In addition, verbal communication assumes a gap between the speakers, a gap to be bridged with words. Thus, any communication has oedipal implications.

The sibling relationship

The progress of the S family was mildly impeded as they went on their way towards establishing a family. However, both Mr and

Mrs S had an unconscious concept of the integral family, an organization that exists to promote the creation, nourishment, and protection of children, either literal or metaphorical. In work with disturbed children and their families we see all kinds of interference with the establishment of external families, which stems from a disturbance (sometimes gross) in unconscious life and the negotiation of the oedipal conflict. What does the negotiation of the conflict entail? We are accustomed to thinking that it entails our relationship with our parents, external and internal. These people, the king and queen of our childhood lives, must be central to the question occupying all children—"who made me?" Not quite so much attention has been paid, though, to the equally important derivative question, "Whom else did they make?" And yet our lives in childhood and as grown-ups depend for their success on our relationship with our peers—classmates, colleagues, friends, acquaintances—in short, our siblings. In work with couples, it is noticeable that the typical features of a sibling relationship also come into play in the couple; not only one's identifications with internal mother and father, but also those with brother and sister are crucial.

Harry

Naturally, these particular identifications tend to be lit up at the birth of a second child, when sibling rivalry enters the scene in a literal way. The first time I noticed this was with a young couple who brought their three-year-old son, Harry, and their six-week-old daughter, Jane, saying that Harry's jealousy was unmanageable and that the family was in uproar. The very first point I noted was that in my room, as the mother and father warmed to their tale, both children were peaceful. Harry played quietly with my toys while Jane slept. I have come to regard this as an indicator that the parents project their conflict into the children, and so it seemed in this case. The parents told me that before Jane was born they had assimilated Harry into their lives, and into their relationship. They had continued, it seemed, to live a little as though they had not quite registered that they were parents. They told me nostalgically how "portable" Harry had been. A cheerful infant, he had travelled on their backs, slept through adult parties, gone up mountains and all over Europe.

However, they knew things would be difficult when Jane was born and they dreaded the change, which turned out to be every whit as bad as they thought. They joined in clamorous complaints; the flat was too small, there was no space to move; the mother described very crossly how she was feeding the baby, getting up at night, doing the washing, trying to soothe the desperate Harry. Her partner countered just as injuredly that *he* was getting up, too, and he was looking after Harry as much as he could, and doing the shopping, *and* he was trying to earn a living for them. There was something so competitive, rivalrous, and self-pitying about them both that they irresistibly reminded me of squabbling children expecting someone to step in and sort them out. It was interesting that when Harry came into action he did a rudimentary drawing—a round face with a huge round mouth, no other feature. This well expressed how the dispossessed Harry was feeling as a small individual, with a dreadful hole in his face, and a sense of having lost something. It also seemed that there was something that the parents could not contain in the way of primitive loss of the object, and being unable to bear the idea, it had gone to somebody else. There was a conviction that there was insufficient good stuff to go round.

There were reasons for the parents' anxieties that we could work on, but the point I wish to stress at present is that they presented as ruthlessly warring siblings; however, they were able to enter into a transference relationship with me as their parent, and very awkward they could be before working through some of their envy and jealousy. The constant problem with them and other parents in this situation is the attraction of ganging up, like destructive siblings in identifications with a sadistic couple, to round on the therapist. Again, I have an example from some time ago, where I saw the parents of an encopretic child. His symptom, as he worked with a child psychotherapist, disappeared. However, the parents, who looked personable, intelligent, and lively, united in their hatred of the combined object. When they found me reasonably resilient, marrying up (as I would hope) the dual aspects of containment, they began a relentless attack. These dual aspects are the embryonic precursors of the concept of mother and father. Containment consists of holding—maintaining receptive, absorbent response with some quality of endurance in it—with the capacity to focus keenly on what is going on. It derives from the primary experience, the infant held securely, surrounded by mother's arms, lap, and encircling attention and simultaneously focusing on the nipple while the mother's eye eventually draws the gaze and invites the child psychically into her mind. This adumbrates the concept of mother and father, vagina and penis, woman and man. The couple I am referring to had all kinds of ways of attacking my power to be receptive, and my power to focus. What stays with me after many years is the excited, would-be jokey, hiss of the mother to her partner, "Keep making the bombs!" There was an irresistible image of rebellion and adolescence, but actually not of a transient, healthy, revolutionary kind. This was envious, mindless rebellion. We were not very satisfied with the progress of the case, but the child was symptom-free and we ended. We were appalled to hear at a later review meeting with the parents that the child was soiling again. The bombs were being delivered. They did not wish for further treatment.

This couple, who had many adjacent problems, was essentially united in a cruel way. Perhaps it is important in family work to be clear-sighted about the balance in a couple: are they more inclined to come together for creative or for destructive ends? In considering the oedipus complex we have to think not only of the setting up of a family (both internal and external) but of its dark reverse: the setting up of an anti-family, where children are not protected, their childish needs are not contained and answered, and they are the recipients of damaging projections. People who have not been in a position to negotiate the essential ambivalence of the oedipal situation have unresolved conflicts not just to bequeath, but to force upon the next generation.

This can be observed in circumstances of severe damage and privation. Frequently one is left with a broken couple and only one piece of it to work with. The pair who created the child is afraid to get together, unconvinced at an unconscious level of the good function of combined parents. Here the child is left to attempt the work the parents cannot manage—a universal phenomenon, but marked and extreme in the clinical population.

Projection into the children

I should like to turn to a family, nominally intact. The children were quite numerous and one was autistic; this child was offered intensive psychotherapy. The parents did not think they would be able to attend meetings with me together, for apparently practical reasons. Therefore, I met regularly with the child's mother. In the sort of work we undertake in the Child and Family Department at the Tavistock Clinic, we try never quite to forget that the parents are here in relation to the child—on the child's ticket, so to speak. This does not mean it is inappropriate to attend to the individual or the couple, but it is important to keep a sense of relationships within the family and an eye on the child. Similarly, if one parent comes, I try to remember that this parent is part of a couple—its representative, perhaps. In the case that I am referring to, I had a strong impression of Mrs G as a parent to the small autistic child, and to her other children. I was in the room with a person who inevitably developed an unconscious transference to me, and brought her own difficulties, either implicitly or overtly. However, I also felt in the presence of the parental couple represented by only one of its members. Mrs G did not speak on behalf of her husband in the ordinary sense. Indeed, there seemed so little agreement between them that such a thing would be unlikely. However, at a deeper level I was naturally able to gain a picture of the nature and function of the couple as an entity, especially as it related to their children.

This mother presented herself as devoted, reasonable, and humorous. She was able to sustain an amiable, even thoughtful relation with me in the context of which I felt able to interpolate some thinking about the children, about her, and about her parents that she accepted, up to a point. However, surging all round the quiet interchanges she and I shared were the waves of her family life. Here, according to her, the children's father lived a separate and cut off existence, descending only to fall into ungovernable rages with her and the children. From time to time he was described as performing eccentric and irrational acts. Gradually, it became clear that my patient was playing her full part in a sado-masochistic relationship. The rages and rows had no resolution. They ended because both sides were exhausted, and started up again under some future stimulus without having changed in the least. This is quite different from the inevitable conflicts and quarrels that take place in families where—at least some of the time—conflict has a resolution, behaviour and attitudes change, and quarrels are at least in part related to argument and debate. This couple was not hoping for a resolution of their differences; at the time of their battles they were unconsciously enacting a fixed phantasy of a cruel primal scene, which nevertheless afforded them unconscious excitement. Though I do not think that Mrs G was always giving me an objective account of her family life, I do believe that the marital relationship had everything in common with those openly engaged in domestic violence. Mrs G, outwardly demure, would madden her husband until he burst. Consciously, she felt her husband's behaviour was a mystery to her; why did he suddenly fall upon her like a thunderbolt? Unconsciously, the shared phantasy of the primal scene was one of a sadistic intercourse, a cruel conflict mistakenly perceived as a sign of life.

Of course, it is more of a sign of death. The sufferers in these rages were (directly and indirectly) the children. While parents' coming together in good intercourse, literal or metaphorical, has the meaning of joining in creative mutuality that can only be to the children's benefit, the sadomasochistic interchange has the reverse intentions. On the one hand, there are all the phantasies of making, nurturing and looking after children; on the other, phantasies of a bad intercourse, the aim of which is to destroy babies.

The G family operated in a way that did not perform the function of fitting its children to participate in real life, and grow towards independent existence. The reverse was true. I was able to catch a glimpse of one child who had phantasies amounting almost to delusions of being grown up. There was scant attempt to restore him to reality; rather he seemed pushed on to ever-greater excesses of projective identification. Another of the children, though of school age, reacted with infantile, uninhibited ferocity when his omnipotence was challenged. I had no doubt but that my patient was using the children as receptacles into which to project unmanageable parts of herself. The roles of husband and wife could be said to be reversible; on the one hand, during the angry outbursts, the husband took the active role and the wife remained passive, a patient Griselda. However, at the level of unconscious projections into the children, the wife was very active, and the husband did nothing to protect them, but remained absent, as passive as she.

Though my patient would have said that she was worried about the children, her attitude struck me often as one of resignation.

Within her was a disturbed infant, child, and adolescent, and it was these figures that were becoming embodied in her children. It was clear that the children caused anxiety at school, tormented each other, and presented constant and unappeasable demands. Mrs G portrayed herself as all providing, at their disposal, patient, cheerful, and up at all hours. She idealized their rebellious and unseemly behaviour, rejoicing in them as what she construed as "free spirits". She consciously took pleasure in the notion that they were not crushed or quelled. There was only one way to say "no" in her unconscious mind; brutally, repressively, and punitively. It could never be a benign and essential aid to the establishment of boundary setting and orderliness.

The parents did not recognize and grapple with their internal states, but projected them into the children. They were none of them in command of their own lives, even to the limited extent that most of us can manage. In fact, the parents were scarcely living their lives at all, as so many of their actions consisted of the dramatization in external reality of their internal situations. The children were drawn into being players in the drama enacted. The parents' attempt to create something new, something that had never existed before, ended in their merely recreating the world as they knew it. In both their cases this was a severely paranoid world, relying on splitting, excessive projective identification with a strong element of confusion. All available adult aspects of the parents were busy with the business of keeping going; they fed and took the children to school, and they worked. However, significant aspects of their personalities were embodied in their children: intolerance for the negotiation of sibling rivalry; omnipotence, whose angry and impetuous commands must be obeyed—in short, a refusal to engage with the ordinary demands of life, shown at its extreme in the autistic child's refusal. The children's preference for the life of omnipotent phantasy naturally put them at odds with school life, and made them unable to get on with the business of growing up.

The family was non-functional, perhaps worse than that. Until the destructive force at work in the central relationship (between father and mother) could be acknowledged, the children were compelled to live in a place where their difficulties were fostered.

This happens when children are emotionally unmanageable for their parents, when (as in the Oedipus myth) something about the child is felt to be unacceptable, thrust out on to the slopes of Mount Cithaeron as dangerous and potentially deathly.

Reclaiming parental authority

I want to describe a case where this seemed true to me. The parents of a five-year-old boy had been worried about him since birth. I saw the whole family first (after a referral from a paediatrician, who queried autism) and concluded that although the two elder siblings might well have plenty of difficulties that were going unannounced, they were not of the same nature as their younger brother's, whom I shall call Jack. Jack's presentation was mildly psychotic. While I did not think he was autistic, I could see that he had difficulties with thinking, with distinguishing between fantasy and reality, that his social relations were impaired and that he inhabited a paranoid world. I also thought the picture was mixed and patchy, with areas of more encouraging functioning, and that it would be worth an attempt at individual work with him to see how far we could get in a year. I offered fortnightly work to the couple while a colleague took on Jack twice weekly, after several further meetings with the parents and Jack in various combinations.

The heartening thing about this couple was that they consciously wanted to work. I had the sense of parents who would like to be able to take charge of their family life, and perhaps people who were at a stage where the change—unspecified but longed for—that they desired could take place.

I should like to describe something of the situation I found, something about the work with the parents and something about Jack's state of mind and how these things link together. The story of Jack's life, as it emerged over time, was not substantially different from the parents' early accounts. They had been in two minds about wanting a third child. Instead of settling philosophically to the fact that Ms X was pregnant again, they started along a difficult road, as the pregnancy was uncomfortable and the birth—unlike the previous two—was traumatic. They repeatedly impressed upon me that the mother had felt shocking extremes of pain and terror, and had been sure she would die. The normal healing of such a wound takes place through the agency of the baby, as the presence of a live, flourishing infant encourages feelings of repair and hope. In this case, the mother did not recover psychologically. The story was fresh when she recounted it to me. After the birth she had fallen into a depressed state. Jack was a baby who "could not be put down". Father took over much of the care. The baby was all-demanding and all-absorbing of the attention they felt he would not let them give to the older children. Mother remained depressed for months, and I had the picture of some lurking fantasy of a monstrous birth, some great lump of a child who, instead of being full of a healthy life of his own, was full of an animation that felt malevolent.

Jack was, by now, and for many months into the treatment, regarded as the sole bringer of discord into the family. A large boy, when I saw him he blundered about bewildered, as though it was hard for him to connect meaningfully with anything. His father found Jack's unfocused and disruptive behaviour unbearable, and behaved as though he expected Jack to burst into flames at any moment. Some fleeting play with toys only demonstrated close encounters of a crashing kind. Father, then obedient and placatory, drew pictures for Jack. When Jack threatened his father with the toy crocodile his father flinched, said, "He knows my weak spot", and said he had a dread of crocodiles. In a meeting with the whole family, a tendency emerged for the older children to laugh at Jack; smirking at his clownishness (which he played up to), and giggling hysterically at his bad behaviour—without anyone getting a proper, serious grip on Jack's aggression, which was either to be feared or mocked. The elder siblings were said to get on very badly with Jack at home.

I had mixed success in seeing Jack on his own, as when his father brought him he hardly dared separate, and father soon had to be included. Father found this terribly trying, and had to control a surge of furious disappointment at my failure and me. I found Jack hard to think about and hard to remember, as though he had difficulty in recognizing me as an object prepared to try to receive him, a process opposed to his projecting into unwilling, uncontaining objects via their weakness, which is what he did.

When his mother brought him, I managed about twenty-five minutes alone with him. He demonstrated his failure to establish a primary split between good and bad or between adults and children. He tried to make animal families—four groups of mixed wild animals. He was vainly trying to divide them up; "Hot and cold," he muttered, and I had a strong impression of faulty thought processes, lack of definition and distinction. He passed on to more openly destructive connections: cars, dolls, toys cannoned into each other. Occasionally, I would catch his attention by taking him seriously, but little lasted, and things seemed profoundly unstable. His mother had to join us. She was full of relief because he had been able to stay for a while and was lavish in praise—how good, how brave he was. Jack sat and did a little drawing. "What is it?" I asked. "Hot dog . . . hot dog . . . hot . . . dog," he answered. I thought some appetite had been kindled in him, but that then the idea slipped away—was the dog hot? What dog? His mother found him funny. I also observed how Jack, like a six-month-old baby, was all over his mother as though to be in touch meant literally to touch physically.

During the third assessment session with his mother, I saw in Jack a sad, feeble child like a despairing outsider who, arriving as a new boy at school, had been much distressed to find that there was no peg for his coat. He was more attentive, leaning against his mother as I talked about how I thought Jack never felt really comfortable or safe, or as if he had a place in the world.

The other significant observation I made was of the quality of his relationship with his mother and her apparent warmth and liveliness mixed with seductiveness. For example, he found a chewing gum bar in her bag. She said he could have half; she broke it and gave him the piece, then he broke his half and gave her a quarter. This was done intimately, teasingly, with Jack passing the gum directly from his mouth to his mother's.

I have said enough to show how identities are blurred, distances unfixed; how Jack was a prey to bewildering rushes of anxiety from without and within. His mind was full of wars and battles where there was no good side. His anxiety was acute, and making connections was a feared activity. The primary connection—first between baby and mother, second between parents—had been interrupted, as with Oedipus himself. The baby was not felt to be a good baby, but a harbinger of disaster. Subsequently, the relationships within the family were disturbed. Father seemed afraid of the son; mother too in a way, but she, despite herself, played a flirtatious part.

Siblings were at war with one another, as in *Antigone*; and the vulnerable side of Jack was still a new boy, an outsider, unacceptable to the family.

His therapist had a difficult job on her hands. Jack turned out to be hard to manage, perverse, and sometimes frankly psychotic and deluded, but she persevered and progress was made. However, what of his parents, when I came to work regularly with them? I had the impression that they were a couple whose worst unconscious fears had been realized. They had been treading very narrow lines, separately and together, probably all their lives. He had left home at sixteen and made his way through university. His own father was a damaged man. She had a father whom she described fleetingly but with vivid detail as sadistic. Late on in the treatment she divulged with great difficulty that her brother had sexually abused her, and this brother is now mentally ill.

However, they had a touching and determined interest in family building. They wanted to do better. They had capacity to observe themselves and, over time, they came to see how, instead of functioning like an adult couple, they readily fell apart into two separate people bemoaning their lots, reproachful, angry, and cruel. I want to pick out the manner of their leaving the treatment. This couple actually made a move. They wanted to move out of London to somewhere they thought was more salubrious. They half-acknowledged that they had been idealizing the inner-city experience the children had had. But the process—finding a house, selling theirs, finding school places—was excruciatingly difficult, taking place as it did against a background of struggling with Jack's statementing procedure, a digestion of the fact that he was really disturbed, and also emerging worry about the two previously faultless children.

I think that when Jack was born both parents began to have a settled unconscious conviction—rather than fleeting phantasies, to be worked through—that their intercourse had produced a bad boy, the envious ghost of the baby they might have had, a destructive creature quite out of their control. This made it impossible to see Jack for what he was, and to feel, contain, and deal with his ordinary aggressive and negative projections.

Part of the hypothesis that I evolved was the idea that Jack was not an easy baby. There must have been something in him that answered to his parents' state of mind—a state of mind unwelcoming to a baby, fearing the worst, confirmed by the traumatic birth. However, although his problems might have been hard to ameliorate, they were definitely capable of being made worse. His parents found themselves in the situation of projecting during times of difficulty and trouble, unable to see the new baby as a blessing taken all in all, unable to grapple successfully with their ambivalence. No baby has the experience of every single piece of distress and dislike being fielded, absorbed, and transformed by its mother or father. However, Jack's experience went beyond one of a failure to contain negative emotion. His unpleasant feelings, projected out into his parents, were not received as a sign that "the baby's feeling unhappy" or "he doesn't like me today". They were interpreted, at an unconscious level, as evidence that he *was* unpleasant. Jack was construed as a baby who brought depression and conflict.

Thus, his parents on the one hand tried to behave positively towards him—with patience, encouragement and helpfulness—but just below the surface there was suspicion and negativity. Jack's father was almost obsequious towards him, but at the same time he simmered with angry resentment beneath. Jack's mother gave way to what must have been a meeting of her confusion with Jack's. I was told that Jack got into bed with her in the morning, and wanted to pretend to be a little dog and lick her all over, a process that overstimulated him and made him impossible to handle. From Jack's point of view, what was supposed to be a good experience, and what a bad one? His parents behaved as though they were in slavery to him; unconsciously, each played out a sado-masochistic union.

The work I did with the parents, as another child psychotherapist grappled with Jack, focused both on their approach to their difficult son, and to their relationship with each other. It became more possible for them to see Jack's behaviour as comprehensible, composed of the impulses and responses of a highly anxious child, rather than incomprehensible, crazy, and visited upon them by blind fate.

Equally, they made a great deal of progress in recognizing two states of mind in themselves as a couple. Broadly speaking, one state was when they could draw together as a parental pair, share their anxieties and ideas about all the children (not only Jack), put aside some time for privacy, and have a clear perception of themselves as adults, and adults in charge for good or ill. The other state was one where disunity ruled. Mrs X fell into depression and Mr X into anger. Each felt resentfully alone, full of self-pity, blaming the other, both fearing the inevitable violent outbursts and quarrels that were the outcome. In this second state, sides were taken. Mother tended to take the children's side, and father was cast as lacking understanding, furious, and somehow ridiculous. (This picture also fits the G couple referred to earlier.) While, when the parents were together, they saw all three children as needing their concern, when they were apart Jack became a kind of scapegoat, a receptacle for their fears of catastrophe and collapse. It is also interesting to note that it was with relief for all the children that they became a threesome. The situation at referral, where the elder girl and boy joined to mock and fear the baby brother, had caused much guilt and anxiety in the children themselves.

Conclusion

I have tried to demonstrate with clinical example and discussion the well-known value of working with the parental couple in conjunction with a referred child in order to bring about change (Barrows, 2003). The child's difficulty can usefully be viewed in the light of the parents' unresolved oedipal conflicts.

With all the couples I have described, the same process is at work. Can the parents draw together as a benign partnership, two people who can manage to reign over their little kingdom without outlawing anyone? Can the family manage to do without a black sheep? Can, indeed, the potential outcasts resist the lure of accepting projections? How do children remain loyal to two parents at once, and how can parents bear in mind the whole range of a child's personality, or the whole range of personalities their family may produce?

In work with children and their parents we see the full range of relationships—parents with each other, with the children; siblings with each other, with the parents—and have much to ponder upon. However, not, perhaps, more than Sophocles did, who watched as events unfolded from the original rejection of Oedipus.

CHAPTER NINE

Oedipus gets married: an investigation of a couple's shared oedipal drama

Joanna Rosenthall

W hat determines our choice of lifelong partner? For Oedipus himself, this is not a valid question because, as we know, he married his mother. His story is about someone who could not give up his primary passion and move on to bear the pain associated with exclusion from the parents' sexual relationship. Oedipus, we could say, acted on a universal longing that, in early life, is a consuming desire—continuing the exclusive possession of our first passionate love, our mother. It is therefore not possible to investigate whom Oedipus would have chosen as a wife if he had been able to relinquish possession of his mother. He is a lost cause. However, the question as to why one partner chooses another, and how the choice is linked to each partner's internal oedipal drama is a valid one, and forms the focus of this chapter.

Sophocles' story of *Oedipus* was revisited and borrowed by Freud, who articulated the oedipus complex—a mixture of impulses, phantasies, anxieties, and defences linked with the change from two-person to three-person relating. Klein and Bion subsequently developed Freud's ideas, and we now recognize the oedipal situation and its resolution as a necessary part of an individual's psychic development. Each one of us has to negotiate a journey from being a babe-in-arms, absorbed with an illusion of being our mother's only love, over a hurdle where the existence of the father and other siblings, either potential or real, is recognized and accepted. First, the possessive and exclusive aspects of the relationship with the mother have to be relinquished. This involves bearing a deep sense of loss and pain. The later stages of the oedipal process involve recognizing the differences between the relationship of child and parent as distinct from that of husband and wife. This recognition comes with a further sense of loss and envy, and results in the child giving up his sexual claim on his parents. The child now understands the difference between the generations—and has managed to recognize that the parents are in a sexual relationship with each other that does not include her/him.

Oedipal development is managed to varying degrees, and, like all psychic processes, it involves a lifelong journey. At any point in this journey each individual has internalized a representation of a couple relationship, "the internal couple", which is based on the experience of the parents, whose qualities have been influenced by projections and distortions.

All individuals, as a result of oedipal development, have an unconscious picture of a couple in intercourse, and this informs their relating style. The partners in a couple must have relating styles that are complementary to each other's, although what we often see is a more complex picture with each partner changing positions at different points. The couple I want to discuss shared material that communicated something essential about the nature of their unconscious phantasies about coupling, which helped me build up a representation of their shared "couple picture".

In my description of the couple and their therapy I have drawn very heavily on my counter-transference experience. The phenomenon of counter-transference has been recognized for several decades to be a crucial tool in psychoanalytic work, if the thoughts and feelings that are evoked in the therapist are detected and turned into interpretations in the clinical situation. Heimann (1950) was among the first to address in detail the use of the counter-transference in formulating interpretations that aim at a deeper understanding of patients' material. She stated that: "The analyst's emotional response to his patient within the analytic situation represents one of the most important tools of his work. The analyst's counter-transference is an instrument of research into the patient's unconscious" (Heimann, 1950, p. 81).

Most of what is described in the clinical material that follows is my attempt to explore and think about a clinical situation with a couple. My experience does not represent an objective truth, but rather is a complex mix of my own reactions with elements of theirs, some magnified and others entirely omitted. This account does not attempt to closely describe a real couple relationship, or the process of therapy, but aims to use parts of an experience to contribute to the thinking about oedipal issues in couple work.

Mr and Mrs Z

The therapy

Mr and Mrs Z came for couple therapy complaining bitterly about their relationship. They quickly conveyed a deep-seated despair about both their relationship and the possibility of receiving any help that was "good enough" for them to use.

They presented themselves as seeking a satisfying partnership, but each felt unappreciated, disregarded and abandoned by the other. They both seemed depressed, and each thought it was the other who needed or ought to change. They both believed that they could have found success and happiness if only they had married someone else. As it was, they were filled with unhappy grievance, and each felt unappreciated and isolated. Both Mr and Mrs Z had always been aware of an enormous discomfort in the presence of the other, which, nevertheless, had not acted as a deterrent to marriage and a long-term relationship. Much of the therapy involved an attempt to make sense of this curious fact. They both felt like misfits, with each other and elsewhere. Each of them presented as an innocent victim of the other, although the "fight" had a lop-sided quality because only Mrs Z tended to give voice to it.

I quickly came to recognize a style that this couple used to communicate. Both partners were reluctant to start speaking but equally seemed to find silence unbearable. Typically, Mrs Z would start complaining angrily about her exhaustion and misery, and then direct or imply accusations against her husband, using recent examples of his behaviour; usually things he had not done rather than what he had. She would present a case for why all the problems were his fault. He would appear phlegmatic, seem to be listening, but in a passive way which conveyed he was unlikely to answer and enter a dialogue. He would often react to her criticisms by nodding readily, agreeing with her diagnosis, apparently admitting his weaknesses and incapacity, but in effect leaving her to have the discussion alone.

More rarely, Mrs Z would make it clear she was exhausted and unwilling to start. This absolutely floored her husband, as if he had no thoughts or dilemmas within himself. He would attempt to turn the enquiry back towards his wife, asking her broad questions, such as "What would you like out of life?' or "What are your aims?" which usually had the effect of deflecting the heat from himself. She would work hard at trying to convey the aspects of her life and their relationship that felt problematic to her, even unbearable, followed by a description of the things she longed for that she seemed to feel he was unreasonably withholding. The discussions always had the same circular quality, as if there was no purpose to the questions other than to be able to ask more questions. In the course of a session, I saw no evidence of them taking things in from each other or of the contact developing. However much they exchanged words and overtly agreed with each other, in fact they each held an unrelenting view of the other and probably experienced themselves as victims.

There were times when I was drawn into their dynamic. I would point out that Mr Z seemed to be avoiding his own thoughts by asking his wife questions, and I then tried to turn Mr Z's questions back on to himself, a thing Mrs Z never did. On several occasions it went something like this:

Therapist: When things get difficult, I've noticed that you start asking your wife questions. Perhaps you have your own thoughts about what you are hoping for in your life, or between you.

Mr Z: What do you think?

Therapist: Are you asking me what I think your thoughts are?

Mr Z: Yes.

Therapist: You seem to be wanting to use my thoughts to have thoughts of your own.

Mr Z: Yes, I think that's right. What's wrong with that? Do you think I do that?

Therapist: Well you seem to turn either to me or to your wife for our thoughts at the moment when you are asked for your own. That's where we started a few minutes ago.

Mr Z: Did I say that? I don't think I said that. No—I don't think that's it at all.

This, and other similar communications between us, resulted in a disconcerting experience for me. On a number of occasions I felt as if I was falling into a dark hole or looking into a hall of mirrors, and would have very much welcomed the presence of a co-therapist. Not only was thinking impossible, but I had a very unnerving and powerful experience of losing the baseline necessary for my own sense of self. This was a powerful counter-transference experience that reflected Mr Z's terrifying feeling that he had no internal resources or markers. He seemed to not know who he was or what he thought, which he managed by asking his wife or myself questions, in an attempt to project the discomfort and disturbance into someone else. These kinds of interactions also had a frustrating quality, as if talking, which involved a lot of hard work on my part, could only end in meaningless circles. It is likely that Mr Z experienced my questions as malicious attacks that terrified and angered him, resulting in the infuriating and frightening experience that I have described. These experiences, however, were relatively rare; mostly Mrs Z expressed her grievance and unhappiness, which filled the space and seemed to relieve Mr Z of the need to know his own thoughts. Arguably, her convictions involved rules and markers in her mind that took the place of her own thinking as well as his.

In the first year of work they were noticeably reserved and wary, and the sessions were taken up with an attempt to establish a relationship of trust. They seemed puzzled about the concept of "help", and, although the trust did grow, they continued to hold cynical views of other people and, more often than not, impute them with unkind or malign motives. On many occasions, Mrs Z spoke freely about different attempts of hers to ask others for help. For example, she had asked a relative to help her organize a party and was refused. This, she was convinced, was not for practical reasons but was simply to give her the message that she wasn't liked, or that she should not expect to be helped because she was in a devalued position. She often talked about other people in a way that indicated they were experienced as takers and users, caring only about themselves and what they could get. These communications were further evidence that my questions or interventions were not experienced as helpful, but rather as attacks designed to humiliate them by exposing their ignorance or vulnerability.

During the second year of therapy there was some movement in how they used the sessions. They were more willing to share details of difficult experiences and to allow some exploration of the dynamics. I suggested that they were both so afraid of making contact with each other that there was a shared preference for being estranged or, at the very best, distant from each other. I also ventured the interpretation that closeness, to them, seemed to mean either one partner having to take responsibility for both, or else having an experience of losing oneself. Mrs Z, especially, seemed to feel able to take more risks, and began to present a deeper picture of herself and the relationship. She also offered more associations to her early experience. She started openly to express her distress and longing for help, at times bringing lively dreams that terrified and confused her. I also noticed, however, that, although there was an increased willingness to discuss complex feelings and motives, and Mrs Z had managed to develop her life more as an individual, they still both insisted that there was no change in the relationship between them. Small gains, they told me, were impossible to maintain.

Mr Z did not seem to have the increased sense of freedom in the sessions that his wife did. He continued to seem empty of himself, he had little to say except that he longed for more sex. He claimed to feel little or nothing. Occasionally he would report a fantasy he had that he would like to become successful in a new field of work, but it seemed to have the quality of a threat. He did nothing about it, nor did he seem to gain any pleasure from these thoughts. Mr Z largely conveyed an unbearable feeling of being utterly stuck, as if there were no future and no recognition of time passing.

I frequently felt invited into a battle where I had to feel I was losing. Much of the time it seemed to be crucial to Mrs Z to paint herself in a perfect light, and convey her husband as the one constantly at fault. She seemed to feel under threat of survival if this view was challenged. Her husband seemed willing to be denigrated as long as her proximity was assured. Later on, we heard more about how he kept her critical attacks at bay and made himself impervious, in order to hold on to his own view of each of them. Their coupling seemed deadly but resilient, and it often felt as if they were pitted against me, hating the possibilities for change that I stood for.

Towards the end of the second year in therapy, Mrs Z had a series of dreams that had disturbed her a great deal. There is one, in particular, which helped me to understand that they shared a difficulty in their oedipal development. It also appeared to offer me a picture of their shared internal couple.

Readers unused to thinking about psychoanalytic couple work may well be startled by the idea that a dream or story told by one individual can be thought about as conveying unconscious meaning for the couple. In couple work, as in group work, there is a change of focus; the two individuals in the room and the material they provide can be thought about primarily as contributing to an understanding of the relationship, rather than simply expressing meaning in terms of them as individuals. This has been expressed most clearly by the idea that in couple work "the couple is the patient" (Ruszczynski, 1993, p. 199). Later on, it should become clearer how the dream helped me to investigate the shared unconscious interaction between the partners in the couple.

Mrs Z's Dream

Mrs Z came into a large government building. It was a big, dark place. It reminded her of the building in which the sessions took place. She had to walk along many dark corridors, and then she saw a couple at the end of one of them. It looked as if they were made of iron. They were white people who were a dark colour. It looked as if they had been painted black. The woman was lying down. She was nearly dead. The man was leaning over the top of her, trying to help. It was an awful sight, absolutely awful. She kept repeating that she couldn't bear to see it.

Then she came out of the building and, near the entrance, she saw her father. He was standing behind a stranger. She told him she loved him, but he shrugged it off. He didn't really acknowledge her. At the end she kept repeating that the whole dream was so awful she could hardly bear to remember it, let alone explore it and allow associations.

What immediately struck me was the dream's relevance and meaning to the unconscious couple relationship that, until this point, had been very difficult to see. In the dream, there are two "couplings" or potential couplings. The first is like the primal scene (Freud, 1919e)—a couple in intercourse watched or seen by a third. In the second, there is a stranger (mother?) who is standing in between her and her father—the dreamer makes an approach to a father/husband and is ignored and rejected.

The first scene takes place inside a building similar to the one the therapy was in. The intercourse has a much damaged quality, in which one partner is dying and the other is desperately attempting resuscitation, but to no avail. The couple look as if they are made of iron, a hard, impenetrable substance, with no human softness, associated with machines. They are white, but they have been painted black, as if something has ruined everything, perhaps envy. The dreamer is looking at the couple and finds it a terrible sight, one that can hardly be borne.

Why is the primal scene depicted in this way? I believe we are learning first and foremost about an internal state of affairs in which there is an internalized couple where the woman is dying, or hardly surviving. The picture implies that sex has damaged, nearly killed her, and the man is desperately trying to resuscitate her and repair the damage. This is a picture of an extremely painful, destructive coupling, in which there is little room for creativity, and separation cannot be envisaged as it threatens to lead to death.

I would like to expand on what I came to know about this couple scenario from three different sources. First, this "damaged couple" from the dream seemed to be similar to each partner's own portrayal of each of their parental couples. Second, it was undoubtedly familiar to each partner, as I have already described and will expand on; and, last, it was congruent with my experience of the relationship with the couple.

The parental couples

There were times in the therapy when Mr and Mrs Z described associations to their early lives and their parents. Mrs Z described her parents as constantly warring. She referred to feeling like a princess during her childhood, as if she felt she came first for each parent. Throughout her growing years she identified closely with her mother, who was ill and vulnerable. At the same time she seems to have managed, while not being close to her father, not to have any battles with him either. Later, her mother left the family home, and Mrs Z's allegiance changed. She now understood things from her father's point of view, and felt so close to him that it became uncomfortable, and she felt forced to leave home prematurely. The parental coupling that she did portray involved one very dominant, lively figure (father) who was constantly having to make up for the other (mother), a vulnerable individual who could barely survive the exigencies of family and of life itself.

Eventually, discussions about this area made it clear that Mrs Z was suffused with persecutory oedipal guilt, unconsciously convinced that she had got rid of her mother and won her father, effectively ruining both of their lives. She quickly recognized these feelings when I explored this with her, and clearly stated that she felt unable to improve her own life when her parents' lives had been so bleak and full of loss. This was a pointer to her unconscious complicity in keeping the relationship with her husband so stuck, hopeless, and full of pain. It assuaged her guilt if her own life was also in ruins, but her anxiety could rise to unbearable proportions if her own life threatened to turn out satisfactorily. It also helps in understanding her need for such deep repression, as portrayed in the setting of the dream—the long dark corridors, the heavy statues made of dark, impenetrable iron—as well as her absolute inability to make associations to her own dream. This atmosphere of suspicion and persecution was shared with her husband, who, as I have already described, could bear neither my questions nor to make contact with his wife or myself.

Mr Z, when describing his parents, immediately said, "they are always together". He described his father as the dominant one, who made decisions on behalf of them both. With the help of his wife, Mr Z conveyed a picture of his mother as someone who didn't really have a mind of her own. She would do and say whatever her husband told her. Mr Z said she had never shown warmth or physical affection. He described her as an iron mother (this made a direct link to the couple in the dream, who also looked as if they were made of iron), mechanical, and as if she had no heart. Mrs Z added to the picture by telling us that relatives, who remembered Mr Z as a baby, had been worried about the way that his mother didn't seem aware of what she needed to do when the baby was crying. Mrs Z implied the likelihood that he had been left crying, unattended, for long periods. The picture I gleaned of his mother was of a woman so damaged, perhaps psychically near-dead, that she needed to "stick herself" on to a husband in order to be able to function. Mr Z seems to have experienced his two parents in precisely this way—as one stuck-together object that would issue orders or instructions but seemed oblivious of him as a feeling, needy being.

Each conveyed a picture of a vulnerable mother who hadn't individuated successfully herself, nor could she bear the ordinary pain and discomforts in life. They also both described domineering fathers who spent their lives trying to make up for the deficit in the women, and who perhaps chose their wives aggressively and narcissistically so that they could be tyrannical and go unchallenged. My patients never seemed to experience their fathers as helping their wives to develop or individuate.

The central near-dead/resuscitator relationship

It was clear from the material, and from the dynamic in the room, that most often Mr Z was like a dying person. He always looked pale, with dark eyes; he moved slowly and seemed depressed. He hardly ever spoke without being addressed directly, and while he would express a desire to develop, change, and start new projects, he was always unable to find the motivation, as if he had no internal motor. His early experience seemed to have left him in a severely undeveloped state, so that his wife's proximity, the presence of her thoughts and feelings and her ability to initiate things, were absolutely crucial to him. His method of attempting to use either his wife's thoughts, or at times my thoughts, so that he too could feel he had thoughts and feelings, and could survive, does at least indicate a primitive ability to use the mother and her thoughts at a very early stage in his development. However, it was disastrously inadequate in the context of an adult marriage.

In one session I gained a clearer picture of how transactions evolved between them. At the time they were starting a family, and needed to move from a flat to a house. As she was pregnant, he was the one who was trying to search for a house, but found himself unable to act. He said that everything seemed too risky. She had heard about a possible property through a friend. She knew he wouldn't go, and went herself to meet the estate agent and visit the house. All the time, she felt it was his job, and probably also felt that the visit wasn't worth it because if something came of it, her husband wouldn't see it through anyway. She almost didn't go, but then thought it was worthwhile, just to see what the house was like, and get a picture of what was available. When she arrived, again she thought she was wasting her time, because she imagined the agent would have already sold the house, or would only want to do business with friends. Then she noticed that the agent was friendlier than she had expected. She came away feeling that he would be good to do business with, and that there was a possibility of their buying the house. She returned home and told her husband that it was a good house and she felt the agent was someone they could trust; she thought they should go ahead. In spite of knowing that her judgement was often sound, he knew he couldn't manage to take the risk, but he thought that perhaps she would do it for them. He gave her all the financial information she would need to go ahead without him, but she felt she couldn't do it alone and the opportunity was missed. It is painfully clear in this example how not only were they competing with each other for the near-dead position, but it might also offer a clear picture of the transference relationship from her point of view. She is probably letting me know that she is willing to do work but she has linked her willingness entirely to his willingness, so that when he feels unable to move, she also refuses/feels unable to move, even though her capacity is greater than his. She is wedded to no-change because of her unmanageable oedipal guilt, and if she links change in herself to change in him, she is on very safe ground as he is more stuck and damaged than she is.

After offering this account, they talked about previous decisions they had tried to make jointly. He described them as times when he had felt very supported by her, knowing they would share the blame if it turned out to be a mistake. He acknowledged sadly that she was unwilling to do that now. She was shocked by his description of the past and convinced that he was either mad or lying. Her view was that she had not supported him but had bullied him until she felt she was going crazy. It had felt too burdensome and weighty, as if she had to find the life in herself and force life into him all at the same time, just like the damaged coupling in the dream.

His version of their interaction also gives us a picture of the transference relationship. He is unable to recognize the object as a separate entity. He receives bullying and resentment as support, as this is the only kind of parenting he knows about. This may go some way to helping us know more about their phantasy of the internal couple. His seems to be a picture of a nearly dead man who appears to be made of iron. He can't think for himself, he doesn't know what to do, he is full of uncertainty, and he needs the woman to breathe life into him—to fire him up with life and energy. However, even when she does he is almost impervious to her efforts, feeling sure that, if she were to be successful, it would lead to a catastrophe. Mr Z's internal world is dominated by a phantasy that intercourse leads to destruction, damage, and maybe death, and his wife shares this view. They both appear to be in the grip of a primitive phantasy about the parental intercourse, which has been coloured by the infant's own projections.

Fascinated by the area of early childhood phantasies, Klein (1929), largely through analysing children and by emphasizing the phantasy content of the instinctual impulses, developed the idea of the "combined parental object". She saw this as a monstrous threatening form made up of the two parents locked together in permanent intercourse, against the child, unmediated by experiences of reality that might have modified or opposed it. These united phantasied parents are extremely cruel and much dreaded assailants (Klein, 1929, p. 213). For some individuals this kind of primitive and terrifying phantasy is not significantly modified, leading to disastrous consequences for the formation of an adult sexual relationship.

Klein saw the child's internal experience as heavily influenced not only by the real external parents, but also by the child's phantasy world. The combined parent figure was seen as a phantasy that emerged from a previous phantasy of penetrating the mother's body, something that Klein saw as one of the infant's most profound wishes. The phantasy involves a wish to penetrate mother's body out of anger and frustration, and do harmful things to the organs and objects found there, partly through jealousy and partly because of a wish to steal them for himself. There is also a phantasy that the mother's body contains father's penis, and then there is an escalating and terrifying phantasy that mother and the objects inside her will retaliate against the infant. Thus, the aggressive phantasies about parental sexual intercourse arouse huge amounts of paranoia from a very early age.

Feldman (1989) shows how individuals who have negotiated the oedipus complex in a relatively healthy way have "an internal model of an intercourse that is, on balance a creative activity. . . . On the other hand, the phantasy that any connection forms a bizarre or predominantly destructive couple seems to result in damaged, perverse or severely inhibited forms of thinking".

Through Mrs Z's dream we catch a glimpse of the shared phantasied internal couple that informs the relationship between Mr and Mrs Z, who have different ways of expressing this phantasy in their relationship. Mr Z lives out the near-dead, or dying position, while Mrs Z carries the energy for her husband. He believes that in order to survive himself he needs her to stay alive, and he is therefore terrified of being abandoned. At the same time, she relies on him to make sure that his efforts are defeated, since if they were successful they would lead to disaster for her in the form of oedipal triumph. She is terrified of being made to experience the guilt attached to her phantasy of having disposed of her mother and won her father.

Mrs Z at different times responded differently to her husband's near-dead stance. She often competed with him for the passive position. She frequently talked about how, when she didn't know what to do in her life, she would talk to her father. He would always know what to do. So she painted a picture of a child/ woman who found it terrifying to stand alone, but who eternally relied on the parent/husband to take decisions and to have the life, as she did when she refused to see through the purchase of the new house. This is very similar to what he felt, and the combination left them in a deadly stalemate in which they were both putting intense pressure on each other to become the lively, active parent/spouse who would take responsibility for everything. When this demand was not met, there was a vicious competition between them for who would occupy the needy, near-dead, but safe—and therefore desirable—position.

At other times Mrs Z seemed to find it unbearable to feel her own vulnerability and need, and this was projected into her husband, a willing recipient. She could at times feel comfortable as a domineering rescuer, full of certainty and moral right. This was probably in accord with the role she took in the "coupling" she made with her mother during childhood, and later with her father, in early adulthood.

Mostly it was Mrs Z who swapped position from resuscitator to resuscitated. In contrast, Mr Z seemed to be stuck in the near-dead position. I never observed him offering help or comfort to his wife, although there were a small number of occasions when she reported that this had happened at home, but would always complain that it hadn't lasted long. What seems important in this context is that the near-dead and resuscitator positions typified their relationship and the "couple picture" emerging from the dream faithfully reflected their relating style.

This kind of intercourse is bleak and disturbing, and Mr and Mrs Z spent many sessions conveying their experience of that. However, it is important to notice that in the dream these white statues had been "painted black". By this time in the therapy I had come to suspect that some aspects of the relationship might have been working better than were ever conveyed, but I was never told directly about these. My information came from feelings the couple expressed, and incidental facts that seemed to slip out unintentionally. The dream seemed to confirm my suspicions that there were more hopeful aspects, both within the relationship and also in the therapy, but that the anxiety aroused in the couple by "good things" was so great that they had to be covered over and painted black. There was some movement on this eventually, but for much of the time it was not possible for them to acknowledge that there were some good things on offer that they felt unable to take. When they did start to interact more, it came with such a flood of emotional pain about what had been missing in their lives previously that they often felt it preferable to receive nothing.

It is also possible to change the focus slightly and think about the statue couple as representing Mrs Z's terrible oedipal triumph, where her coupling with father leaves her mother virtually dead. The second scenario in the dream, where she sees father and tells him she loves him, would then express the hoped-for situation where father comes to her for comfort and love, installing her in mother's place. Instead of this wish-fulfilment scenario, she gets its opposite; a father who ignores her, treats her like a stranger, and acts like a stranger. This is the bitter fruit of her oedipal long-ings, perhaps the result of her persecutory guilt. She ends up in a terrible place, with no live and loving mother *or* father.

There is another element that has enormous importance in working through oedipal longings, and that is the capacity of the child to be on the outside the parental couple and to envisage and subsequently manage standing alone. In the second dream scenario, Mrs Z is left alone as a person in her own right. It is possi-ble that the first couple is the one she feels herself to be in, and the second is one she can envisage for the future, once outside of the building, after the end of therapy, so to speak. It is possible that, at this point in the therapy, she has started to entertain the possibility of moving further away from the damaged couple and managing to exist alone as a person in her own right.

If the dream does represent this more hopeful possibility for Mrs Z, I believe it might also contain more sinister overtones, carried by Mr Z. In the second scenario there is no mother: she doesn't appear to exist. Father stands for mother and father stuck together, and the child is left unable to make contact. There is a dynamic within the couple between these two interpretations. The more Mrs Z devel-oped the capacity to exist as a separate person psychically, the more depressed and deathly Mr Z became, which tended to stimulate her role as resuscitator. A point was reached in this way where couple therapy could no longer contain this dynamic between them, and it was an important outcome of the therapy that Mr Z was referred for individual help.

Counter-transference

As I discussed earlier in this chapter, the main source of under-standing during the therapy came from my experience of being with this couple. In the first year of therapy I was often drawn into a battle that seemed never-ending, and without resolution. Each partner invited me in to a "coupling" that felt stagnant and non-developmental. Although they both talked about a desperate longing for change, in fact the desire for change and knowledge seemed to be lodged entirely in me, leaving the two of them free to fight against me. I was left to experience a barren and hopeless intercourse. At times, in order to avoid complete despair, I would find myself being abrasive or overly insistent. At other times I would feel in a trance-like state from which I could make intellectual comments that kept me distant and safe from the emotional contact that felt too dangerous and painful. I was experiencing in turn various states of mind and roles in which they each found themselves. It was as if it wasn't enough for them to tell me about these frustrating experiences—they could only trust me to know about them if they could get me, quite concretely, to have these experiences myself.

Everything I said, Mrs Z argued against and angrily rejected. Alternatively, Mr Z wholeheartedly agreed on the surface, but secretly disagreed, or did not engage with what I said, and then forgot it moments later. Though their methods looked different, for each of them as individuals, and certainly as a couple, I was usually in the "resuscitator" position. I tried to maintain my sense of hope for them and their relationship, while they both reclined, so to speak, near-dead, as resistant as iron, to their many attempts to move or change anything. At times, they conveyed that I had become a cold, harsh figure, imposing this nasty experience of thinking upon them. I should understand that, really, underneath their iron fortifications, they were so frail and delicate, all they could bear was to be loved unreservedly and fed only very easily digestible, tasty morsels.

I was also made to feel indispensable, in that their attendance could feel interminable and yet, I often felt useless and in despair about making any significant impact. It could feel as if there was no real contact between them and me, just words or angry rebuffs. So there was a cold "iron" quality, a feeling that I could never give or receive genuine contact. The result was that I could feel hard-worked but resentful and reluctant, as if I was being used and not appreciated, just as each of them felt about the other. The marriage and the therapy sometimes felt like a hospital for chronic illness, and I was left feeling as if I was forcing unwanted hope and therapy upon them.

As the therapy progressed, though, there were moments of real contact with Mrs Z, where she seemed able to engage in a creative intercourse. On one occasion she was able, for the first time, to share real feelings of guilt about the destructive part she had played in the relationship. Other times she talked more freely about her early experiences, and was able to develop a less idealized picture of her family. Initially, she would often forget or have obliterated these experiences by the following week, and it took some time before she was able to hold them in her mind and build on them. Eventually, there was a sense of something cumulative developing within her, and she was able to show some appreciation and gratitude. As Mrs Z changed, I noticed that my emotional repertoire with them also changed. I felt warmer and more connected, and the flow of my thoughts became less stilted.

There was a paradox here, in that the more it was possible to make contact with Mrs Z, the more Mr Z became remote and harder to reach. This increased my anxiety. There were times when I found myself imagining that he might die. This, I think, reflected a shared longing of the couple to be in a fused, blissful state where intercourse was repudiated and differences hated. They were, I think, also defending against hope and the promise of reparation turning out to be yet again a cruel mirage. Not only that, but there was an eroticization of this defence, so that it gained a life and momentum of its own, complete with its own gratification. This element of their shared situation, a constant attempt to return to a primal state of fused togetherness with a primary object, helped to explain why it looked as if there was no oedipal material with this couple. They couldn't bear to know that they were separate, nor that there was "a third" with which to contend. Staying as they were, maintaining a phantasy that they didn't have to be separate people, was always preferable to the experience of standing alone, taking risks and suffering pain.

Discussion

Feldman's (1989) paper, "The oedipus complex: manifestations in the inner world and the therapeutic situation", highlights how patients bring oedipal dilemmas into the analysis in a way that draws the analyst into a re-enactment of the child's original dilemma. He demonstrates the close relationship between the way patients have negotiated the oedipus complex and the quality of their thinking. It is clear from the paper how the analyst is bound to be drawn into oedipal re-enactments. It is also true that partners in a couple relationship subtly pressure each other into re-enactments of their original, and as yet unresolved, oedipal drama.

When forming a couple relationship, each partner comes unconsciously armed with a complex picture of what a couple looks like, a kind of template for an intimate adult relationship. The partners individually have an unconscious capacity to recognize something shared in the other's internal couple picture, in each other's oedipal configuration. It is likely that these factors create a resonance for each of them, which seems to contribute towards the "draw" that the individuals feel for each other at the start. After some time in therapy, it should be possible to attempt to elaborate the nature of the couple's shared unconscious couple phantasy, and how it informs their interactions with one another.

Partners in a couple will subtly nudge and pressure each other until they are in a position which is close enough to a shared unconscious phantasy about coupling. Therefore, we shouldn't be surprised that as soon as Mrs Z became more open and developed herself in various ways, it had a powerful impact on her husband. The more she gave up the role of resuscitator, the more lifeless and depressed he became. The more she moved towards life and health, the more vulnerable he became, and she found herself under pressure to regress and reconstitute a static, psychic relationship with him that reflected the picture in the dream.

Britton points out that "external reality may provide an opportunity for benign modification of such phantasies, or it may lend substance to fears" (Britton, 1989, p. 93). Unhappily for Mrs Z, her oedipal phantasy of victory over her parents was confirmed in the external world when her parents separated and her mother removed herself from the picture. The "missing mother" left scope for the phantasy that she had won her father away from her mother, damaging her mother so badly that, like Oedipus, she would forever feel burdened with the guilt of the most terrible crime. This resulted in Mrs Z becoming someone who needed not to achieve a satisfying adult relationship, for fear that this would stimulate intense persecutory guilt for the "crimes" against both parents that she was unconsciously convinced she had committed.

Mr and Mrs Z were in a position with regard to each other that made it very difficult for them to change. They were in the grip of a shared oedipal phantasy in which two people ganged up against a third, catastrophically. In Mrs Z's phantasy, she gangs up with father, and mother is banished and disappears as if dead. Mr Z's phantasy consisted of an earlier, more primitive, and even more serious triangle. He conveyed that, when he was a baby, his mother's preoccupation with depression—almost as if the depression constituted a third object in its own right—meant that the infant's terror of being left alone to die was strengthened by his experience of his mother being unavailable right from the start—an iron mother. Bion (1962a) coined the term "nameless dread" to denote the appalling "black hole" experience of the infant who is left alone to manage his own terrors on too many occasions. He desperately needs the mother to take in and bear his projections, thereby conveying an experience back to him that these kinds of terrors can be mentalized and borne. "If the mother does not accept the projection, the infant feels that its feeling that it is dying is stripped of such meaning as it has. It therefore reintrojects, not a fear of dying made tolerable, but a nameless dread" (Bion, 1962a, p. 116).

Later on, Mr Z's awareness of father coincided with an experience of both parents being locked in a fused coupling that was impenetrable to him, confirming the phantasy of the "combined parental object"—which implies that intercourse has deadly consequences as the two partners do not survive as separate individuals. This scenario also rendered both parents unavailable to any sort of flexible relating that would have enabled him as the child to experience and move through his painful oedipal feelings. This level of exclusion and the lack of real contact and understanding for him underscored his terror of being asked direct and personal questions, which he seemed to experience as if they were cruel instruments of torture designed to expose him to contempt.

Perhaps it was the differences between their individual oedipal phantasies that provided the hope for intercourse between them. Mr Z did convey, through his urgent pressure to find out my thoughts and those of his wife, that he had managed to find some life in his mother, albeit at a very early stage. It must have been this early success that helped him find a wife who could battle through, in the hope that she could help him battle through as well. He seemed to hope that, as he didn't know his own thoughts, she would give him hers. However, as we have seen, she was convinced that her fighting spirit was disastrous and led in unconscious phantasy to her mother leaving and to the unforgivable crime of her own tragic oedipal triumph. It then becomes clear that it was this pulling in two different directions that drew them to seek help, as they were each desperate to gain support for their own positions. Each felt these longings and fears intensely, which led to an extremely painful and destructive dynamic between them.

By the end of therapy, Mrs Z was managing to take more risks. She was leading life with more vigour and vitality, although it was kept within its limits and she still suffered enormously from fear. However, her shift away from her husband created a greater separation between them which, while it gave her more hope and a vision for the future, left him more desolate. Although Mr Z would mouth a hopeful stance, he became less and less able to act or think for himself. Greater separation, and less safety from their stuck-togetherness, seemed to leave him defeated by his own fears, which had a catastrophic intensity, and also left him exposed to an unmediated experience of his own cathected death-like state.

For some time, the oedipal elements in Mr and Mrs Z's dilemma were not obvious to me. Gradually, however, it became possible to understand something of the complex interweaving and dynamic interaction of their inner worlds. Mr Z, in particular, remained depressed, but he conveyed that his depression was made more bearable by feeling that he understood a little more about what he and his wife had been caught up in; and he also felt, and was, less blamed. While the therapy could not claim to have dramatically and positively transformed the couple's lives, it seemed that they at least experienced a quieter quality of containment by being attended to and thought about closely over a sustained period of time. This helped them to tolerate their situation and to begin to get some distance from it and to reflect on it, which in itself modified and softened the former deadly, over-entangled and rigid internal structure of their marriage.

CHAPTER TEN

No Sex couples, catastrophic change, and the primal scene*

Francis Grier

Introduction

Acommon presenting problem to the marital psychotherapist is that of No Sex. Sometimes a couple names this as
their principal problem at a first interview. Often, however,
they will be too embarrassed to be so frank, but it will soon become
apparent that there is this crucial absence in their relationship. In
this chapter I propose to attempt to make some inroads into understanding this situation. I want to concentrate, in particular, on how
such difficulties often arise when the partners share a history of
inadequate working through of certain aspects of the oedipus
complex.

I will use three clinical illustrations, which represent variations
on a theme. The variations are, I suspect, quite commonplace,
although the particular version that any couple develops is their
own. The underlying theme consists of the dynamic relationships

---

*This paper was presented at a Scientific Meeting of the Tavistock Clinic on
8 May 2000. It was published in the *British Journal of Psychotherapy* (2001), Vol.
17(4).

between the child and the parents in intercourse in the primal scene. The three variations represent typical defence systems erected by couples against the psychic pain evoked in attempting to accept the reality of the primal scene. The variation of my first couple, the Flints, consists of their not being able to bear the fact that it is the parents who couple. They insist on a version in which the child and one of the parents come together, the other parent becoming the excluded one. The Grays, my second couple, did not dispute that it was the parents who were intimate, but they could only conceive of the excluded child being cruelly deprived. This justified their complaining about this forever and ever. The variation or solution of my third couple, the Forsyths, was to eliminate the child in the triangle and hence to construct a non-procreative version of adult intercourse. There was to be no problem or pain, because no demanding child would eventuate from the intercourse. For all three couples, their coming to therapy was evidence that they knew something was seriously wrong and that they needed to change. However, when confronted with the reality of the demands made by psychic development, they reacted as if faced with a catastrophe.[1]

Theories of the primal scene and catastrophic change

In his paper "The oedipus situation and the depressive position", Britton explores the great developmental significance of the child's unconscious phantasies about the parents' sexual intercourse. He comments that, though Freud explored the primal scene to some extent,

> he never incorporated the primal scene and its associated phan-
> tasies as a principal component of the oedipus complex. In contrast
> to this, Klein not only did so but made it central in her account of
> what she called the 'oedipus situation' (Klein, 1928, 1945). [Britton,
> 1992, p. 36]

My purpose in this chapter is to show examples of the pathology that can ensue in adult heterosexual relationships when individuals couple who have not been able to adequately work through this all-important aspect of the oedipus situation. Not that any individual or couple can ever fully meet this challenge as, by its very nature, it is a life-long task. I hope to show that, if two individuals come together who have been overwhelmed by its difficulties and opted for maintaining rigid defences against working through the oedipus complex, rather than continuing the struggle, they will almost inevitably encounter serious relationship problems. Often these will erupt, appropriately enough, in the arena of sex.

One might say that it is precisely because of the impossibility of full working through of the oedipus complex during the growing child's developmental phases that continued engagement becomes a universal aspect of the motivation for adult sexual relating. What has not been processed in the turbulent periods of infancy, childhood, and adolescence remains to be engaged with as an adult sexual being, in addition to those new tasks which are specific to this epoch. If one thinks in terms of each new stage of the life-cycle throwing up developmental crises, challenges, and opportunities, then adult sexual relating offers the chance to engage fully with one's oedipal difficulties and dilemmas. For all of us, this chance is like a double-edged sword, as seizing it offers the opportunity for growth, but it also forces one to engage with one's unresolved nightmares. Small wonder, then, that some partners, who may often have unconsciously chosen each other in the hope that the complementarity of their problems may help each to become allies of the other in taking up the developmental challenge, instead unconsciously prioritize, work out, and put into practice a strong, combined, anti-developmental defence.

One of the difficulties with this strategy is that it can only work (if at all) on a short-term and superficial basis. The psychic subset of the potentially mature, developmental couple within what one might refer to as "the total couple" becomes increasingly frustrated with this anti-developmental strategy. They know that something is terribly wrong, particularly if it results in symptoms like the non-occurrence of sex. However, not only do they not know consciously how to engage with the problem, but unconsciously they fear that were they to do so, the consequences would be catastrophic.

It was to describe just such situations, with their attendant anxieties, that Bion (1965) coined the term "catastrophic change". My understanding and application of this core theoretical concept in terms of the couple is as follows. A psychologically healthy part of the joint couple ego—the couple analogy to what Bion (1957) referred to with regard to the individual as the "non-psychotic part of the personality"—wishes to develop, but its dilemma is that it simultaneously fears change. When that fear becomes strong enough, it induces regression in the couple psyche, and joins forces with the anti-developmental aspect of the couple—the psychotic part of the couple personality—that actively hates truth and psychic reality. Psychic reality at this point would entail recognition of the need to risk taking up the challenge of change and development. A lie is preferred over this truth, the deceit being that maintaining the *status quo* is better and wiser than taking the unknown step into the future, portrayed as leading inevitably to catastrophe.

This version contains much truth, which is why it is so beguiling. It is highly likely that taking the developmental step will result in major, probably terrifying, internal turbulence, leading to a need to work out all over again the partners' understanding of themselves in relation to each other and the world. So, "better the devil one knows". The forces ranked in triumphant opposition against it may now defeat the "developmental couple". It is crucial that, if such a couple manages to get to therapy, the therapist tries to link with this "developmental couple", who correspond to what Rosenfeld (1987) called in the individual "the sane, dependent part of the patient"; but if he does so, he can expect to become an object of suspicion, resentment and hatred to the dominating, allied forces of fear and hatred within the couple.

The Flints: the myth of the excluded parent

The Flints presented with a case of no sex after the birth of their one and only child, a daughter. They were in their thirties, they had married in their early twenties, and their child was four years of age at the start of therapy. They both agreed that their earlier married life had been quite satisfactory, both emotionally and sexually. However, the birth of their child had presented them with a tornado. Elizabeth had a puerperal psychosis. Andrew had to look after his wife and their child for many months. Sometimes he had to take the child away from Elizabeth for a couple of days, for fear that she might kill her. Elizabeth's psychosis took the form of immensely strong manic-depressive swings of mood, and it was when she was at her lowest that she would think it in her baby's best interests to kill her rather than let her suffer the cruelties of life. With the help of psychiatric medication, her mental state improved, and things gradually got better for the couple. By the time they came to us, they were happier and able to live a more normal life. Elizabeth was intensely conscious of all that her husband had heroically done. She was very grateful to him. However, he had only coped so well by becoming quite split off from many of his emotions, so that he could concentrate on doing his duty. Now, when circumstances allowed it and his wife required it, he could not retrieve his former warmth, emotional or sexual, towards Elizabeth. In addition, she, despite and because of her indebtedness, became furious with him for his coldness; and her rage was massive.

The couple engaged in their therapy, and fairly soon their relationship ameliorated in many areas, but not sexually. As therapists[2] we had constantly borne their unresolved sexual abstinence in mind, and had often suggested that material which was not overtly sexual (e.g. their anger, need to control, emotional withdrawal) was played out in the sexual arena.

Over the course of time, we became aware of some important similarities in their individual relationships to us. They both tended to engage in a more adventurous, sometimes excited, manner with me, while they could be subtly dismissive and less vital towards my female therapist partner. This dynamic also influenced our therapist relationship, so that I could become rather full of myself at my colleague's expense, and she could become too backward in coming forward. We then noticed that I would be rather patronizing towards her, and for her part, she would feel not only resentful but, not in accordance with her usual professional character, also rather impotent towards me. This counter-transference experience was disruptive, painful and difficult to process. However, we persevered, and gradually discovered how this linked with the deeply held attitudes of both Andrew and Elizabeth towards their parents, and of their internal parents towards each other. Thus, Elizabeth idealized her energetic and potent father, and denigrated her mother—not openly, but subtly, by disparagement. She also felt that her father related similarly to his wife, yet could get excited about his relationship with her, his daughter. Andrew spoke of giving up on his rather depressed mother who never experienced anything in her life with enjoyment and eagerness, including him, her only child. He had turned to his father, a rather wordless, but very competent and warm-hearted man, with whom he had forged a strong bond. He thought his father had given up on women from his disappointing experience with his wife.

Much of the content of the therapeutic process flowed from this. We explored Elizabeth's oedipal phantasy of vanquishing the mother and gaining the father; and we realized that she risked catastrophically losing this special place by becoming a mother herself, especially since she had produced a daughter. We noted her extreme reluctance to relinquish the gratification of excitement that came with hanging on to this position. We saw this re-enacted in the transference to me, and to other men in their current lives. We understood that part of their marital problems also lay in her constantly comparing Andrew with her father unfavourably, partly because in making the choice for a husband the inevitable consequence would be to lose her phantasized incestuous relationship with her father. We began to understand that Andrew contributed to all of this. By modelling himself on his own father and modelling his relationship with his wife on his parents' relationship (as he perceived it), he made himself rather wordless and competent, not exciting, and he denigrated and patronized his wife. Severe problems were bound to ensue.

Nevertheless, there was a further counter-transference experience, much less frequent, which challenged this set of relationships. On odd occasions, Andrew clearly felt special warmth towards my co-therapist. He would miss her if she had to miss a session. Whereas Elizabeth would set up a triumphantly exciting relationship with me, Andrew never quite conquered my co-therapist in this overt manner. He would tend to build up a warm relationship with me (very importantly, for here we could see for ourselves his capacity for warmth and vulnerability) and then apparently feel rather sorry for my co-therapist who was left out of this—not always patronizingly, but sometimes with a sense of affection and concern. This was hard to process, because almost all of Andrew's emotional activities towards my colleague were exclusively non-verbal. However, we began to find ourselves giving more weight to certain parts of their narrative than hitherto. For example, Elizabeth told how Andrew would sometimes telephone his mother secretly. Then, in one session, they brought together two incidents, apparently unrelated. They had actually had sex, and good sex at that, initiated by Elizabeth, but which Andrew had then asked her not to repeat. They had also had a row, because Elizabeth was furious that Andrew wanted to celebrate his birthday by having his mother to stay.

The first point seemed almost unbelievable. Here was a couple who had both yearned to get back into a sexual relationship; the man had had huge problems with impotence, to the extent of having medical examinations and advice. Yet when confronted by the evidence that he could not only get an erection but also use it, experience pleasure, and give his wife satisfaction, his response was to ask his wife not to stimulate him again. In explanation and defence, Andrew could only say that he thought his wife was offering him sex without love, yet he himself realized immediately that this was not true.

The couple regarded the matter of the invitation to his mother as an entirely separate matter. It had occurred a few days later. However, to us it seemed that they were managing to bring to our notice the intimate unconscious relationship between these two instances, dynamically powerful in the extreme. For, just as the exclusive dyadic unconscious relationship between Elizabeth and her father attacked the couple's adult sexual relating, so did Andrew's relationship with his mother. It began to become clear that, internally and unconsciously, underneath his warm man-to-man son–father relationship, which included a sad and worried casting off of the mother, paradoxically and simultaneously there existed a strong phantasy of an exclusive, dyadic union with his mother. Elizabeth was right to be jealous. And just as it was hard for Elizabeth to contemplate losing her exciting relationship with her father for an ordinary adult partner, so for Andrew it was felt as too much to lose that special closeness with his internal mother, particularly as she was depicted there as so depressed that to separate from her would undoubtedly cause him great anxiety and guilt, both depressive and persecutory in tone.

After nearly two years of steady therapeutic work, in which the couple really began to internalize and digest different ways of understanding their relationship, a period of some months followed that was characterized by a flat, depressed, and hostile tone. They voiced their doubts as to whether they any longer loved each other at all, and as to whether it was worth continuing the struggle to develop their relationship. It was a depressing period for all of us, but there followed a time of greater stability in the marriage. The couple began to find more happiness together, including sexually, and they even began to contemplate the possibility of having a second child.

I think this flat, hopeless period was a symptom of anxiety about catastrophic change. It was as if, as a result of their engagement with their therapy, the couple found their ability continually and repetitively to substitute omnipotent phantasies for disappointing realities was fast waning, and so they found themselves faced with the unwelcome fact that the only way forward was to take up the developmental path of attempting actually to form an adult—including sexual—relationship with each other. But this step seemed catastrophic, as it entailed trying to deactivate their previous defensive strategies and investing energy into something they had written off long ago: the possibility of two adults engaging in a mutually satisfying, potentially procreative, relationship. The hopeless period perhaps consisted of the time spent between these two alternatives.

A session

An example of these different progressive and defensively regressive trends, oscillating and vying with each other for supremacy, came in a session during the period in which they were beginning to contemplate whether to try for a second child. They had introduced this important idea and we had discussed their feelings about it for a couple of sessions. For the next session, I was absent; for the following one, some of which I will report here, my co-therapist was absent. Both these absences were unavoidable, and we had warned the Flints about them well in advance.

> Andrew started by telling me all about the previous week's session. After some time, I pointed out that he had a picture of my co-therapist and me in which we seemed to be like parents. Either we did not have

"intercourse" at all or, if we did, our relating did not apparently include ordinary care and concern for our children. In his mind, I had not met with my co-therapist, or, if I had, I had not asked her about the session, nor had she any wish to tell me about it. Elizabeth said she thought differently from Andrew in one respect, as she would expect the two therapists to liaise in a quick, generalized way, not bothering with the detail of the session.

They then went on to tell me about another potential project. Andrew said that he had for a long time wished to develop his own business in a particular line, and he had recently been seriously wondering if now might not be a good time to give up his job and try to make his dream an actuality. Of course, he could only do it if they were prepared to cope with a sizeable drop in income and financial security in the short term, and Elizabeth's help would be vital. She appeared to be very much in favour. During the last week, she had moved out with their daughter and stayed with friends for a couple of days so that Andrew could formulate some practical plans, undisturbed by family. When she returned she discovered that, although he had done a lot of good groundwork, including arranging a meeting at the end of the week with potentially interested financiers, he had also dramatically lost confidence in himself. So she put Humpty-Dumpty together again, partly by reassuring him emotionally but principally by becoming very practical. She examined all his notes and ideas, found unrecognized flaws and constructively criticized his work, adding her own thoughts, finally helping him to put together an even better package of initial ideas for his important meeting. Andrew had quite recovered his confidence through Elizabeth's helpful interventions, and the financial meeting had gone well.

They themselves referred in passing to this project as "Andrew's baby", an accurate interpretation in my opinion. However, they then continued talking to me about their lack of confidence concerning these two projects, the actual baby and the potential new business. The more they talked, the more anxious and depressed about the future they became, and the more certain that if they actually tried to put these ideas into effect, they would surely come to nothing or eventuate in a disaster. It was as though they were beseeching me for help as a good figure, but simultaneously I was also becoming contaminated by the evolving gloom.

I think the couple was showing me the way their minds often worked together as a combined unit. Through their narrative, they told me a story that demonstrated the way they *could* work well as a couple. It was an impressive story of purposive complementarity. There was a mixture in it of ideas and fantasies (about the potential business project), and evidence of their capacity to transform these into practice, in reality. Plans had been written down, and a meeting with real financiers had been organized, well prepared for, and had taken place successfully. An inextricable part of the story was their emotional duet: Andrew's desire to act on his dream; Elizabeth supporting him at some cost to herself (her moving out); his emotional collapse; and her successful repair of him. It was a picture of satisfactory adult intercourse. However, they had then continued talking to me about the future as if none of us had attended to this narrative. We were all expected to believe that their plans would come to nothing, fizzling out or erupting in chaos; that Andrew would be incapable in the business world and Elizabeth would again prove a catastrophic mother.

I was experienced ambiguously. I had started by being predominantly a good, helpful figure, but as they felt themselves becoming more acutely dependent on me they seemed to become resentful, as if I were turning in their eyes into someone who had contempt for their neediness. Finally, I seemed to have evolved into a figure who had no doubt that they were arrogant, stupid, and wrong to imagine they could actually carry off these two creative projects. This was a verdict they hated me for, but which they themselves seemed fully to endorse. Nor had they themselves given any weight to a most significant detail in the real event they had narrated, that it was Andrew, not Elizabeth, who had psychically collapsed; and it was Elizabeth, not Andrew, who did the repair work. This was a conspicuous reversal of their habitual and fixed picture of who was strong and who was weak in their relationship.

Later in the session, they spoke about having enjoyed watching *Mission Impossible* on the TV together. They described the heroes and heroines of the drama in tones that seemed to me to be clear pointers to rather excited identifications. It seemed that one strategy for coping with the huge internal attack on the developmental processes we had just witnessed was to "ride high", to picture their projects to themselves as "Missions Impossible", and themselves as the protagonists. What was avoided and pictured as far more alarming was taking on "Mission Possible", i.e., portraying to themselves their projects of having a baby or running a business as quite possible, potentially within their grasp, even if difficult. When I interpreted this, the couple said they felt "depressed", but to me they seemed more grounded and thoughtful, and less manic. I thought one of the reasons they lost heart and needed to "ride high" was because they felt they lacked internal parents who would back them up, bear them in mind and be interested in them when tackling the ongoing problems of ordinary life.

I think the act of telling me this story of a successful creative and cooperative intercourse immediately provoked an internal, envious attack on the parental couple. They attempted to protect themselves from attack, firstly by giving up, and subsequently by adopting a manic defence. However, after this was interpreted, they seemed more grounded, more realistically depressed and more potentially creative.

Their case illustrates Britton's (1989) thesis, that crucial in working through the oedipus situation is the development of what he terms "the third position"; in which one can know one is excluded from the parental couple, and yet still know oneself to be loved by the parents, so learning to tolerate this position. Both Andrew and Elizabeth were possessed by a variation on the primal scene in which they were *not* excluded by both parents; instead, each excitedly phantasized that he or she was in an exclusive dyad with one parent, while the other parent, not the child, was in the intolerable cast-out position. This position itself was bad enough, but to contemplate trying to alter it provoked anxieties of catastrophic proportions—which had, in the first instance, necessitated psychiatric treatment.

The Grays: the myth of the excluded child

A different dynamic obtained in the case of the Grays. They also had an only child, and had not had sex together for many years, except for isolated instances.

Their chief complaint was the state of nearly unremitting war that existed between them. This situation had been chronic, lasting many years. This couple had seemed to use therapy quite well, in the sense that gradually they had used us to help them to listen to each other, begin to hear each other's point of view, and so on. Their relationship did get better. However, it would constantly threaten to slip back into mindless warfare, and all too frequently it did. On those occasions, it would usually take a long time for their relationship to improve again. The wife tended to sit around (literally) at home, fuming when her husband was absent and attacking him with the utmost ferocity when he was present; the husband would abscond hopelessly to the pub. If, when things got better, he spent more time with her, she would then find a different pretext for attacking him (with which he would comply by providing her with the opportunity for just such pretexts); consequently he would abandon her again for the pub. With regard to the sexual arena she would complain that she did not want him coming in to her bed late at night smelling of beer, having abandoned her to her rage earlier. She demanded a separate bed in a separate room. When things got better, they sometimes even managed to get together sexually. However, not for long: these disquieting and unwelcome outbursts of peace and harmony were soon quelled by a victorious recall to war.

In the transference, my co-therapist and I realized that we were being consistently idealized. It was not just that neither spouse became angry with us even when we gave just cause for anger (e.g., through ordinary mistakes), but that even when we made deep interpretations that must have caused pain, this pain was denied. Moreover, the couple's chronic tendency easily to slip back into war indicated that these interpretations were not being metabolized and digested. As therapists, we were increasingly frustrated by this too frequently repeated negative therapeutic reaction.

It became clear that each cherished a grudge. Their actions proclaimed that, despite their conscious desire to get better, they continually preferred to nurse their grievance. In their marriage, their grievances were against each other; but the depth and dynamism of these grudges suggested that these were new editions of what they had originally brought to their relationship from childhood. We first recognized this when Florence underlined her diagnosis of their problem. She said that they had never had a good, romantic period when they first went out together. We gradually realized that these words had a deeper significance.

On the face of it, each came from quite different families. Florence was an adopted child in a small family; Tony one of many children. However, similarities began to emerge in their experience of their families. Florence's adoption had taken place immediately after birth, and she was never told about it until, as a teenager, someone in the town mentioned it to her in the assumption that she knew about it. She told us that when she approached her mother about this news, her response was to demand Florence's sympathy for *her* predicament and difficulties. Florence felt that her mother apparently did not think she needed either sympathy or an explanation. To Florence, this made sense of some of her earlier childhood experiences: her own sense of never quite belonging and her intense jealousy of her father playing with the other child, a natural daughter born soon after Florence's arrival. For his part, Tony was the sixth child of many, all born fairly close together. Family life was regimented like an old-fashioned boarding school. In this way, all the children were adequately looked after by their parents and by each other. They could talk about this, but could not contemplate or voice thoughts and feelings about not getting any individual attention from the parents, in particular the mother. Both felt that their individual histories were marked by a real degree of psychological deprivation. Florence's view was that her parents could not empathize with what the experience of a baby torn at birth from her biological mother might be. Similarly, it felt to Tony that his parents could never imaginatively enter their son's experience of a genuine lack of enough individual love, care, and attention.

Tony and Florence met each other in their early twenties, and soon married. It is not difficult to see that each of them brought a basic attitude of grievance towards their parents. However, what they also shared was that they felt their grievances to be quite unjustified. After all, Tony's parents could justifiably answer him that they had done their best, and Florence's similarly. How could the child ever complain? Therefore, the characteristic form their resentment took was of guilty, passive aggression. In addition, the narrative of their marriage suggests that they continued along these lines, combining their forces. The psychological events of their years in marital therapy, particularly their continual backsliding and defeating of the therapists' and their own best endeavours to improve matters, suggest that there was something quite strongly and actively anti-developmental operating in addition to their understandable previous repetition of these dynamics, which up to now had been unconscious. It was as though there was a secret gratification at work in each of them, destroying any good links between them that might develop, including the good sexual intercourse they occasionally managed to re-establish.

Discussion

This case underlined for us the therapeutic importance of trying to understand the couple's shared unconscious phantasies. When Florence complained that they had had no real romance at the start of their relationship, she could be heard as voicing a deep grievance on behalf of both spouses that each felt he/she had had no good or long enough period of idealization or special individual attention from the parents, especially the mother. But what was more malignant was the unspoken and deeply unconscious vow that, since their romantic start to life had not been as desired, then, rather than make use of the marriage as a second opportunity to make good a flawed beginning, the marriage would be used to repeat the bad experience, to harbour an everlasting grudge about this and, in "justified" retaliation, to wreak eternal vengeance on the parents, in the forms of the partner and the couple. The marriage had become so internally organized around these grievances and the gratification of nursing them that it was almost impossible to think of giving them up, to bear their loss. The rewards of development, by contrast, seemed much more uncertain and perhaps less exciting. Thus, the upholding and repetition of their grievances also protected them from unconsciously feared further disappointments.

Like the Flints, the Grays could not bear to work through their combined oedipal development. They apparently found that the degree of mental pain they would need to tolerate was too great. In eternally justifying their grievance, they were defending themselves from this pain by clinging to the omnipotent position of the young child who is always in the right, and who can only deal with frustration by accusing and hating his objects, taking up a superior, righteous position. Their developmental challenge consisted partly in bearing the pain of relinquishing this position, through mourning what they felt they had never had. However, this development was feared as catastrophic because it would entail their stepping out of such familiar, well-worn grooves towards quite unknown, frightening territory. Above all, it would entail at its core the surrender of the enormous gratification of the justified, superior position.

The Grays seemed to share a basic unconscious phantasy of the primal scene as consisting of parents engaged in an intercourse that utterly—and intentionally—deprived their children of their love, which they hogged all to themselves. Tony and Florence therefore felt they were entitled to feel constant resentment against such depriving and abusive parents. Yet, this version did not quite fit with other perceptions of their parents or their therapists, who at their core felt not greedy and evil, but loving. So the "developmental couple" within the Grays longed to recognize another version of the primal scene in which the parents had a right to private sexual love from which they would properly exclude the children without depriving them of their love. The Grays sometimes imagined that we therapists might well often be too busy, whether with each other or attending to the demands of other patients, to be constantly thinking specifically about them; and yet that did not mean that we had utterly withdrawn our interest and concern from them. They also occasionally slipped—as it were, by mistake—into just such a satisfactory intercourse themselves, both sexual and emotional, but after a while they would usually regress to their old, sterile warfare. Life was much more exciting here. Both they and their objects tended to be very high or very low—and it seemed that they were too addicted to this excitement to bear parting from it.

The Grays' way of handling their difficulties and defending against the oedipal challenges posed by development illustrates a couple version of what John Steiner (1993) has called a "psychic retreat". They often tantalizingly demonstrated their capacity to enter upon a much more developmental oscillation between the paranoid–schizoid and depressive positions; but then they would slide into this dead-end, anti-developmental warfare as a place in which the pain, uncertainty, and tasks of the depressive position were avoided. Their particular psychic retreat was characterized primarily by their preference for nursing their grievances (Steiner, 1993) rather than relinquishing them.

The Forsyths: the myth of the non-existent children

I have tried to illustrate some of the complex and powerful unconscious oedipal dynamics that can be operating when a couple complains that they can no longer make love. I would like to end with a short example of a situation that can apparently turn this clinical picture on its head, and yet can illustrate similar psychic defences against oedipal working through.

Jessica and Mark Forsyth encountered intense difficulties soon after the arrival of their two children, especially after their second. They were fairly typical problems (although, of course, not typical to them), consisting of two main strands. They had conceived their children sooner than expected, so that, although there was no doubt that they were loved, their early arrival also made them resented. The resentment of spouses was re-directed from their children on to each other. The second strand was interconnected, as both parents were ambitious and career-minded. Severe quarrels arose over the balance between them of child-care and professional work. They fought bitterly, and contemplated divorce as a despairing solution to their problems.

After we had seen them for some months, we realized that they had never spoken about their sexual relationship. We imagined it might well be impaired by their problems, especially as these were directly linked with their procreativity. We had also noticed a quality of excitement in their fights, which suggested that their sexual energy might be finding a sublimated outlet there. We wondered if they were abstaining from sex for long periods, and whether this factor might be exacerbating their problems. To our surprise, the couple told us that sex between them was good, and in fact, was the only good thing that they could consistently rely on. Shortly after this, they left the therapy rather suddenly. We had a sense that there was a connection between what they had said and their leaving.

We were curious as to why this intelligent and reflective couple were themselves not more curious, as well as anxious, about the paradox of their sexual relationship flourishing in the midst of their other difficulties. We did not think they were deceiving us about the satisfactory quality of their sexual love. They did not remain in therapy long enough for us to follow this through, but it would seem that they had managed to split off and encapsulate their sexual relating from the rest of their relationship. This meant that it could not be harmed by the poison in the rest of the system, but it also meant that whatever was genuinely dynamically loving and developmental in their love-making was not given the chance to have a constructive effect upon the impaired aspects of their relationship.

Discussion

Britton writes:

> The oedipal phantasy may become an effort to . . . deny the reality
> of the parental sexual relationship. . . . The oedipal romance may be
> preserved, by splitting it off into an area of thinking protected from
> reality and preserved, as Freud described, like Indians in a reser-
> vation (Freud, 1924). This reservation . . . can become the place
> where some people spend most of their lives, in which case their
> external relationships are only used to enact these dramas to give
> a spurious claim of reality to their fantasies which lack "psychic
> reality". [Britton, 1992, p. 40]

The Forsyths, like the Flints and the Grays, were taking steps to
avoid meeting their developmental oedipal challenge. Part of the
oedipal reality is that, when the parents do couple in the primal
scene, they may produce real babies—who, once born (and even
before), demand to be looked after and insist that the family is
reshaped to include them. The Forsyths tried to construct a version
of the primal scene that would protect them from this procreative
reality. Psychically it was probably not wholly true that they had
initially desired children but then found it difficult to cope with
them, although this is, of course, how it felt to them consciously. On
a different, unconscious plane, however, it seemed as though they
had continuously been collaborating in maintaining this psychic
retreat—consisting of encapsulated, romantic, non-procreative
intercourse—from reality. This retreat was rudely shattered by the
arrival of real children with real demands. The Forsyths faced the
painful need to get to know their intensely narcissistic aspects if
their adult, parental relationship was to develop. Their reaction to
this inexorable, developmental demand for change, which felt catastrophic to them, was to opt decisively to maintain their psychic
retreat. Accordingly, they left therapy.

One could so easily imagine this couple presenting, like the
others, as a No Sex couple if their bad relationship had affected
their sexual intercourse. Clearly, the fact that it hadn't gave this
couple a lifeline. They didn't use it for life, however, but to avoid
being more fully aware of the impact of their difficulties. And yet,
it would only be through allowing their difficulties to impact upon

them, which might well have involved pain in their sexual relating, that their development would have been spurred on.

Conclusion

In this chapter, I have tried to illustrate some of the consequences that can befall couples who have got together on the basis of a shared, complementary, and inadequate working through of primal scene aspects of the oedipus situation. Their combined defensive, regressive, and anti-developmental characteristics, strategies, and actions have, in the event of their marriage, proved stronger than their combined developmental and progressive forces, resulting in their sexual relating—as well as other aspects of their relationships—being drastically affected.

I have illustrated some of the events that can consequently occur in the therapeutic arena. My last two couples, the Grays and the Forsyths, show how defences and anti-developmental forces can strive with a high degree of success against development in therapy. I suggest that an enormously strong factor in all such cases is each couple's different capacity to tolerate the anxieties associated with change, feared as catastrophic. The desire to change is not enough in itself. Actually to change, to move into new, unknown territory, can be so alarming as to keep the couple continually oscillating between development and a more fixed position, a psychic retreat; or very high anxiety coupled with a real hatred of reality and development can compel a couple into an even more drastic flight from development into the reassuring arms of an even more rigid and enduring pathological solution. However, my first couple, the Flints, show most clearly a couple that have been able slowly to begin to bear the—often terrible—mental pain of having their inner world scenarios become conscious through reflection and interpretation. They have been able to move towards the much more desirable outcome of a creative relationship, possibly even a procreative one.

Note

1. I have tried to disguise my patients' material so that, I hope, only pertinent aspects remain accessible for discussion. In all three cases my

understanding of the clinical material has developed largely through discussion with my co-therapists and supervisor, to all of whom I would like to express my gratitude, while absolving them of responsibility for the particular opinions expressed here.

2. For this therapy, as with both the other clinical examples discussed in this chapter, I was co-working with another therapist, in each case a different co-therapist.

REFERENCES

Barrows, P. (2003). Change in parent—infant psychotherapy. *Journal of Child Psychotherapy, 29*(3): 283–300.

Bergman, I. (1982). Full-length version of the film entitled *Fanny and Alexander*.

Bergman, I. (1988). *The Magic Lantern*. London: Hamish Hamilton, Penguin Group.

Bick, E. (1968). The experience of the skin in early object relations. *International Journal of Psycho-Analysis, 49*: 489–486 [reprinted in A. Briggs (Ed.), *Surviving Space: Papers on Infant Observation*. London: Karnac, 2002].

Bion, W. R. (1957). Differentiation of the psychotic from the non-psychotic personalities. *International Journal of Psycho-Analysis, 38*: 266–275.

Bion, W. R. (1959). Attacks on linking. *International Journal of Psycho-Analysis, 40*: 308–315.

Bion, W. R. (1961). *Experiences in Groups and Other Papers*. London: Routledge.

Bion, W. R. (1962a). A theory of thinking. *International Journal of Psycho-Analysis, 43*: 306–310.

Bion, W. R. (1962b). *Learning from Experience*. London: Heinemann.

Bion, W. R. (1965). *Transformations*. London: Heinemann.

Bion, W. R. (1967). *Second Thoughts*. London: William Heinemann Medical Books [reprinted London: Karnac, 1984].

Bion, W. R. (1970). *Attention and Interpretation*. London: Tavistock Publications.

Birkstead-Breen, D. (1996). Phallus, penis and mental space. *International Journal of Psycho-Analysis*, 77: 649–657.

Boswell, J. (2001). The oedipus complex. In: C. Bronstein (Ed.), *Kleinian Theory—a Contemporary Perspective*. London: Whurrs Publishers.

Britton, R. (1989). The missing link: parental sexuality in the oedipus complex. In: J. Steiner (Ed.), *The Oedipus Complex Today: Clinical Implications* (pp. 83–101). London: Karnac.

Britton, R. (1992). The oedipus situation and the depressive position. In: R. Anderson (Ed.), *Clinical Lectures on Klein and Bion* (pp. 34–45). London: Routledge.

Britton, R. (1995). Foreword. In: S. Ruszczynski & J. Fisher (Eds.), *Intrusiveness and Intimacy in the Couple*. London: Karnac Books.

Britton, R. (1998a). *Belief and Imagination: Explorations in Psychoanalysis*. London: Routledge.

Britton, R. (1998b). Subjectivity, objectivity and triangular space. In: *Belief and Imagination: Explorations in Psychoanalysis* (pp. 41–58). London: Routledge.

Britton, R. (2000). On sharing psychic space. *Bulletin of the Society of Psychoanalytic Marital Psychotherapists*, May 2000: 10–16.

Britton, R. (2003). *Sex, Death and the Superego: Experiences in Psychoanalysis*. London: Karnac.

Canham, H. (2003). The relevance of the Oedipus myth to fostered and adopted children. *Journal of Child Psychotherapy*, 29(1): 5–20.

Chasseguet-Smirgel, J. (1985). *Creativity and Perversion*. London: Free Association Books.

Dicks, H. (1967). *Marital Tensions: Clinical Studies Towards a Psychoanalytic Theory of Interaction*. London: Routledge & Kegan Paul.

Edwards, J. (2003). The elusive pursuit of insight: three poems by W. B. Yeats. In: H. Canham & C. Satyamurti, (Eds.), *Acquainted with the Night: Psychoanalysis and the Poetic Imagination* (pp. 167–187). London: Karnac.

Eliot, G. (1872). *Middlemarch* [reprinted Harmondsworth: Penguin, 1985].

Feldman, M. (1989). The oedipus complex: manifestations in the inner world and the therapeutic situation. In: J. Steiner (Ed.), *The Oedipus Complex Today: Clinical Implications* (pp. 103–128). London: Karnac.

Fisher, J. (1993). The impenetrable other: ambivalence and the oedipal conflict in work with couples. In: S. Ruszczynski (Ed.), *Psychotherapy with Couples* (pp. 142–166). London: Karnac.

Fisher, J. (1995). Identity and intimacy in the couple: three kinds of identification. In: S. Ruszczynski & J. Fisher (Eds.), *Intrusion and Intimacy in the Couple Relationship* (pp. 74–104). London: Karnac.

Fisher, J. (1999). *The Uninvited Guest: Emerging from Narcissism towards Marriage*. London: Karnac.

Freud, S. (1950a). Extracts from the Fliess papers: Letter 71. *S.E., 1.*

Freud, S. (1900a). The interpretation of dreams. *S.E., 4.*

Freud, S. (1905d). Three essays on the theory of sexuality. *S.E., 7.*

Freud, S. (1905e). Fragment of an analysis of a case of hysteria. *S.E., 7.*

Freud, S. (1909b). Analysis of a phobia in a five-year-old boy. *S.E., 10.*

Freud, S. (1909d). Notes upon a case of obsessional neurosis. *S.E., 10.*

Freud, S. (1916–1917). Introductory lectures on psycho-analysis. *S.E., 15–16.*

Freud, S. (1918b). From the history of an infantile neurosis. *S.E., 17.*

Freud, S. (1919e). A child is being beaten. *S.E.*

Freud, S. (1923b). The ego and the id. *S.E., 19.*

Freud, S. (1924d). The dissolution of the oedipus complex. *S.E., 19.*

Freud, S. (1924e). The loss of reality in neurosis and psychosis. *S.E., 19.*

Freud, S. (1928b). Dostoevsky and parricide. *S.E., 21.*

Freud, S. (1930a). Civilization and its discontents. *S.E., 21.*

Gittings, R. (Ed.) (1987). Keat's Letter to Reynolds (1818). In: *Letters.* Oxford: Oxford University Press.

Glasser, M. (1979). Aggression and sadism in the perversions. In: I. Rosen (Ed.), *Sexual Deviation* (pp. 279–299). London: Oxford University Press.

Heimann, P. (1950). On countertransference. *International Journal of Psycho-Analysis, 31:* 81–84.

Horrox, A. (1988). *Ingmar Bergman: The Magic Lantern* and *Ingmar Bergman: The Director*. Thames TV productions, first shown on ITV and Channel 4 in May 1988.

Hughes, L., & Pengelly, P. (1997). *Staff Supervision in a Turbulent Environment*. London: Jessica Kingsley Publishers Ltd.

James, H. (1897). *What Maisie Knew*. London: Penguin Modern Classics, 1966.

Johns, M. (1996). Why are three-person relationships difficult? In: C. Clulow (Ed.), *Partners Becoming Parents*. London: Sheldon.

Kernberg, O. (1993). The couple's constructive and destructive superego functions. *Journal of the American Psycho-Analytic Association*, 41(3): 653–677.

Kernberg, O. (1995). *Love Relations—Normality and Pathology*. New Haven: Yale University Press.

Klein, M. (1927a). The psychological principles of early analysis. *International Journal of Psycho-Analysis*, 7: 25–37 [reprinted in *Love, Guilt and Reparation*. London: Hogarth Press, 1975].

Klein, M. (1927b). Criminal tendencies in normal children. *British Journal of Medical Psychology*, 7: 177–192 [reprinted in *Love, Guilt and Reparation*. London: Hogarth Press, 1975].

Klein, M. (1928). Early stages of the oedipus conflict. *International Journal of Psycho-Analysis*, 9: 167–180 [reprinted in *Love, Guilt and Reparation*. London: Hogarth Press, 1975].

Klein, M. (1929). Infantile anxiety-situations reflected in a work of art and in the creative impulse. *International Journal of Psycho-Analysis*, 10: 436–443 [reprinted in *Love, Guilt and Reparation*. London: Hogarth Press, 1975].

Klein, M. (1930a). The importance of symbol-formation in the development of the ego. In: *Love, Guilt and Reparation and Other Works*. London: Hogarth Press, 1975.

Klein. M. (1930b). A contribution to the theory of intellectual inhibition. *Love, Guilt and Reparation and Other Works* (pp. 236–247). London: Hogarth Press, 1975.

Klein, M. (1935). A contribution to the psychogenesis of manic-depressive states. *International Journal of Psycho-Analysis*, 16: 145–174 [reprinted in *Love, Guilt and Reparation*. London: Hogarth Press, 1975].

Klein, M. (1940). Mourning and its relation to manic depressive states. *International Journal of Psycho-Analysis*, 21: 125–153 [reprinted in *Love, Guilt and Reparation*. London: Hogarth Press, 1975]

Klein, M. (1945). The oedipus complex in the light of early anxieties. *International Journal of Psycho-Analysis*, 26: 11–33 [reprinted in *Love, Guilt and Reparation*. London: Hogarth Press, 1975].

Klein, M. (1946). Notes on some schizoid mechanisms. *International Journal of Psycho-Analysis*, 27: 99–110 [reprinted in *Envy and Gratitude*. London: Hogarth Press, 1975].

Klein, M. (1952a). The origins of transference. *International Journal of Psycho-Analysis*, 33: 433–438 [reprinted in: *Envy and Gratitude*. London: Hogarth Press, 1975].

Klein, M. (1952b). Some theoretical conclusions regarding the emotional life of the infant. In: *Developments in Psycho-Analysis*, with Heimann, P., Isaccs, S., & Riviere, J., London: Hogarth [reprinted in *Envy and Gratitude*. London: Hogarth Press, 1975].

Lanman, M., Grier, F., & Evans, C. (2003). Objectivity in psychoanalytic assessment of couple relationships. *British Journal of Psychiatry, 182*: 255–260.

Langer, S. (1953). *Feeling and Form: A Theory of Art*. London: Routledge.

Laufer, M. (1975). *Adolescent Disturbance and Breakdown*. London: Penguin Books.

McDougall, J. (1986). *Theatres of the Mind*. London: Free Association Books.

Mattinson, J. (1975). *The Reflection Process in Casework Supervision* (2nd edn, 1992). London: Tavistock Marital Studies Institute.

Mattinson, J. (1981). The deadly equal triangle. In: *Change and Renewal in Psychodynamic Social Work*. London: Group for the Advancement of Psychotherapy in Social Work [reprinted in *The Deadly Equal Triangle*. London: Tavistock Marital Studies Institute, 1997].

Money-Kyrle, R. (1971). The aims of psychoanalysis. *International Journal of Psycho-Analysis, 52*: 103–106 [reprinted in D. Meltzer & E. O'Shaughnessy (Eds.), *The Collected Works of Money-Kyrle*. Strath Tay, Perthshire: Clunie Press, 1978].

Morgan, M. (1995). The projective gridlock: a form of projective identification in couple relationships. In: S. Ruszczynski & J. Fisher (Eds.), *Intrusiveness and Intimacy in the Couple* (pp. 33–48). London: Karnac.

Morgan, M. (2001). First contacts: the therapist's "couple state of mind" as a factor in the containment of couples seen for consultations. In: F. Grier (Ed.), *Brief Encounters with Couples*. London: Karnac.

Morgan, M., & Ruszczynski, S. (1998). The creative couple. Unpublished paper presented at the Tavistock Marital Studies Institute 50th Anniversary Conference.

O'Shaughnessy, E. (1989). The invisible oedipus complex. In: J. Steiner (Ed.), *The Oedipus Complex Today: Clinical Implications* (pp. 129–150). London: Karnac.

Pullman, P. (1995). *Northern Lights*. London: Scholastic Books Ltd.

Quinodoz, J. M. (2002). *Dreams That Turn Over A Page: Paradoxical Dreams in Psychoanalysis*, P. Slotkin (Trans.). London: Routledge.

Rey, H. (1994). *Universals of Psychoanalysis in the Treatment of Psychotic and Borderline States*. London: Free Association Books.

Rilke, R. M. (1987). *The Selected Poetry of Rainer Maria Rilke*, S. Mitchell (Ed. & Trans.). London: Pan Books.

Rosenfeld, H. (1987). The narcissistic omnipotent character structure: a case of chronic hypochondriasis. In: *Impasse and Interpretation* (pp. 63–84). London: Tavistock.

Rusbridger, R. (1999). Elements of the oedipus complex: building up the picture. In: *British Journal of Psychotherapy*, 15(4): 488–500.

Rustin, M., & Rustin, M. (2003). Where is home? An essay on Philip Pullman's *Northern Lights*. *Journal of Child Psychotherapy*, 29(1): 93–105.

Ruszczynski, S. (1992). Some notes towards a psychoanalytic understanding of the couple relationship. *Psychoanalytic Psychotherapy*, 6: 33–48.

Ruszczynski, S. (1993). Thinking about and working with couples. In: S. Ruszczynski (Ed.), *Psychotherapy with Couples* (pp. 197–217). London: Karnac.

Ruszczynski, S. (1995). Narcissistic object relating. In: S. Ruszczynski & J. Fisher (Eds.), *Intrusiveness and Intimacy in the Couple* (pp 13–32). London: Karnac.

Ruszczynski, S. (2003). States of mind in perversion and violence. *Journal of the British Association of Psychotherapists*, 41 (July): 87–100.

Ruszczynski, S., & Fisher, J. (1995) (Eds.) *Intrusiveness and Intimacy in the Couple Relationship*. London: Karnac.

Segal, H. (1957). Notes on symbol formation. *International Journal of Psycho-Analysis*, 38: 391–397.

Segal, H. (1988). *Introduction to the Work of Melanie Klein*. London: Karnac.

Segal, H. (1989). Introduction. In: J. Steiner (Ed.), *The Oedipus Complex Today: Clinical Implications*. London: Karnac.

Sophocles (1986). *Oedipus the King*. D. Taylor (Trans.). London, Methuen.

Steiner, J. (Ed.) (1989). *The Oedipus Complex Today: Clinical Implications*. London: Karnac.

Steiner, J. (1990). Pathological organisations as obstacles to mourning: the role of unbearable guilt. *International Journal of Psycho-Analysis*, 38: 87–94 [reprinted in Steiner, J. *Psychic Retreats*. London: Routledge, 1993].

Steiner, J. (1993) *Psychic Retreats*. London: Routledge.

Steiner, J. (1996). Revenge, resentment and the oedipus situation. *International Journal of Psycho-Analysis*, 77: 433–443.

Törnqvist, E. (1995). *Between Stage and Screen*. Amsterdam: Amsterdam University Press.

Waddell, M. (1991). George Eliot: The unmapped country. In: M. Harris

Williams & M. Waddell (Eds.), *The Chamber of Maiden Thought: Literary Origins of the Psychoanalytic Model of the Mind* (pp. 143–169). London: Routledge.

Waddell, M. (1998). *Inside Lives: Psychoanalysis and the Growth of the Personality*. London: Karnac.

Winnicott, D. W. (1958). The capacity to be alone. *International Journal of Psycho-Analysis*, 39: 416–420.

Winter, S. (1999). *Freud and the Institution of Psychoanalytic Knowledge*. Stanford, CA: Stanford University Press.

INDEX